"I've had the pleasu   :s,
which are strongly   d.
This book does a gre.   ,   ₅ ₅ ₕₑ₀ᵣy ᵢₙ ₚᵣₐ......, ₍₀ ......ers
finish the book feeling confident not only about the 'whys' of MEMI,
but also the 'hows.' In this book, he shares with readers the techniques
he taught me, and skillfully develops a trauma therapy rooted in brain
science, theory, and practice. It is a must read for mental health clinicians
looking to bolster their competence in treating trauma, and is sure
to be used as a reference guide, workbook, and instruction manual for
years to come."

—Jennifer Sweeton,
PsyD, MS, MA, author of *Trauma Treatment Toolbox*

"With this book, Mike Deninger introduces Multichannel Eye Movement Integration, an innovative, science-based approach to PTSD unlike conventional therapies. Its clear-cut theoretical model, protocol, and procedures will appeal to practitioners frustrated with the complications of EMDR. I learned how simple, safe, and effective this therapy is after completing a MEMI seminar led by Mike. And because I've referred PTSD clients to him for treatment, I can attest to the superior results he invariably achieves with MEMI. If you are a therapist who works with clients with trauma histories, or would like to, this is a book you will want on your shelf."

—Jeffrey Lewis,
Ph.D., licensed psychologist

"An exceptionally clear and jargon-free guide on the leading edge of trauma treatment. Readable and practical; more immediately useful than other eye movement therapy texts. A well-organized approach that can be used with any theoretical orientation."

—Steve Andreas
(based on his review of a prepublication manuscript draft),
psychotherapist, pioneering author and developer of NLP models,
master trainer, and cofounder of Real People Press

MULTICHANNEL EYE MOVEMENT INTEGRATION

The Brain Science Path to Easy and Effective PTSD Treatment

MULTICHANNEL EYE MOVEMENT INTEGRATION

The Brain Science Path to Easy and Effective PTSD Treatment

Mike Deninger, PhD

Gracie Publications

Copyright © 2021 by Mike Deninger, PhD
Published by Gracie Publications
(202) 468-8633
www.multichanneleyemovementintegration.com

All rights reserved. No part of this book may be reproduced, stored in a retrieval system, or transmitted in any form or by any means—electronic, mechanical, photocopying, recording, or otherwise—without the prior written permission of the publisher, with the exception of brief excerpts that may be used in articles and reviews.

The author of this book is not dispensing medical advice or prescribing the use of any technique as a form of treatment for physical or mental health problems without the advice of a qualified mental health provider, either directly or indirectly. This book is intended as an educational tool to acquaint the reader with and help them better understand, assess, and choose the appropriate course of treatment for themselves or for their clients and perhaps improve their well-being.

The information in this book should not be substituted for the advice and treatment of a qualified and/or licensed mental health professional. It's up to the client and healthcare provider to discuss suitable treatment methods available to the client. The author and publisher shall not be held liable or responsible to any person or entity regarding any loss or damage incurred, or alleged to have incurred, directly or indirectly, by the information contained in this book.

Editor: Ilene Stankiewicz
Cover design and layout: Sean Graham
Cover model: Ivy Graham

Printed in the United States of America
First Printing

Publisher's Cataloging-In-Publication Data
Names: Deninger, Mike, author.
Title: Multichannel eye movement integration : the brain science path to easy and effective PTSD treatment / Mike Deninger Phd.
Description: [Tucson, Arizona] : Gracie Publications, [2021] | Includes bibliographical references and index.
Identifiers: ISBN 9781735151502 (softcover) | ISBN 9781735151519 (Kindle-MOBI) | ISBN 9781735151526 (Nook-EPUB)
Subjects: LCSH: Post-traumatic stress disorder--Alternative treatment. | Psychic trauma--Alternative treatment.
Classification: LCC RC489.E98 D46 2020 (print) | LCC RC489.E98 (ebook) | DDC 616.852106--dc23

       ISBN: 978-1-7351515-0-2 (softcover)
       ISBN: 978-1-7351515-2-6 (e-book)

This book is dedicated to Mary Ellen Robinson, my soul sister, who never met a wounded person or critter she couldn't heal, and to the survivors of all types and stripes who have crossed my path, and those yet to come. You continue to inspire me with your courage in the face of horrendous experiences, with your dignity and your determination. As our cadre of survivors grows, so will our ability to shed light in even the darkest corners.

CONTENTS

ACKNOWLEDGMENTS xvii
FOREWORD xix
PREFACE 1
INTRODUCTION 7

PART I
CONTRADICTIONS IN TRAUMA TREATMENT AND RESEARCH 19

CHAPTER 1
Posttraumatic Stress Disorder — Science, Symptoms, and Treatment 21

CENTRAL NERVOUS SYSTEM 21
PERIPHERAL NERVOUS SYSTEM 22
    Somatic Nervous System 23
    Autonomic Nervous System 24
LIMBIC SYSTEM 26
    Thalamus 26
    Amygdala 27
    Hippocampus 29
    Hypothalamus 30
    Cingulate Cortex 31
    Anterior Cingulate Cortex 31
    Insula 32
LIMBIC SYSTEM RESEARCH 33
PTSD SYMPTOMS 37
PTSD INCIDENCE RATES 38
PTSD DIAGNOSTIC CRITERIA 39

PRACTITIONER PREPARATION AND
  TRAUMA TREATMENT 41
  Practitioner PTSD Preparation 42
  PTSD Treatment 43

CHAPTER 2
Policy Disputes in PTSD Research and Practice 47

THE BIOMEDICAL MODEL – A BRAIN DISEASE
  THEORY OF MENTAL ILLNESS 49
RANDOMIZED CONTROLLED TRIALS – THE
  "GOLD STANDARD" CONTROVERSY 52
ORIGINS OF EVIDENCE-BASED PRACTICES
  IN MENTAL HEALTH 56
EVIDENCE-BASED PRACTICES – THREE
  CONTROVERSIES 59
THE PERVASIVENESS OF EVIDENCE-BASED
  PRACTICES 63

CHAPTER 3
Are Evidenced-based Practices Really More Effective? 67

SYSTEMATIC DESENSITIZATION AND
  EXPOSURE THERAPIES 67
A CLOSER LOOK AT COGNITIVE BEHAVIORAL
  THERAPIES FOR PTSD 72
PSYCHOTHERAPEUTIC FACTORS AND
  TREATMENT EFFECTIVENESS 76
THE PATH FORWARD 77

PART II
MEMI HISTORY AND DEVELOPMENT 79

CHAPTER 4
The First Two Eye Movement Therapies 81

BRAIN RESEARCH – SPRINGBOARD FOR
   EYE MOVEMENT THERAPIES 81
NEURO-LINGUISTIC PROGRAMMING
   EYE MOVEMENT MODEL 83
THE INTRODUCTION OF EMDR 90
EMDR CONTROVERSIES 93
EYE MOVEMENT INTEGRATION (EMI) – AN
   NLP-BASED MODEL 101
EYE MOVEMENTS ARE PURPOSEFUL
   AND UNCONSCIOUS 103
EMI AND EMDR – SIMILARITIES AND DIFFERENCES 106
   EMI and EMDR Similarities 106
   EMI and EMDR Differences 110

CHAPTER 5
The Creation of Multichannel Eye Movement Integration 117

MEMI PRESUPPOSITIONS AND
   THEORETICAL MODEL 121
MEMI INNOVATIONS 131
   Visual Reframe 133
   Temporal Reframe 134
   Spatial Reframe 134
   Direct and Embedded Commands 135
MEMI CLINICAL OBSERVATIONS 137

PART III
MEMI PROTOCOL, PROCEDURES, AND RESULTS 141

CHAPTER 6
MEMI Basic Eye Movements 143

EYE MOVEMENT 1 – "ABOVE THE HORIZON" 147
EYE MOVEMENT 2 – "STANDING TRIANGLE" 149
EYE MOVEMENT 3 – "SITTING TRIANGLE" 150
EYE MOVEMENT 4 – "FIGURE 8" 151
EYE MOVEMENT 5 – "SHRINKING CIRCLES" 152

CHAPTER 7
MEMI Protocol Steps 1-5 155

PTSD CHECKLIST 156
DESIGNING THE THERAPY SPACE 157
PROTOCOL STEPS 1-5 158
STEP 1. ADMINISTER PCL-5 AND
    ESTABLISH RAPPORT 160
    Administer the PCL-5 160
    Establish Rapport 161
STEP 2. SECURE AGREEMENT TO CHANGE 162
STEP 3. PRETEST ELEMENTS OF STRUCTURE 164
    MEMI Does Not Use Systematic Desensitization 165
    When to Avoid the Most Distressing Memory 166
    Selecting the Problem State 168
    Intensity Scale (I-Scale) 169
    Subjective Units of Distress Scale (SUD Scale) 170
    Pretesting the Elements 172

STEP 4. ANCHOR A RESOURCE STATE 175
    Anchoring Instructions 178
STEP 5. INTRODUCE THERAPEUTIC DISSOCIATION 181
    Associated versus Dissociated View 181
    Visual Kinesthetic Dissociation 183
    Therapeutic Dissociation Instructions 184
    Adding Gestures and Vocalizations 185

CHAPTER 8
MEMI Protocol Step 6 189

STEP 6. CONDUCT EYE MOVEMENTS 190
    Set 1 Eye Movement Sweeps 192
    Set 1 Scripts and Tips 196
    Set 2 Eye Movement Sweeps 198
    Set 2 Scripts and Tips 202
    Set 3 Eye Movement Sweeps 204
    Set 3 Scripts and Tips 207
    Set 4 Eye Movement Sweeps 209
    Set 4 Scripts and Tips 213
    Final Tips 216

CHAPTER 9
MEMI Protocol Steps 7-10 219

STEP 7. TEST STRUCTURE OF EXPERIENCE ELEMENTS 220
    Context 220
    Thoughts 222
    Sensory Information 223
    Feelings 225
    Posttest Questions 228

STEP 8. TAKE I-SCORE AND SUD SCORE READINGS 231
    Intensity Scale Score (I-Score) 231
    Subjective Units of Distress (SUD) Scale Score 233
STEP 9. RECORD RESULTS ON MEMI WORKSHEET 238
    Recording Changes to Context or Thoughts 239
    Recording Changes in Sensory Information 241
    Recording Changes in Feelings 241
    Recording SUD Scores 243
STEP 10. CONDUCT FUTURE REHEARSAL AND
SELF-APPRECIATION. 244
    Future Rehearsal 244
    Self-Appreciation 245

CHAPTER 10
MEMI Facts and Features 249

"THOUGHTS" IN MEMI VERSUS COGNITIVE
RESTRUCTURING 249
DEFINITION OF MEMI TREATMENT SUCCESS 253
EYE MOVEMENTS ELICIT TRANCE STATES 256
HANDLING ABREACTIONS 257
THE IMPORTANCE OF EYE CONTACT 264
WHEN REPRESSED INFORMATION EMERGES 264
USING MEMI WITH DEAF AND HARD
OF HEARING CLIENTS 269
OTHER MEMI TIPS 272
    Phobias 274
    Personal Failures, Slights, or Affronts 275
    Substance Abuse 275

CHAPTER 11
MEMI Case Reports 281

CASE 1. "REBECCA" – RAPE AND STALKING 282
CASE 2. "KEVIN" – CHILDHOOD PHYSICAL
    AND SEXUAL ABUSE 292
CASE 3. "ASHLEY" – SEXUAL ASSAULT AND
    ABANDONMENT 306
CASE 4. "MIGUEL" – WITNESS TO DAUGHTER'S
    OPIOID OVERDOSE 319

APPENDIX A: PCL-5 (DSM-5) 329
APPENDIX B: MEMI WORKSHEET 331
**APPENDIX C: MEMI PROTOCOL AND EYE
    MOVEMENT SUMMARY** 333
**APPENDIX D: MULTICHANNEL EYE
    MOVEMENT INTEGRATION EFFICACY
    USING PCL-C** 335
APPENDIX E: PCL-C (DSM-IV) 345
REFERENCES 347
INDEX 365
ABOUT THE AUTHOR 373

ACKNOWLEDGMENTS

Writing a book is a solitary endeavor, unless you have people who provide assistance along the way, as I did. Of the many friends and colleagues who have been a part of this book's development, I would like to acknowledge several individuals who provided particular insight, advice, or support.

First and foremost, to Michael, my husband and partner, who listened patiently as I explained my day-to-day progress over lunches at Subway, who edited many sections of the book, who made insightful suggestions, and who has been my anchor for over 20 years. Without a doubt, you're the best thing that's ever happened to me.

To Ron Klein, my teacher and mentor, whose expertise and guidance provided me the knowledge, skill, and confidence to challenge the existing order, and the motivation to seek safer, more effective solutions to the problems all humans encounter.

To Connirae and Steve Andreas, who created the original EMI procedure and who graciously shared their history and accomplishments with me as I was researching this book. A special thanks to Steve, who reviewed an early draft of the manuscript.

To Jennifer Sweeton, for teaching me the real facts about EMDR, for taking the time to learn MEMI, and for allowing me to incorporate her neuroscience information into this book.

To Ned Geraty, therapist *par excellence*, for modeling serenity and for guiding me through recovery from PTSD.

To Ilene Stankiewicz, the book's editor and so much more. My sincere appreciation for the skillful way you marshaled every aspect of this book. Your perceptive questions and suggestions provided the guidance I needed to transition this product from an imperfect draft into a glossy galley proof. Because of your standards and your abilities, I am now a better writer.

To Sean Graham, this book's graphic artist, who masterfully translated sometimes cryptic ideas into visual representations of concepts very difficult to display in static images. Your patience and insistence on flawless, final illustrations were noticed and appreciated.

To Jeff Lewis, my friend, colleague, and fellow traveler, for his encouragement, wisdom, and heartfelt support as we walk the path together. Namaste!

To Phil Mackall and Marty Noretsky, for editing an early draft of this book and helping me refine its purpose and message.

FOREWORD

I first met Mike Deninger at an EMDR workshop I was teaching in the fall of 2019. While talking to him, I was immediately struck by his depth of knowledge about PTSD and trauma treatments, and we agreed to keep in touch to discuss more about the role of eye movements in trauma therapies, including EMDR and his burgeoning therapy, Multichannel Eye Movement Integration (MEMI).

Over the last several months, I've had the pleasure of meeting with Mike to learn MEMI techniques, which are strongly evidence-informed and surprisingly straightforward. In this book, he shares with readers the techniques he taught me, and skillfully develops a trauma therapy rooted in brain science, theory, *and* practice.

While the use of eye movements in psychotherapy is not new, the author does what no one else has—he details specific eye movement patterns that have been shown to facilitate the processing and desensitization of distressing events in a fast, simple manner. Moreover, readers will appreciate the author's historical summary of other trauma treatment therapies, and a discussion of the common discrepancies and conflicts in the trauma treatment world.

Finally, this book does a great job of merging theory and practice, so that readers finish the book feeling confident not only about the "whys" of MEMI, but also the "hows." This is the first book of its kind to verbalize and organize eye movement integration strategies for trauma resolution, drawing from theories and skills used in EMDR, hypnosis, Eye Movement Integration™, and Neuro-Linguistic Programming. It is a must read for mental health clinicians looking to bolster their competence in treating trauma, and is sure to be used as a reference guide, workbook, and instruction manual for years to come.

—Jennifer Sweeton, PsyD, MS, MA, Kansas City, 2020

PREFACE

I was impressed the first time I saw Ron Klein demonstrate his Eye Movement Integration™ (EMI™) technique at a one-day seminar in 2002. I'd never observed a method so simple, yet so fast and effective at alleviating posttraumatic stress disorder (PTSD) symptoms. To the uninformed observer, Klein's version of the approach was almost indistinguishable from the original technique invented by Steve and Connirae Andreas in 1989. It was Steve who coined the term *eye movement integration* (EMI) and taught the technique to Klein and many others. Klein's signature improvement to EMI was his emphasis on client safety and security during trauma re-exposure.

While I was preparing this guide, and prior to Steve Andreas's passing, I was able to interact via video chat with him and his wife, Connirae. They are recognized Neuro-Linguistic Programming (NLP) innovators who have authored numerous publications—books, articles, videos, and pioneering human change models. They were a great help to me during my research, gracious in their support, and generous with their information. Although EMI has only a few pages of print support materials, the technique lives on in a video of Steve using the original technique with a Vietnam veteran. A trailer for that demonstration can be found on YouTube. A copy of the entire video can be purchased from Real People Press. I've watched the demonstration dozens of times, and on each occasion I've seen something I'd previously overlooked.

I was eager to begin using this approach with clients, but neither EMI nor EMI™ had written procedures of any measure. To overcome this deficit, I began developing procedures of my own, which I eventually began to compile into a practitioner's guide for the technique. At the outset, I envisioned a task of manageable proportions. That was not to be, however.

Similar to the way I tend to clean a cluttered closet, I began digging into cracks and crevices, as it were: pulling dog-eared books off shelves; scouring historical records; conducting first-person interviews; testing different eye movement patterns; reviewing PTSD treatment studies; investigating the traumatized brain; doing more research than expected; and taking much more time than anticipated. In the end, a new brain-based therapy for PTSD emerged—drawn from earlier EMI versions—but enhanced, limbic, dynamic, multifaceted, and comprehensive. From the time of Klein's demonstration in 2002 until the publication of this guide, what I call Multichannel Eye Movement Integration (MEMI) has been 18 years in the making! I even took intensive training in Eye Movement Desensitization and Reprocessing (EMDR) so I could compare what I had developed with that approach. MEMI proved to be much easier to learn and use, and every bit as effective.

Because I've worked with trauma survivors for over 20 years, and trained more than a thousand practitioners, I've developed a keen interest in PTSD research, policy, and practice. Yet my pursuit of safe and effective treatment methods has been propelled as much by personal experience as by professional interests. At the age of 45, and almost a year to the day after I began recovery from tobacco and alcohol addictions, I was confronted by memories as alarming as they were staggering. I was working full-time as a research scientist and pursuing graduate studies in mental health counseling when I began treatment for PTSD from childhood trauma. It would take several years to sort through those experiences and to heal in the aftermath of their unmasking. I would learn "from the inside out" what it was like to recover from incest (Deninger, 2011).

As both patient and student, I was uniquely positioned to evaluate the counseling approaches used as part of my treatment: client-centered therapy (both individual and group), cognitive behavioral therapy (CBT), hypnotherapy, exposure therapy, EMDR, and antidepressant therapy—with less established techniques occasionally added to the mix. After a few false starts, I found a therapist with both the temperament and skill to guide me from that PTSD netherworld back to normalcy. He was not a trauma therapist by training, but he'd overcome severe agoraphobia as a young man, a byproduct of growing up in an alcoholic household. He was a wise, patient, open-hearted fellow, well versed in traditional as well as alternative, nontrauma therapies. When I became a practicing therapist, I found myself emulating his methods, his serenity, and his compassion. His approach became a benchmark for my own performance as a trauma professional. From that time on, every PTSD study I read and each presentation I attended were viewed with a steely, existential eye, particularly when one approach was judged more effective than others.

After commencing work as a private practice therapist, I attended more than 250 hours of training at the American Hypnosis Training Academy (AHTA) under the direction of Ron Klein, a consummate teacher. With his expert guidance and my own ardent interest in safe and effective approaches to trauma treatment, I earned advanced certifications as a trainer in three disciplines: Ericksonian Hypnotherapy, NLP and EMI™. And I now maintain certification as a Clinical Trauma Professional in order to stay abreast of developments in PTSD treatment.

This practitioner's guide to MEMI is a product of all my experiences.

I believe it's important to facilitate positive change. When I observe human problems, my mind seeks possible solutions. When I perceive injustice, I think of ways to right the wrong. I'd like to think that at every stage of my life, I've tried to make a difference, to advance the common good. I approached writing this book with that mindset. As someone who has recovered from PTSD, and out of concern for others in my tribe, it was my desire to verify that the PTSD treatments being promoted as most effective were as superior as promised. When I concluded that the written history of eye movement therapies was inaccurate, I sought to correct that record. And when I determined that MEMI was as effective as EMDR and traditional PTSD therapies, but faster, easier to learn, science-based, and much safer for survivors, I resolved to develop MEMI into a fully documented therapy and bring it to a larger audience.

Preface

I have advocated for the use of eye movement therapies for more than a decade by giving demonstrations and presentations at regional, national, and international conferences; training mental health professionals; teaching graduate courses; and collaborating with trauma experts. As a leading proponent of the use of eye movement integration techniques, and based on years of clinical experience, I can attest that the therapy described in this book is a safe, efficient, effective, multiuse, brief therapy for PTSD and lesser traumas.

—Mike Deninger

Multichannel Eye Movement Integration

INTRODUCTION

For those living with PTSD, everyday experiences can instill fear. The sound of a spoon dropped on a restaurant floor, the honk of a horn, or a light finger tap on the shoulder can trigger an overreaction. When ordinary events like these are perceived as threats by trauma survivors—as if something horrible is about to happen—the brain's amygdala triggers a rapid-fire, systemic reaction. Bursts of the neurotransmitters adrenaline and norepinephrine pulse into the bloodstream and help activate the sympathetic nervous system's fight or flight response. Pupils dilate, sweating and heart rate increase, and blood pressure elevates (Lanese, 2019).

There are many methods for treating trauma symptoms—cognitive and cognitive behavioral approaches, somatic techniques, narrative procedures, neuro-linguistic strategies and eye movement therapies, to name only a few. The best method for calming these PTSD overreactions has been the subject of much research. It is my contention, as described in this book, that limbic hyperreactivity and the resulting body dysregulation must be targeted in early stage PTSD treatment, not a trauma's cognitive correlates.

Although this book's main purpose is to present the theoretical model, protocol, and step-by-step procedures for conducting Multichannel Eye Movement Integration (MEMI) treatment sessions and evaluating the results, an overview of trauma science, research, policies, and practices is presented first to establish a context within which MEMI therapy can be understood. As I was reading studies evaluating the effectiveness of trauma methods, I quickly learned there are many disputes over the best treatments for PTSD. And although I was concerned that a deep dive into the research might be unnecessary, fearing a tumble down a rabbit hole, I did discover why eye movement therapies receive scant recognition. More importantly, my review of numerous studies, books, and commentaries unearthed an even more serious concern: The superior effectiveness claims of the most popular PTSD therapies are not supported by available evidence. After considering all important factors, I was struck by a discrepancy between the evidence I was finding and the inflated success claims about cognitive behavioral therapies. Although leading professional organizations declare these methods are the most effective, this assertion is now being actively contested. Because I was disturbed by what I found, I spent a year investigating how this came about—how, after thousands of PTSD studies, the evidence does not match the rhetoric. A deeper understanding of the research also prompted me to look more closely at the neurophysiology of trauma.

Our knowledge of what happens in the brain following traumatic experiences has come a long way since Cannon (1915) first coined the term *fight or flight* when describing the brain-to-body reactions following threats to our survival. In the postmodern era, after tens of thousands of veterans returned stateside from Vietnam with severe psychological impairments, out of necessity, the study of the brain's reactions to trauma accelerated. And when the third edition of the *Diagnostic and Statistical Manual of Mental Disorders* was published five years after the war's end, a new diagnosis called posttraumatic stress disorder (PTSD) was added to the manual (American Psychiatric Association, 1980).

While gathering source material for this book, and in search of credible descriptions of the human response to trauma, a flyer for an intensive eye movement desensitization and reprocessing (EMDR) certificate course arrived in the mail. My decision to attend was auspicious, perhaps even providential, for four reasons. For one, I was able to verify several assumptions I'd always had about EMDR but was previously unable to confirm. Second, after this practical training in EMDR's use and recent trends, I was able to add the therapy to my trauma treatment repertoire.

Third, I learned valuable information about the brain's processing of traumatic experiences vis a vis the eye movements used in MEMI and EMDR. The neuroscience presented applied equally to both therapies because they have so many features in common, and each of them uses guided eye movements as the principal therapeutic intervention. Fourth, and finally, insights gleaned from the seminar, coupled with previous research I had conducted into the origins of eye movement therapies, affirmed my belief that EMDR must have been based on Neuro-Linguistic Programming (NLP) principles and strategies. I build a case for this assertion in Chapter 4.

The seminar was taught by Jennifer Sweeton, who later graciously agreed to write the foreword for this book. Jennifer is a prominent trauma expert, neuroscientist, and author of the bestselling book *Trauma Treatment Toolbox* (2019). With advanced degrees in affective neuroscience and clinical psychology, and many honors to her credit, the skills and insights she was able to convey to participants as an EMDR trainer were exceptional. More than that, the scientific information she presented was as digestible as it was relevant to understanding how MEMI works. For these reasons, I requested and received permission to reference her neuroscience information in this book (J. Sweeton, personal communication, November 4, 2019).

Chapter 1 lays the groundwork for a discussion of trauma treatment controversies by describing the nervous system's neurophysiological responses to traumatic experiences. Special attention is paid to the brain's limbic system and its role in the fight or flight response. Descriptions of PTSD diagnostic criteria, trauma-informed care, practitioner PTSD preparation, and a treatment overview from the National Institute of Mental Health (NIMH) follow. Ironically, although the Institute recommends flexible, individualized, and client-centered PTSD treatment, this is not what the American Psychological Association PTSD treatment guideline recommends.

The reasons for this are clarified in Chapter 2, where three factors affecting PTSD treatment practices are profiled: the biomedical model, randomized controlled trials (RCTs), and evidence-based practices (EBPs). The origin of each factor is described and the impact each has had on trauma research and treatment is examined. Three problems inherent in EBP policy definitions are also raised, as are the ways in which each one confounds interpretations of PTSD treatment effectiveness research. Surprisingly, despite these documented flaws in the design of EBPs, their elevated status in trauma treatment research and policies is now endemic.

Because cognitive behavioral therapies are now considered synonymous with evidence-based treatments for PTSD, Chapter 3 explores whether these approaches are actually more effective than other methods. And because they are also considered exposure therapies—meaning clients must repeatedly re-experience the offending trauma as a part of treatment—concerns about client safety and elevated dropout rates in studies are also investigated. A number of PTSD treatment effectiveness studies and associated commentaries are analyzed, which provide persuasive evidence, despite the claims, that cognitive behavioral therapies for PTSD are no more effective than other approaches.

There has also been a great deal of confusion over who deserves the most credit for the development of eye movement therapies. The history was unrecorded for the most part, kept alive in brief written vignettes or via oral histories. In Chapter 4, the origins of the first two techniques (EMI and EMDR) are chronicled, including new information that provides a more authentic portrayal of their inception than previous accounts. An argument is made for how the genesis of these revolutionary techniques can best be understood when viewed in light of four endeavors: studies of eye movements and brain hemisphere activation, groundbreaking NLP principles and practices, the NLP eye movement model, and a single innovation by Shapiro (1989).

John Grinder and Richard Bandler developed NLP—a collection of sensory-based counseling strategies and modeling techniques—in the 1970s. NLP tenets were derived from the therapeutic patterns of master therapists Milton Erickson, Fritz Perls, and Virginia Satir (Bandler & Grinder, 1979; Dilts et al., 1980). Bandler and Grinder detected a number of unifying beliefs powering the successful methods of these three masters. Operating principles called *presuppositions* were fashioned from these beliefs and provided the basis for the development of subsequent NLP strategies.

Since the introduction of EMI and EMDR three decades ago, several other eye movement techniques have emerged, all of which have had an influence on one another. Three of them were derived from EMI (Austin, 2020; Beaulieu, 2003; Klein, 2015) and two were developed by EMDR trained therapists (Grand, 2013; Rosenzweig, 2020). Although the approaches employ different procedures, all use eye movements as the active component in alleviating trauma symptoms. While descriptions of each approach are beyond the scope of this book, an online search of these interventions will reveal obvious cross-fertilizations. History shows us that successful approaches are often adopted or modified by others. Innovations without merit tend to be abandoned; those that work survive. That's the way it should be—as long as credit is given where it's due.

Chapter 5 summarizes the development effort I undertook to create a comprehensive therapy from earlier eye movement integration techniques. Five NLP *presuppositions* are introduced, which serve as the foundation for the *Structure of Experience* theoretical model. Together, they provide the framework for MEMI's protocol, procedures, and instructions. The two safety mechanisms appended to EMI by Klein (2015)—namely NLP *anchoring* and *therapeutic dissociation*—are explained, as is the fact that, unlike in earlier versions, MEMI specifies which eye movements to use and their order of presentation. Fixed eye movement patterns proved to be more effective than a random approach, and standardization of the eye movements made more formal evaluations of the therapy feasible.

Chapter 5 also describes how therapist-verbalized metaphors, reframes, and hypnotic suggestions were added to the eye movements as a result of the many experiments I conducted. These were designed to stimulate shifts in limbic reactions to targeted traumas and represented a dynamic enhancement to earlier versions. With these additions, MEMI became a multidimensional therapy—at least 5D! Those dimensions are as follows:

1. *Testing* and *retesting* the cognitions, sensory characteristics and feelings associated with the recalled traumatic experience
2. *Projecting* an image of the trauma onto a surface across the room

3. *Following* the movement of a pen with the eyes while thinking about the image
4. *Listening* to the therapist reframe the cognitive aspects of an experience
5. *Listening* to embedded commands intoned with provocative (auditory) vocalizations

In a real sense, when eye movement integration was transformed into MEMI, it became a multisensory method and a "multichannel" approach.

In chapter 6, MEMI's five basic eye movements are introduced, with illustrations and instructions for their execution. The development of these movements was guided by NLP eye movement research and principles. They are the result of years of experimentation. Practitioners are encouraged to master these basic patterns with volunteers or clients prior to attempting the more intricate eye movement *sets* introduced in Chapter 8. The sets are actually combinations of the basic eye movements, strategically joined together to enhance therapeutic effects.

The first five steps in the MEMI protocol are described in Chapter 7. They do not involve any eye movements. Instead, they form the introductory phase of the therapy, during which clients are administered a standardized PTSD checklist, a client-therapist working alliance is established, an agreement to change the reaction to the traumatic experience is secured, a pretest of trauma symptoms is conducted, clients are anchored in safety, and therapeutic dissociation is explained. A rationale is provided for each step, as are therapist instructions and recommended scripts.

Chapter 8 begins with a preview of what is to come in the second half of the therapy by listing Steps 6-10 in the MEMI protocol. The rest of the chapter is devoted to Step 6, which explains how to perform the four combinations of the basic eye movements called *sets*. After extensive experimentation with the basic movements, these four sets, accompanied by strategic reframes, metaphors, and embedded commands spoken by the therapist became the nucleus of the therapy. Illustrations depict how to perform the sets, along with instructions, scripts, and tips explaining how to synchronize the spoken part of the protocol with the eye movements.

Although the choice of which eye movements to use was left to the therapist in eye movement integration, in MEMI the sets are predetermined, ordered, and systematic. Therapist comments were only added after each set's structure had been determined. Clinical experience has shown that when the basic eye movements are combined into carefully sequenced sets and the comments are added, treatment outcomes improve. If this seems unclear to you at this point, rest assured that complete explanations are provided in each chapter.

The last four steps in the protocol (7-10) are described in Chapter 9. For obvious reasons, the proficient execution of each eye movement set is critical to achieving positive treatment outcomes. However, the procedures explained in Steps 7-9 are equally important because they are the mechanisms for collecting and recording response data before and after treatment. To begin, Step 7 explains how to test for the Structure of Experience elements—the context, thoughts, sensory information, and feelings related to a traumatic experience. This is followed in Step 8 by descriptions of the Intensity Scale (I-Scale) and the Subjective Units of Distress (SUD) Scale, which are two in-session assessments measuring the strength of client reactions to the targeted traumatic memory. In Step 9, instructions are provided for recording before and after treatment results on the MEMI Worksheet. Examples illustrating how to record responses to the elements in a memory's structure, as well as I-Scale and SUD Scale scores, are also provided.

Chapter 10 presents a number of additional facts, features, and clarifications about MEMI not addressed in previous sections of the book. Further clarification is offered about the differences between MEMI's "thoughts" and cognitive restructuring, specifically how changes in cognitions are viewed in each approach. Tips and guidance for treating phobias and additions, handling abreactions, and an explanation of how repressed information sometimes emerges during treatment are also addressed in this chapter.

In Chapter 11, four individual case reports summarize the use of MEMI with actual PTSD subjects treated in a private practice setting. One subject had been a victim of sexual assault and stalking, one experienced childhood sexual abuse and was addicted to methamphetamines, one had been sexually assaulted at school and was abandoned by a parent, and one had witnessed his daughter's overdose on opioids. In each case, the subjects recovered and no longer qualified for a PTSD diagnosis.

Although large-scale treatment effectiveness studies of MEMI have not yet taken place, a small clinical study using this therapy with PTSD clients was conducted. The purpose of the study was to determine whether a validated PTSD self-report instrument would be compatible with the MEMI protocol. All subjects in the trial were diagnosed with PTSD based on results from the PTSD Checklist (PCL-C) developed by the U.S. Department of Defense's PTSD Center, and the PCL-C proved to be a good fit for use with the MEMI protocol. Further, none of the subjects qualified for a PTSD diagnosis following treatment. A summary of the MEMI study is included as Appendix D. Due to the small sample size, the results cannot be generalized. However, when larger studies are conducted, there is every reason to believe the results will demonstrate a similar level of effectiveness.

This guide to planning, executing, and evaluating MEMI's use in trauma treatment provides the working therapist with a simple but clear blueprint for assessing and treating clients with acute stress or PTSD. It's also important to note that the therapy is equally effective when used with many other disorders, some of which are described in Chapter 10. Although care has been taken to make this guide as comprehensive as possible, practitioners are encouraged to attend in-person seminars, online trainings, or to view video demonstrations of this dynamic, new therapy to supplement this book's contents.

PART I

Contradictions in Trauma Treatment and Research

"HYPERAROUSAL—after a traumatic experience, the human system of self-preservation seems to go onto permanent alert, as if the danger might return at any moment. Physiological arousal continues unabated."

—Judith Lewis Herman
Trauma and Recovery: The Aftermath of Violence

CHAPTER 1

Posttraumatic Stress Disorder — Science, Symptoms, and Treatment

The human nervous system is composed of the brain, the spinal cord, and an additional 86 billion neurons, each one networked with thousands of others. The system's initial response to traumatic events is managed by the brain's limbic system, a set of structures above the brain stem and beneath the cortex. From an evolutionary perspective, this is a much older part of the brain. While the limbic system is responsible for interpreting emotions, facilitating memory storage, and regulating hormones, its most noteworthy function is to detect and act on threats to our being. What actually happens in this system to accomplish these tasks has been the subject of a host of research studies. But first, in order to establish a context within which the limbic system's role in processing traumatic events can be discussed, it would be helpful to review the major parts of the nervous system itself.

CENTRAL NERVOUS SYSTEM

The *central nervous system* (CNS) is one of two main branches of the human nervous system shown in *Figure 1.1*. Composed of the brain and spinal cord, the CNS functions as a data processing, decision-making, and action-oriented communications network. The purpose of the brain is to receive sensory input from sources within the body, integrate this information with thoughts and emotions, and coordinate responses back to the organs, muscles, and limbs. The spinal cord serves as an information highway, shuttling neural impulses back and forth between the brain and internal organs via its network encased within the spinal column. For example, if you were to sit on a sewing needle protruding from a spool of thread (people used to sometimes absentmindedly leave these things on chairs), tactile sensations at the puncture site would be transmitted via neurons over to the spinal cord and up to the brain, interpreted as pain, and signals would be returned, prompting you to distance yourself from the needle!

PERIPHERAL NERVOUS SYSTEM

The billions of neurons found outside the brain and spinal cord make up the *peripheral nervous system* (PeNS). Shown in *Figure 1.1*, it is so named because its nerve bundles branch out from the spinal cord in the direction of muscles, organs, and limbs on the periphery of the body. The PeNS has two functions: to facilitate complex physical movements and to stimulate neurochemical actions within the muscles and organs by connecting the CNS to the rest of the body. The two subdivisions of the PeNS are the *somatic nervous system* (SoNS) and the *autonomic nervous system* (ANS).

The Nervous System

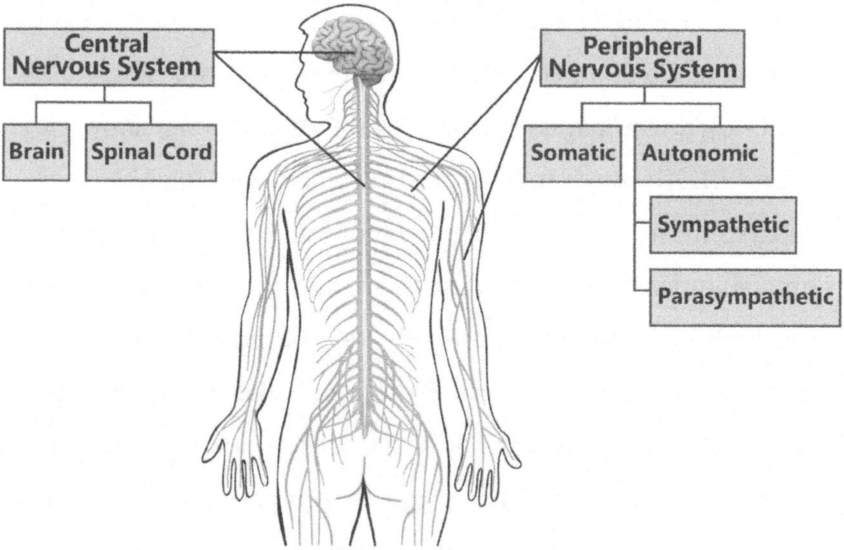

Figure 1.1

Somatic Nervous System

The SoNS regulates <u>voluntary</u> movements, such as walking, dressing, and posture. Its purpose is to connect muscles to the CNS in order to facilitate these intentional actions. If I decide to pick up an apple, for example, sensations are sent from the skin and muscles in my hand, through the CNS, to the brain via *sensory neurons*, and messages stimulating the affected muscles to grasp the apple are returned via *motor neurons*. Although this function is obviously basic to everyday life, it does not play a significant role in the processing of traumatic experiences. Its ability to function may even be stalled if we "freeze" or become immobile in response to a threat.

Autonomic Nervous System

The ANS, on the other hand, governs <u>involuntary</u> bodily functions, such as heart and respiratory rates and digestion, all performed without our conscious awareness. It has two subsystems of its own, the parasympathetic and sympathetic, shown in *Figure 1.1*. Although independent of each other, together these subsystems maintain a stable metabolic balance in our cells and organs under normal circumstances, and if necessary, prepare our bodies to respond defensively when threatened. Basically, when one system becomes activated the other deactivates. The ANS achieves these actions by automatically adjusting the ratio of water, minerals, and chemicals within and among internal organs. We never have to remind ourselves to breathe or take our pulse, these functions are regulated unconsciously.

Parasympathetic Nervous System

The first subsystem of the ANS, the *parasympathetic nervous system* (PaNS), controls what Benson (2000) called the *relaxation response*. If you meditate, or practice self-hypnosis or mindfulness, you are undoubtedly aware of your ability to return your body's internal systems from an aroused state to a resting calm—the balanced condition known as *homeostasis*—where we find ourselves most of the time. Although these are conscious and deliberate actions we sometimes take to relieve stress, PaNS actions are usually unconscious and automatic. For instance, when the danger of a threat is removed, parasympathetic activation of the relaxation response returns the organs from an alert state to their "rest and digest" condition (homeostasis) by increasing saliva and digestive secretions, constricting the pupils, slowing breathing, and reducing heart rate. Benson's discovery of this process was a determining factor in shifting the medical profession's outlook on wellness and disease.

Sympathetic Nervous System

The second subsystem of the ANS, shown in *Figure 1.1*, the *sympathetic nervous system* (SyNS), activates what's commonly known as the "fight or flight response" whenever threats are encountered. As many as 1,400 biochemical and psychophysiological changes are triggered: blood pressure elevates, heart rate and blood flow to the muscles increase, pupils dilate, saliva production is restricted, breathing becomes rapid, digestion deactivates, and immune capabilities are enhanced—all in order to bring us to a hyperalert state. This full-body, all-systems response following actual or perceived threats of harm, also known as the stress response, makes us faster, stronger, and more vigilant—physically and mentally more prepared to react in dangerous situations. The stress response, when enacted by the SyNS, is the end result of a process that began only seconds earlier in the brain's limbic system. A PTSD diagnosis is given when elements of this response persist months or even years after a threat is no longer present.

The Limbic System

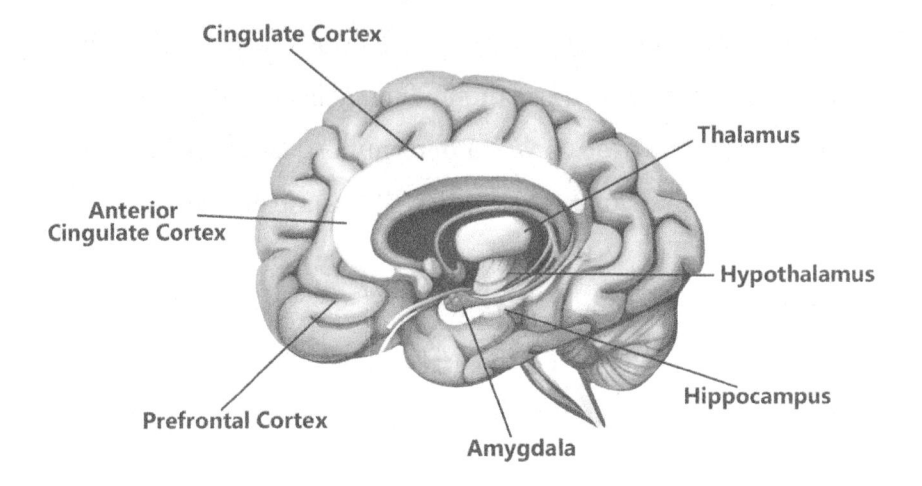

Figure 1.2

THE LIMBIC SYSTEM

Disagreement exists over which components of the brain actually make up the *limbic system*. Although the four most frequently mentioned are the thalamus, the amygdala, the hippocampus, and the hypothalamus, as seen in *Figure 1.2*, other parts of the brain are sometimes included in limbic system descriptions because of the important roles they play in the fight or flight response. The anterior cingulate cortex, prefrontal cortex, and insula are examples.

Thalamus

The *thalamus* is a mass of grey matter located just above the brain stem and adjacent to the hypothalamus. It acts as the gateway through which all sensory information (except smells) passes as it enters the brain. The primary function of the thalamus is to share sensory data with the rest of the brain as quickly and completely as possible. For example, signals transmitted from the thalamus to the cortex at the top of the brain arrive in just .5 milliseconds. Even more rapid are the signals from the thalamus to the *amygdala*, which arrive after only .25 milliseconds. The speed of this signal supports the amygdala's primary role as the initiator of the fight or flight response.

Amygdala

Immediately detecting the presence of danger is the amygdala's major purpose. After receiving sensory input from the thalamus, this almond-shaped cluster of neurons at the base of the limbic system performs several actions. It sends a quick message to the hippocampus seeking an immediate assessment of the sensory input's threat level, as if asking, "How serious is this?" Because the hippocampus encodes emotional and contextual information as *explicit memories,* ones that we can consciously recall, it compares this new sensory information with stored, factual memories and sends a message back to the amygdala with its threat assessment. At the same time, the amygdala reviews its own depository of *implicit memories*—unconscious impressions from stored sensory experiences—which also helps to determine whether to trigger the stress response.

An example will help clarify the differences between these two types of memories. Imagine that it's midnight and your car is idling at a red light. Suddenly, you hear high-pitched screeching sounds behind you. These sounds are transmitted to the thalamus, where they are quickly jettisoned to the amygdala as neural signals. Upon arrival, the sounds are compared to unconscious impressions of similar sounds (implicit memories) from previous sensory experiences. Even before the meaning of the sounds has been determined, if they are assessed as dangerous, based on these subliminal comparisons, the amygdala triggers the stress response.

On the other hand, suppose after hearing the sounds you glance over at your rearview mirror, and see you are about to be hit from behind by a car swerving back and forth. The amygdala quickly queries the hippocampus for more information about the sounds and images, and compares them to any explicit memories with particular relevance. If you were rear-ended once before, information from that conscious memory is bundled with the new sensory information and messaged back to the amygdala with a risk assessment.

When reacting to a threat, the amygdala also distorts the sensory signals from the thalamus to the cortex, thereby interfering with the proper encoding of the sensory information into accurate, long-term memories. Parts of the memory may be missing, or in extreme cases the entire memory may be blocked, as in repressed. And research tells us that when trauma-related sensory information is not adequately encoded by the cortex, a person is more likely to develop PTSD and its symptoms are more difficult to resolve.

One other factor affecting the persistence of PTSD symptoms is the amygdala's baseline activity level—its default setting. When a person is relaxed, the amygdala is activating normally. This is the opposite of its hyperactive response when facing a threat. If a boy has been sexually abused a number of times by a family member and believes it will happen again, this may cause his amygdala's baseline activity level (default) to increase and stay fixed at a hyperactive level. As a result, he is more likely to overreact to noises or the touch of another person. This is one reason why PTSD symptoms, such as hypervigilance and the startle effect, are so difficult for survivors to resolve. Although evidence is emerging that eye movement therapies appear to help reset amygdala activity levels, further research is needed to confirm the hypothesis.

Hippocampus
This small horseshoe-shaped part of the brain beside the amygdala plays an important role in memory and learning. When functioning normally, the *hippocampus* "time stamps" panoramic images of our experiences—indicating when they happened and how long they lasted—and acts as the repository of autobiographical memories. It encodes both emotional and contextual information and serves as the explicit memory center of the brain.

For obvious reasons, we want our memories to be accurate and clear, but when the stress response is triggered, the hippocampus absorbs the stress hormone cortisol and stops functioning normally. Images become distorted, blurry, no longer panoramic, and PTSD is more likely to develop. For this reason, trauma treatments that resolve image distortions and improve signals from the hippocampus will be more effective. Therapies using eye movements as a principal intervention actually help to reset the hippocampus and have been described by Sweeton (J. Sweeton, personal communication, November 4, 2019) as a "memory reconsolidation tool."

Hypothalamus

The *hypothalamus* is located below the thalamus and just above the pea-sized pituitary gland. Its purpose is to regulate heart rate, breathing, perspiration, fluid levels in organs, blood flow, and other SyNS functions. Once the amygdala has confirmed the existence of a threat, it signals the hypothalamus to accelerate these functions by initiating the stress response along the hypothalamic/pituitary/adrenal (HPA) pathway. Successive actions over this route from the brain to the body's extremities convert neural impulses into stress hormones that alter the neurochemistry of the cells, muscles, and organs.

The hypothalamus secretes *corticotropin-releasing hormone* (CRH) into the bloodstream, which increases SyNS activity and signals the pituitary gland to release *adrenocorticotropic hormone* (ACTH) into the bloodstream. After a few seconds, ACTH enters the adrenal glands at the top of the kidneys where, following complex cellular interactions, stress hormones like *cortisol* are released into the bloodstream. Cortisol stimulates an increase in blood pressure, cardiac performance, and blood flow to the muscles. These intricate brain to body actions along the HPA axis begin with a signal from the amygdala to the hypothalamus and end with a whole body, heightened state of alert.

Cingulate Cortex
The *cingulate cortex* is involved in processing cognitive information in addition to its role in monitoring emotions and conflict. It is located beneath the cortex and runs front to back along either side of the midline of the brain. With roles in both cognition and emotions, it's often considered a limbic *and* a cortical structure. The purpose of the cingulate cortex appears multifaceted and is still somewhat of a mystery, but the activity of one of its sections has been studied extensively in connection with its role in the fight or flight response.

Anterior Cingulate Cortex
Located at the front of the cingulate cortex is a section called the *anterior cingulate cortex* (ACC), with connections to the amygdala, the hypothalamus, and the frontal cortex. Although commonly referred to as the emotion regulation center, the ACC does much more than control emotional states. During the stress response, it also activates the SyNS and aids in the secretion of stress hormones by the endocrine system. Under normal circumstances, the ACC assists the *prefrontal cortex* (PFC)—also shown in *Figure 1.2*—with memory development. But when the amygdala reacts to a threat, it suppresses that

activity of the ACC, causing further disruption in memory development by the PFC.

As previously stated, when sensory information is not encoded accurately by the PFC, posttraumatic stress disorder is more likely to develop. The suppression of the ACC and PFC operations by the amygdala each correlate with the development of PTSD and the persistence of its symptoms over time. The extent to which eye movement therapies are instrumental in reversing these reactions when a serious threat is encountered is a subject ripe for investigation.

Insula

The *insula* is not depicted in *Figure 1.2* due to its location in small crevices between the frontal, parietal, and temporal lobes of the brain. Although it's considered a cortical and not a limbic structure, it does play a role in the determination of emotional states, hence its importance to the stress response.

The insula is thought to be the part of the brain responsible for *proprioception* and *interoception*—the former being our ability to determine body position (sitting, turning, or crouching) and the latter our awareness of internal physiological states (nausea, lightheadedness, or pain). With regard to its role in interoception, the insula also allows us to translate somatic sensations into emotional experiences. Pain from a broken arm could engender sad feelings, or paralysis from a stroke could generate fear. As will become clear in later sections of this book, somatic sensations and emotional feelings associated with traumatic events play very important roles in the diagnosis, treatment, and resolution of PTSD symptoms with MEMI.

LIMBIC SYSTEM RESEARCH

Several research studies reinforce the involvement of the limbic system and other parts of the brain in the stress response. Wlassoff (2015) found that certain neurophysiological and neurochemical changes occur in the brain following traumatic events and reoccur when the experiences are recalled. In response to overwhelming stressors, hormonal secretions alter the function of the limbic system's amygdala and hippocampus, as well as the frontal lobe's ventromedial prefrontal cortex (all of which play a role in memory formation). The three organs begin responding differently when processing trauma-related information, and over time, the amygdala and hippocampus even grow or shrink in size.

Another study determined that the neurohormones norepinephrine and corticosterone alter interactions between the amygdala and hippocampus in ways that impair memory development of traumatic events. The authors hypothesize this discharge of neurohormones and the physical reactions in these organs may be one reason why they grow or shrink in size (Akirav & Richter-Levin, 2002).

A brain imaging study conducted by Bremner et al. (2008) found heightened amygdala reactivity when PTSD patients re-experience a trauma, as well as a failure of the ventromedial prefrontal cortex to activate. The authors hypothesize that this heightened amygdala reactivity and deactivation of the prefrontal memory function correlate with the inability to extinguish PTSD symptoms like flashbacks, somatic reactions and startle responses.

Heightened amygdala reactivity to trauma was reaffirmed by a more recent study (Stevens et al., 2017) reporting a relationship between decreasing ACC activity and the persistence of trauma symptoms. In the study, approximately one month after traumatic civilian incidents and then three more times over a 12-month period, subjects viewed threatening facial images while brain activity was measured using functional magnetic resonance imaging. To quote the study's lead author:

> *People with a greater amygdala response to fearful faces had greater initial symptom severity and were more likely to maintain PTSD symptoms over the following year. Additionally, those with a sharper drop in ventral ACC activity over repeated viewings of fearful images, called habituation, showed a poorer recovery trajectory. The findings suggest that amygdala reactivity and ventral ACC habituation to a threat predict the emergence of PTSD symptoms after trauma.* (Stevens, 2017).

Considered as a whole, these studies provide important evidence of a biological relationship between limbic system anomalies following traumatic experiences and the development of PTSD. However, the results are not directly applicable in therapeutic settings because the data were gathered in lab settings using MRI technology. Consequently, they are not considered *biomarkers* of the disorder. Biomarkers are easy to use, clinical assessments for diagnosing, monitoring, and evaluating appropriate therapeutic treatments for diseases (Mandal, 2019). Blood pressure readings for heart disease and PSA blood tests to detect prostate cancer are good examples. No purely biological biomarkers (like a blood test) have been discovered to detect the presence of PTSD and researchers have predicted it will be a long time before that ever happens (Schmidt et al., 2013; Morgan, 2017).

Nevertheless, we should not discount the clinical relevance of limbic system reactivity findings when assessing the appropriateness of PTSD treatments. Although equipping each therapy room with an MRI machine is hardly practical, making informed decisions about treatments using the best available science is imperative. In keeping with this premise, Stevens and her colleagues (2017) recommend the development of new treatments designed to reduce amygdala reactivity and restimulate ACC function immediately following traumatic incidents. If successful, early interventions of this sort could foster a paradigm shift and revolutionize the treatment of PTSD.

Under the current paradigm, the most frequently recommended PTSD therapies (cognitive behavioral approaches), require clients to repeatedly re-experience traumatic events—live them over and over—in the belief that this is the most effective way to resolve symptoms. These re-exposures usually take the form of numerous, first-person retellings of trauma stories—a task clients find extremely distressing.

While contemplating this aspect of treatment orthodoxy, I was struck by the similarities between repeated exposures in cognitive behavioral therapies and the habituation to a threat finding reported in the Stevens et al. study (2017). If survivors who go on to develop PTSD exhibit greater amygdala reactivity and have a harder time recovering when exposed to threatening images, why would practitioners want to repeatedly expose clients to their traumatic experience during early stage treatment? Other problems associated with the use of cognitive behavioral therapies for PTSD will be explored in the next two chapters.

Whether repeated exposures are effective or efficient in resolving limbic system anomalies—like amygdala reactivity, prefrontal cortex deactivation, and ACC habituation—or are actually counterproductive during early-stage treatment should be investigated. If repeated exposures prove to be counterproductive, new methods more effective at targeting limbic abnormalities could replace exposure approaches altogether.

A case presented later in this book will show how MEMI provides superior protections to clients during what are very brief, nonrepetitive exposures to traumatic experiences. The results are fast and long-lasting, and the procedures are much easier on the client than cognitive behavioral therapies. If limbic system anomalies do correlate with the persistence of PTSD symptoms, as theorized by Bremner and his coauthors (2008), then rapid resolution of symptoms using less harsh procedures may also help to rebalance limbic system functions. This is what I believe happens with the use of MEMI.

Conversely, repeated exposure during early-stage treatment with cognitive behavioral therapies could exacerbate PTSD symptoms and perpetuate limbic system abnormalities. What's most concerning is the possibility that repetitive exposure without adequate protections during early-stage treatment actually makes matters worse for clients, causing them to become overwhelmed, discontinue therapy, and end up more despondent than when treatment began.

As the path to understanding the human brain's responses to life-threatening experiences continues to unfold with research, so will our ability to target and more efficiently resolve the neurological and physical reactions associated with PTSD. Although what happens in the brain following perceived threats to survival is currently only detectable with an MRI, the cognitive, sensory, and somatic reactions are either observable or can be obtained simply by asking clients about their experiences. And these are the reactions that form the basis of the PTSD criteria in the *Diagnostic and Statistical Manual of Mental Health Disorders*.

PTSD SYMPTOMS

When individuals living with PTSD re-experience a trauma, they respond as if what happened is still a threat. Their reactions from the time of the event are replayed in the form of somatic symptoms (shortness of breath, heart palpitations, numbing, or other physical discomforts) and sensory distortions (threatening images or sounds). Thoughts about the event are often negative or self-limiting. Given the neuroscientific information discussed in the previous section, one can now assume these reactions are associated with limbic system anomalies. These individuals can be burdened with incapacitating symptoms for months, years, or even decades after an event. They can become reckless and irritable, with concentration problems and sleep disturbance. They can suffer from hyperarousal when a touch or a noise triggers an extreme reaction. They can feel detached or estranged from family and friends, develop negative attitudes about self and others, even lose the ability to experience happiness or satisfaction. However, not all people develop PTSD following life-threatening events.

PTSD INCIDENCE RATES

Of the millions of Americans exposed to traumatic experiences, less than 10% develop the severe, anxiety-producing reactions associated with PTSD. A woman threatened with sexual violence, a senior citizen who suffers a near-fatal heart attack, or a teenage witness to a brutal mugging might all develop PTSD, but chances are they will not. Why certain individuals develop the disorder and others do not after very similar experiences is not known. The study by Stevens et al. (2017) sheds some neurological light on this question. Individuals with greater amygdala reactivity and ACC attenuation in the months following exposure are more likely to develop PTSD and recover more slowly. However, it's unclear at this time whether genetic or environmental factors, or a combination of the two, play a role in the development of PTSD.

Although half of the U.S. population faces at least one traumatic event during their lifespan, only 7-8% will subsequently develop PTSD. Notwithstanding this low percentage, estimates are that five to eight million people in the U.S. struggle with PTSD in any given year (Kessler et al., 2005; American Psychiatric Association, 2013; U.S. Department of Veterans Affairs, 2020a). Prevalence rates are higher for veterans, law enforcement officers, firefighters, and emergency first responders who risk greater exposure to trauma. The highest rates of PTSD—30-50%—occur after exposure to rape, war, captivity, or genocide (American Psychiatric Association, 2013). Basically, the more frequent, more violent, and more heinous the experience, the more likely it is a person will develop PTSD.

PTSD DIAGNOSTIC CRITERIA

The *Diagnostic and Statistical Manual of Mental Disorders*, fifth edition (DSM-5) designates two specific trauma-related disorders: acute stress disorder and PTSD (American Psychiatric Association, 2013). To confirm a diagnosis, both disorders stipulate a person must be exposed to actual or threatened death, serious injury, or sexual violence, either firsthand or as a witness to such events. Each also requires the presence of essentially the same cognitive, physical, and sensory impairments to confirm a diagnosis:

- Re-experiencing the trauma in the form of intrusive thoughts, nightmares, or flashbacks
- Avoidance of memories, thoughts, feelings, and situations that remind a person of the trauma
- Changes in cognition or mood (memory loss, negative beliefs about self or others, estrangement from family and friends)
- Arousal and reactivity (hypervigilance, angry outbursts, self-destructive behaviors)

The major distinction between acute stress disorder and PTSD involves the amount of time elapsed between exposure to the trauma and the emergence or persistence of symptoms. Acute stress disorder is diagnosed when the onset of symptoms occurs within three days and one month of the event. PTSD is diagnosed when symptoms commence or persist after one month has passed.

To become comfortable with diagnosing acute stress disorder and PTSD, I recommend you do two things: First, read the diagnostic criteria for both disorders in the DSM-5 until you understand how they work. Second, learn how to use the PTSD Checklist for DSM-5 (PCL-5) developed and validated by the U.S. Department of Veterans Affairs National Center for PTSD (Wortmann et al., 2016). The Center's website provides a summary of the disorder's DSM-5 diagnostic criteria, as well as instructions for administering and scoring the PCL-5 to endorse or reject a PTSD diagnosis (U.S. Department of Veterans Affairs, 2020b). At a minimum, every mental health practitioner should have this level of familiarity with these two trauma-related disorders.

PRACTITIONER PREPARATION AND TRAUMA TREATMENT

During the last two decades, much more attention has been paid to the importance of trauma-related information in mental health treatment—ever since the groundbreaking Adverse Childhood Experiences (ACE) Study established a connection between childhood events and the leading causes of death in American adults (Felitti et al., 1998). The study's results stunned the medical world, finding that negative childhood experiences (physical, emotional, or sexual abuse; divorced parents; substance abusers in the home; or incarcerated family members) correlate with the development of medical and mental illnesses. Strong associations were found between these factors and the development of cancer, heart and lung disease, substance abuse, PTSD, depression, and anxiety. The finding that childhood trauma was associated with the development of physical diseases like cancer came as a surprise to health professionals.

Kaiser Permanente and Centers for Disease Control (CDC) collaborated in this study of over 17,000 adults who gave retrospective views of their childhood experiences during an annual wellness check. The study was a rarity, one with results so profound it altered the approach to patient care around the world. Its results challenged conventional conceptions of disease development. Brandings like "trauma informed care" and "trauma focused therapy" found their way into the medical and mental health treatment vernaculars, and trauma history became an important topic in nature versus nurture discussions.

This study's significance cannot be overstated, and a thorough reading of its results is a "must do" for the practicing therapist. Given the subject of this book, the findings raise an obvious question: How prepared are mental health practitioners to adequately treat patients with adverse childhood histories?

Practitioner PTSD Preparation

The number of mental health professionals in the U.S. has been estimated at 577,000, based on numbers reported by the Bureau of Labor Statistics. Sixty-seven percent are masters degree level social workers, mental health therapists, marriage and family therapists, or substance abuse counselors. The rest are clinical or counseling psychologists (28.3%) or psychiatrists (4.3%) (Grohol, 2020). Although the academic preparation of practitioners to treat PTSD has been reported as markedly insufficient (Courtois & Gold, 2009; DePrince & Newman, 2011), patients in public as well as private practice settings frequently present with the illness. The number of people living with PTSD and the implications of the ACE Study results confirm the extent of this problem.

With five to eight million people suffering from PTSD, and an ill-prepared mental health workforce providing therapy, it seems certain that many individuals with trauma-related disorders will receive substandard care or will go untreated. Many other individuals without PTSD, but with psychological disorders like depression, anxiety, or substance abuse stemming from adverse childhood events are also in need of trauma informed care. In short, there simply are not enough adequately trained practitioners to meet the demand. Considering the number of Americans without access to healthcare, the problem is even more severe than this information suggests. The need for brief, simple, safe, and effective therapies for PTSD and trauma-associated disorders during early-stage treatment is evident.

PTSD Treatment

The National Institute of Mental Health (NIMH) is the federal agency monitoring research and reporting trends in mental health practice. The two general approaches to treating PTSD described by the Institute, and recommended for use separately or in combination, are medication (primarily antidepressants) and individual or group psychotherapy (NIMH, 2020). The Institute states that individual therapy for PTSD can continue for 6 to 12 sessions or more, depending on client needs. The Institute does not recommend one particular therapy over any other. In fact, it notes providers commonly combine several different therapies when treating PTSD, depending on the client. Because PTSD affects people differently, NIMH recommends individualized treatment. The Institute confirms many trauma and nontrauma approaches can be of benefit, so it suggests clients try different treatments until they find one that works best for them. NIMH also recommends that practitioners who treat trauma clients have PTSD experience.

According to the NIMH website, effective talk therapies for PTSD generally emphasize three key components: 1.) client symptom education; 2.) skill development in identifying symptom triggers; and 3.) training in symptom management. These components are common to many therapies for PTSD and are often used in conjunction with medication.

Cognitive behavioral therapies are mentioned as "helpful" PTSD approaches, but are not cited as any more effective than other therapies. Moreover, the NIMH website notes "a treatment that works for one person may not work for another." Cognitive behavioral therapies, the website states, may include both *exposure* and *cognitive restructuring* components. Exposure is a technique for slowly and repeatedly exposing clients to memories of an experienced trauma, supported by a belief the repetition will diminish reactions and help clients overcome symptoms. Cognitive restructuring assists clients in examining their thoughts about a trauma with the goal of replacing unrealistic thinking with more realistic views of what happened. This is sometimes described as changing irrational thoughts about what transpired to more rational thinking.

NIMH confirms nontrauma therapies can also effectively reduce symptoms, although they do not name those therapies: "Many types of psychotherapy can help people with PTSD. Some types target the symptoms of PTSD directly. Other therapies focus on social, family, or job-related problems. Clients are advised to discuss all PTSD treatment options with their providers."

PTSD research funded by NIMH, or reported as underway, appears to align with the Institute's emphasis on individualized PTSD treatment and the consideration of all options in the pursuit of treatment success. The topics include:

- The characteristics of patients whose symptoms improve naturally
- How fear memories are affected by learning
- Changes in the body and sleep
- How to prevent the development of PTSD soon after trauma exposure
- Factors influencing whether someone will respond better to one treatment or another
- Gene research and brain imaging studies to determine what happens in the brain when PTSD develops

Although the PTSD treatment practices reported by NIMH accurately reflect the approaches therapists are using in the U.S., some experts and professional organizations discount the need for an individualized approach and lobby vociferously for the exclusive use of cognitive behavioral therapies instead. Other experts argue the success claims about cognitive behavioral therapies for PTSD are grossly overstated, that they are no more effective than nontrauma therapies. To understand the nature of this debate, three factors significantly influencing the conduct of mental health research—the biomedical model, randomized controlled trials (RCTs), and evidence-based practices (EBPs)—are explored in Chapters 2 and 3.

CHAPTER 2

Policy Disputes in PTSD Research and Practice

While an academic Dean at Gallaudet University, I had occasion to mediate discussions between researchers and elementary classroom teachers engaged in cooperative studies. When it came to educational research, the two groups did not see eye to eye. Teachers believed they were in the best position to evaluate instructional approaches because "they knew what worked and what didn't." In their opinion, researchers (some of whom had never taught children) couldn't really understand classroom learning. And they objected to classroom disruptions caused by research procedures.

Researchers, on the other hand, were committed to closely following study protocols for the sake of reliable results. In their view, the benefits of research outweighed what they thought were minor classroom disruptions. They were more interested in procedures, data, statistics, and significant findings. The overriding concern of teachers was the welfare of their children. Conflict was inherent in the process, simply because the two groups had opposing perspectives about research and classroom learning. This kind of tension exists wherever groups with competing interests are involved in research. Friction of this sort has also been reported between researchers and mental health practitioners with regard to effective treatments for PTSD.

These role conflicts among professionals represent just one of many disputes associated with the research and treatment of trauma. Topics of disagreement easily identified by the reader of published research include:

- Arguments over what research methods should be used to evaluate mental health treatments (randomized controlled trials or a variety of research methods)
- Disagreements over whether biomedical remedies or psychotherapeutic treatments will produce better results
- Disputes over the validity of evidenced-based practices (EBPs) as defined in the PTSD treatment guideline enacted by the American Psychological Association
- The definition of effectiveness in PTSD research
- The most effective therapies for PTSD
- Whether research tested procedures or client-therapist factors contribute more to treatment outcomes
- Whether any particular trauma therapy can be judged more effective than others

In this chapter and the next, these controversies are examined from a therapist's point of view. Although this analysis is not intended as an exhaustive review of the trauma literature, it was nevertheless important to accurately reflect the theories, methods, and conflicts found in existing research and practice. This account begins with an analysis of a theoretical model confounding the conduct and interpretation of trauma treatment research—the biomedical model.

THE BIOMEDICAL MODEL – A BRAIN DISEASE THEORY OF MENTAL ILLNESS

Medical research and treatment practices have been guided for a century by sustained adherence to a theoretical paradigm known as the biomedical model. This concept of disease relies primarily on biological factors when diagnosing and treating illness, with little influence attributed to social and psychological factors.

The following is a definition of the model and its influence on psychological research reported by Deacon and McKay (2015):

> *The central tenet of the biomedical model is that psychological problems are literal diseases of the brain. This model has dominated mental health research, policy, and practice in the United States for more than three decades. During this time, federal agencies like the National Institute of Mental Health (NIMH) and the National Institute on Drug Abuse (NIDA) have focused their grant funding initiatives on biomedical research, medications have replaced psychosocial interventions as the modal treatment for psychological problems, "brain disease" and "chemical imbalance" explanations for mental disorders have been heavily prompted [sic] by the pharmaceutical industry and academic psychiatry, and the general public has come to regard mental disorders as diseases of the brain caused by biogenetic abnormalities* (p. 231).

Two examples will help elucidate the model's influence on current mental health research. The first appeared in a commentary by National Institute of Drug Abuse (NIDA) Director Nora Volkow (2016) when she declared: "addiction is not just 'a disease of the brain,' but one in which the circuits enabling us to exert free will no longer function as they should." Without free will, she alleges, addicts are incapable of choosing sobriety. Therefore, only treatments like medications that target the brain's faulty circuitry or compromised neurochemistry can resolve the problem at its source. Psychotherapeutic treatments like client-centered therapies, which do not directly address brain anomalies, miss the mark. However, there is no credible evidence to support this theory with regard to mental health disorders (Abramovitch & Schweiger, 2015).

With these beliefs guiding this agency, it's no surprise NIDA has supported biomedical investigations of brain function and pharmaceutical remedies, and not biopsychosocial research. In effect, psychotherapeutic approaches have been marginalized due to the influence of this paradigm.

The Director of NIMH (like his NIDA counterpart) also claims mental health problems are caused by defective brain circuitry. He refers to abnormal thoughts and behaviors associated with mental health problems as symptoms arising from malfunctions in the brain and not the result of behavioral or psychological factors (Insel, 2015). In the same editorial however, the director admits that no clinically useful information has been obtained from thousands of biomedical studies in search of mental health disorder biomarkers. Oddly, he uses evidence from this failure in biomedical research to justify the need for *more* biomedical research.

Deacon and McKay (2015) view the NIMH director's belief in brain disease as the cause of all mental health problems and his flat admission that brain studies have yielded no evidence in support of this proposition as "advancing incompatible claims." Strong objections to a biomedical focus in mental health research have been reported by several other investigators (Abramovitch & Schweiger, 2015; Kinderman, 2015; Lacasse & Leo, 2015; Moncrieff, 2015; Peele, 2015; Whitaker, 2015).

Other agencies and patient advocacy groups reflect the same brain disease thinking, among them the National Institute on Alcohol Abuse and Alcoholism (NIAAA), the National Alliance on Mental Illness (NAMI), the Depression and Bipolar Support Alliance (DBSA), and the organization known as Children and Adults with Attention Deficit/Hyperactivity Disorder (CHADD) (Deacon, 2013).

Deacon and McKay (2015) also chastise biomedical model proponents for predicting in 2005 that the future discovery of biomarkers for mental health disorders would revolutionize psychiatric treatment within 10 years. When that time had elapsed, not one biomarker had been identified. The authors further report the promised destigmatization of mental illness and predicted improvements in mental health outcomes from new pharmaceuticals had not materialized either. They call for a dialogue about the biomedical model because of its singular focus on the brain as the root of all mental health problems.

This steadfast assertion that brain abnormalities are the sole cause of all illness has undoubtedly swayed the course of mental health research. However, the allegation that social and psychological factors contribute little to the development of mental disorders is undermined both by logic and overwhelming evidence to the contrary from powerful epidemiological research like the ACE Study reported in Chapter 1 (Felitti et al., 1998).

RANDOMIZED CONTROLLED TRIALS – THE GOLD STANDARD CONTROVERSY

In addition to the biomedical model, one other force has significantly influenced the direction of mental health research and practice—the widespread use of a research method called randomized controlled trials (RCTs). For centuries medical scientists have promoted the development of objective, bias-free research techniques. Procedures like blind experimental studies, the use of treatment and control groups, and the development of more powerful statistical methods were adopted decades ago. By the beginning of the 20th century, the inclusion of these procedures in research protocols had become routine (Bothwell et al., 2016).

As reported by Bothwell (2014), a standardized approach called the randomized controlled trial (RCT) was introduced by British researcher Austin Bradford during the 1940s. When conducting RCT studies, subjects are randomly assigned either to an experimental group where they receive the treatment under investigation, or a control group where they receive no treatment, an alternate treatment, or a placebo. Group assignments are also balanced, based on race, age, gender, socioeconomic status, and other variables believed to affect results. By the beginning of the 21st century, the RCT was being referred to as the *gold standard* in medical research, even though several of its limitations had been well-documented (Bothwell et al., 2016).

Since its inception, the RCT has received mixed reviews. When it was introduced, concerns were expressed by some researchers about the generalization of RCT results. Ethical questions were also raised about the practice of withholding promising treatments from control groups. Although the RCT continues to be called the gold standard, its widespread use is nonetheless heavily criticized. And although RCTs have been favored by academics, researchers, and policy makers, this is not true of medical providers. In fact, evidence of this discrepancy in RCT support, based on professional role, has remained a constant in the literature over time and created a scientist versus practitioner mindset (Deacon, 2013), similar to the aforementioned teacher/researcher role conflict.

Nevertheless, RCT use rose dramatically in both medical and mental health research, due in part to a sharp increase in the number of new medications being evaluated and introduced (Bothwell et al., 2016). The method happens to be a very good fit for testing pharmaceuticals. This research model received even more support in 1970 when the Food and Drug Administration (FDA) issued a guidance recommending RCTs be used in all pharmaceutical trials (Carpenter, 2010).

Although well suited to drug evaluations, problems were encountered when the method was applied to other areas of medicine. Frieden (2017), the director of the Centers for Disease Control (CDC) during the Barack Obama administration, cites several "substantial limitations" of RCTs. In addition to complications encountered when the method is applied to disease outbreaks and psychological disorders, Frieden reports three other problems: they are expensive, the research takes years to complete, and the findings may not be valid beyond the populations studied.

Instead of endorsing RCTs as the gold standard, he argues the method's overall influence on medical practice has not been significant, given the fact that most modern clinical care is not based on RCT results and probably never will be. He contends that traditional research methods (e.g., observational studies using epidemiological information or patient case studies) produce equally sound data when compared to RCTs, but are actively discounted. He concludes there's no best method for collecting data to evaluate interventions, advising policy makers, researchers, and evidence grading systems to use other research methods in addition to RCTs.

Clay (2010) corroborates Frieden's concern about the generalization of RCT results, basing her objections on deficiencies in the method's representative sampling procedures. She also reports psychologist and researcher disagreement with the "one-size-fits-all mentality" of the procedure and criticizes the Food and Drug Administration (FDA) and National Institutes of Health (NIH) for using the gold standard label. Like other investigators, she recognizes the value of RCTs, as long as data from other methodologies are used to supplement findings.

Bothwell et al. (2016) also report RCT limitations, citing several of the same shortcomings noted by Frieden. They confirm RCTs have not been central to the production of new medical knowledge, arguing a scan of published research would support this contention. Like Frieden, the authors report RCTs are difficult to apply when evaluating health interventions other than pharmaceuticals. Most pertinent to the subject of this book, they conclude RCT evaluations of long-term psychological treatments are at least inappropriate, perhaps even impossible. And, like Frieden and Clay, they report other research methods (e.g., case reports and observational studies)—used alone or in combination with RCTs—are equally valid. They also caution researchers to avoid overapplication of the procedure.

When capping off concerns about the preponderant use of RCTs in research, Frieden (2017) concludes: "Glorifying RCTs above other approaches, even when these other approaches may be either superior or the only practical way to get an answer, relegates patients to receiving treatments that aren't based on the best available evidence." Although RCTs were created to reduce bias in research, these escalating disagreements about their applicability in many situations (particularly psychological studies) point to the need for policy reconsiderations.

As might be predicted from the information cited above, disputes about the gold standard status of RCTs in mental health research are rife, as are concerns that strict adherence to this policy may actually be harming clients. More specifically, assessing to what extent the use of RCTs may be adversely affecting PTSD treatment practices requires exploration of yet another topic: an outgrowth of RCTs, known by its buzz phrase *evidence-based practices* (EBPs).

ORIGINS OF EVIDENCE-BASED PRACTICES IN MENTAL HEALTH

The EBP movement in mental health had its origins in American Psychological Association (APA) committees in the 1990s. Organization pronouncements from that period declared only therapies demonstrating efficacy (significant *reductions* in symptoms based on RCT investigations) should be endorsed as evidence-based (McFall, 1991). In other words, a therapy could only be called evidence-based if randomized controlled trials showed it significantly *reduced* symptoms associated with a disorder. Therapies deemed successful based on other research methods could not be considered evidenced-based. Other research methods were thus deemed invalid for that purpose and disavowed.

The EBP movement in mental health was inspired by a similar initiative called evidence-based medicine (EBM) underway at the same time in general medicine. Both were efforts to base clinical practice on the most recent scientific evidence. The two movements may not have gained footing, however, had it not been for a young school of medicine faculty member who coined the catchphrase *evidence-based medicine* (Guyatt, 1991).

In a short history of that movement, Zimerman (2013) referenced a succinct definition of EBM (Sackett et al., 1996): "The conscientious, explicit, and judicious use of current best evidence in making decisions about the care of individual patients."

It appears the APA was attempting to mirror what was happening in the EBM movement by adopting RCTs as its own gold standard, and by designating EBPs as an extension of that policy. In so doing, the APA was aligning its own approach with the medical profession's research paradigm and standards. This affiliation with medical policy may even have been a conscious attempt to bring greater validity, respect, and authority to mental health investigations.

Ever since that APA decision established the EBP standard, RCT studies of trauma method effectiveness have also discounted the importance of interpersonal and therapeutic factors in determining PTSD treatment outcomes. These are, of course, two areas of particular interest to practicing therapists. Instead, the research became method-centered and shifted to the study of approaches considered more "quantifiable"—RCT-tested procedures drawn predominantly from cognitive behavioral theoretical models. This has been true even though other studies (to be discussed in Chapter 3) have found the most important factors contributing to PTSD treatment outcomes are not related to the method used.

At the same time, evidence-based policies have been just as controversial among mental health practitioners as they have been within the medical community, and for the same reasons.

Both well-intentioned and ill-advised, the focus on EBPs in mental health research has caused rifts within the APA and across the entire mental health profession. When RCT findings were used to declare certain PTSD therapies evidence-based—suggesting other methods were not—the results were vigorously contested.

Following an interview with the president-elect of the American Psychological Association in 2004, a *New York Times* journalist defined this controversy as a struggle over the very nature of psychotherapy: whether to view the patient-therapist relationship as important to treatment success, or to expect therapists to strictly follow RCT tested procedures (Carey, 2004). An example of the heated rhetoric from that time occurred when Tavris (2003) condemned practitioners who were resisting the large-scale adoption of evidence-based protocols based on RCTs. She rebuked psychotherapists for failing "to understand their own biases of perception," or "to test their own ideas empirically before running off to promote new therapies or wild claims" (p. 3). She even accused practitioners of "psychological warfare." What is most interesting is the fact that Tavris was reportedly reacting to Shapiro's development of EMDR!

In referencing McGlynn et al. (2003) and Goodman (2003), Tanenbaum (2005) notes how evidence-based authors denounced therapists for not using EBPs, calling them "uninformed" and "unethical" practitioners providing "inadequate clinical care." Statements like these have only fueled academic researcher versus mental health provider disputes over the escalating use of approved EBPs.

On the other hand, in referencing Chambless et al. (1996), Tanenbaum (2005) reveals evidence of bias in the EBP movement: "Findings favor the behavioral and cognitive psychotherapies, where technique is paramount and more easily codified in treatment manuals." RCT methodology has also been described as ill-suited to investigations of psychodynamic and humanistic psychotherapies, two approaches emphasizing patient-therapist relationships (Bohart et al., 1998). RCT research, by design, has been method-focused, without sufficient attention to relationship factors in the therapeutic process. Thus, from its outset, this methodological approach to mental health research has demonstrated bias in favor of treatments compatible with the RCT model—like an answer in search of the right questions.

This disharmony among researchers and practitioners has done nothing for those suffering from trauma. It has, however, demonstrated the need for meaningful collaboration between researchers and therapists and an unbiased research-to-practice model that ensures therapist participation. Only then will EBPs be better received by practicing therapists.

EVIDENCE-BASED PRACTICES – THREE CONTROVERSIES

In a compelling article exploring the EBP model, Tanenbaum (2005) describes how APA committees had originally "gone to war" over whether benefits derived from psychotherapy were due more to scientifically tested procedures or to certain client-therapist factors. The author identifies three controversial aspects of the EBP movement: 1.) how the term *evidence* is defined; 2.) disagreements over applications of research in clinical practice, and 3.) what the term *effective* treatment means. Her concern over the definition of evidence is straightforward. She questions whether the standard for determining treatment efficacy should be limited to RCT results, or whether practical clinical trials involving a variety of practice settings, diverse populations, and based on a broad range of health outcomes should also be an acceptable standard. The importance of practical clinical trials in making treatment decisions was also supported by Tunis et al. (2003). This controversy is at the heart of the overall dispute.

The second controversy concerns whether clinical practice in mental health can or should be restricted to research derived protocols, or whether the ability to modify procedures and individualize treatments to fit client needs should be honored. Tanenbaum argues research findings alone cannot determine with any certainty how to treat individual patients, regardless of scientific rigor. "Research pertains," she writes, but "the attempt to substitute research for discretion is futile." This belief parallels Carey's (2004) characterization of the controversy as a tug of war over who controls what happens in the therapy room. In the end, this struggle for dominance has raised a critical question: Do RCT tested procedures or client-therapist factors contribute more to client outcomes? This question frames the debate between RCT proponents and others who are convinced therapeutic factors contribute more to treatment success than the choice of method.

The third controversy concerns what *effectiveness* means and who should define the term. Tanenbaum reports the APA's Division 12 definition of EBP equates effectiveness with symptom relief (*reduction* in symptoms). Applying this definition to trauma treatment, effective PTSD therapies are those demonstrating more significant *reductions* in symptoms, but only if based on RCT results. Research findings from case studies or other research methods are not considered valid. In addition, broader outcomes, like complete symptom remission, improvements in quality of life, and patient satisfaction with treatment are viewed as less important. Symptom *reduction* becomes all-important in determining effectiveness, which is a narrow view of treatment success.

Ironically, however, Tanenbaum also reports treatments endorsed as effective based on RCT results often "produce only partial relief"—successful, but only marginally so. For example, although group mean scores in a study might show modest but statistically significant *reductions* in symptoms, many subjects could still qualify for a PTSD diagnosis! She draws a distinction between the terms *efficacy* (defined as *some* relief from symptoms) and *effectiveness* (e.g., when clients completing treatment no longer have PTSD or believe their remaining symptoms will be manageable going forward). This flaw in the model is the *Achilles heel* of the EBP movement.

And although the definition of EBP effectiveness is considered self-evident by the APA, it's determined largely by researchers without input from patients or practitioners. The notion that a group of researchers could determine ahead of time whether a treatment will be effective for an individual client is a *non sequitur* and ignores the pivotal role of therapist in the process. Nevertheless, efficacy and effectiveness are now used interchangeably in mental health discourse, agency policy manuals, legislation, and promotions for PTSD therapies.

Based on these and other concerns, Tanenbaum broadly questions whether translating research findings into clinical practice in the manner professed by EBP proponents is even viable. This problem, she concludes, could result in inadequate patient care by delegitimizing truly effective treatments and adversely affecting patient care, a prediction confirmed by Frieden (2017) 12 years later.

Although Tanenbaum's article was written in 2005, her portrayal of the EBP movement is by no means dated. Her analysis of the movement's controversies remains the clearest and most farsighted description of problems engendered when scientific procedures discount therapeutic factors in treatment. In mental health care, she argues, "turning research findings into clinical directives is fraught with difficulties." The extent to which these practices are affecting PTSD treatment and the problems encountered when research protocols dictate clinical practice must receive greater scrutiny.

THE PERVASIVENESS OF EVIDENCE-BASED PRACTICES

Despite these active and unresolved concerns over mandating EBPs based on RCT results, Tanenbaum warned how extensive the use of these practices might become when she wrote the following in 2005: "The policy train is leaving the station." Now, 30 years after the EBP movement's inception, its impact on mental health practice is well-known.

- In graduate education classes, professors emphasize the "practices"; certification and licensure exams test knowledge of the practices.
- Continuing education classes advertise the evidence-based characteristics of promoted programs.
- Insurance companies require the use of the practices in their contractual agreements with providers.
- National and international conferences limit presentations to EBP topics; and federal and state priorities, budgets, and grants all favor evidence-based themes.

By any measure, the RCT policy train is still on the move.

One example of the far-reaching impact of the EBP movement can be viewed in an advertisement for a cognitive behavioral therapy book about PTSD treatment, published by the APA (Monson & Shnaider, 2014): "Backed by decades of research, cognitive behavioral therapy is the intervention of choice for clients with post-traumatic stress disorder (PTSD), regardless of their age, gender, ethnicity, or source of symptoms." This declaration leaves little room for debate and has the backing of the premier psychological association in the country. Sweeping statements like this are quite common and, for the most part, unchallenged. They also contradict the position of NIMH regarding client treatment choice and the exploration of all therapeutic options, including client-centered therapies.

The PTSD Center of the U.S. Department of Veterans Affairs had always used the term *evidence-based practices* (EBPs) to describe the therapies it recommended for PTSD (Cognitive Processing Therapy, Prolonged Exposure, and EMDR)—until its PTSD Clinical Practice Guidelines (CPG) were revised in 2017 (Norman et al., 2020). Although the precise term EBPs is no longer used on its website, the same therapies are recommended for PTSD. And abandoning the term may have been a deliberate attempt to avoid the evidence-based practices disputes evident in the research literature. Nonetheless, the Center still recommends trauma-focused treatments that are evidence-based. Furthermore, the Center continues to advocate for manualized treatments, based on RCT results that use exposure and cognitive restructuring, the two main components of cognitive behavioral therapies. In other words, nothing of substance has changed at the Center with regard to evidence-based practices.

The American Psychological Association (2019) followed by developing its own PTSD practice guideline with strikingly similar recommendations. Three therapies were "strongly recommended" for use with adult patients with PTSD: cognitive behavioral therapy (CBT), cognitive processing therapy (CPT) and prolonged exposure (PE)—all of them considered cognitive behavioral therapies. Three other therapies were recommended on a conditional basis: brief eclectic therapy (BET), eye movement desensitization and reprocessing (EMDR), and narrative exposure therapy (NET). APA promises reconsideration will be given to the latter three therapies, pending further research. No other therapies warranted a recommendation.

In a blistering condemnation of the publication of this guideline, Shedler (2017) criticizes the APA for ignoring all scientific evidence except for studies using randomized controlled trials. Like Frieden (2017) and Bothwell et al. (2016), he concludes that most advances in science do not rely on RCT generated results. And after summarizing studies conducted by Schnurr et al. (2007) and Steenkamp et al. (2015) revealing cognitive behavioral therapy shortcomings, Shedler questions the truthfulness and ethics of the APA for strongly recommending these therapies. As evidence of his disdain for the PTSD guideline, he even advises patients and therapists to ignore the recommendations altogether.

The predominant use of RCTs in PTSD research and the EBP movement have radically altered mental health research and practice over the last 20 years. Cognitive behavioral approaches are now advertised as more effective than all other therapies. They are called "evidence-based" and "best practices" simply because they are based on RCT results. A million-dollar question begs a response: Do these therapies actually result in better client outcomes?

CHAPTER 3

Are Evidence-based Practices Really More Effective?

The umbrella term *cognitive behavioral therapies* describes a category of trauma methods cited frequently as the best bet for evidence-based PTSD treatment. Whether this is actually supported by available research is the subject of this chapter. The three most frequently recommended therapies in this category are cognitive processing therapy (CPT) (U.S. Department of Veterans Affairs, 2020c), cognitive behavioral therapy (CBT) (American Psychological Association, 2019) and prolonged exposure therapy (PE) (McSweeney et al., 2020). CBT, it's important to note, is a specific therapeutic method in its own rite, in addition to being considered one of several in the category of cognitive behavioral therapies. These therapies blend the use of techniques from cognitive as well as behavioral treatment methods, hence the name. They are also considered exposure therapies.

SYSTEMATIC DENSENSITIZATION AND EXPOSURE THERAPIES

The term *exposure*, as it relates to trauma interventions, refers to moments in therapy when clients are asked to talk or think about a traumatic experience. Exposure therapies employ the use of this technique throughout treatment, believing repeated, conscious focus on a traumatic experience will desensitize its effects. One cannot discuss exposure therapies without paying homage to Joseph Wolpe. The cognitive behavioral therapies described above all use adaptations of Wolpe's (1958) work on systematic desensitization (SD). This extensively researched, three-step procedure for overcoming anxiety was a precursor to several exposure therapies currently in use, including the ones mentioned in the previous paragraph.

In step one of SD, clients learn relaxation techniques to offset the negative reactions they will experience when exposed to a feared object or situation. Called *reciprocal inhibition*, this is a theory from behavioral psychology asserting that a relaxed body will weaken the link between a stimulus and its fear response. In the second step of SD, the client develops a graduated hierarchy of trauma-related objects or situations, starting with the least distressing and leading to the most distressing. And in the third step, while relaxation is encouraged, the client is repeatedly exposed to each feared object or situation, beginning with the least difficult, until all have been desensitized (Head & Gross, 2008). What is actually meant by "desensitized" varies, but in general, the goal is to bring an individual's reaction to a trauma-related stimulus into a manageable range.

Underlying SD itself, and trauma therapies employing this procedure, are two assumptions. The first is that multiple exposures to traumatic memories will be effective in diminishing client reactions to a feared event. The number of exposures is one reason these therapies require multiple sessions. In PE, for example, as many as fifteen 90-minute sessions are required to achieve a *reduction* in symptoms. The website of the Einstein Healthcare Network (2020) explains how weekly PE therapy for PTSD at their center continues for 12-15 sessions. This represents 18-22.5 patient contact hours, which necessitates a significant commitment of client time. In another example, a study from the Naval Center for Combat and Operational Stress Control (Abou & Goldwaser, 2010) reports fifteen 90-minute PE sessions are required to achieve PTSD symptom *reductions*.

Important note: Both of the references cited in the previous paragraph imply symptom reduction (as in the EBP definition) is synonymous with treatment success. However, this does not take into account broader outcomes, like client satisfaction with treatment, manageability of symptoms, or ruling out a PTSD diagnosis. The significance of this distinction when evaluating treatment success will become evident in this chapter.

A second assumption underlying SD is that exposure should begin with the least disturbing situation before working up the hierarchy. If, for example, a client develops a hierarchy of eight separate anxiety-generating situations resulting from a single trauma, and is exposed to each situation multiple times over several sessions, the total number of exposures could approach 50 or more! This takes time and, make no mistake, it's hard on clients. This is one reason why cognitive behavioral approaches using exposure require so many sessions—and why clients demonstrate resistance to these therapies.

Although SD is an empirically tested method proven to *reduce* symptoms (Corey, 2013; Cormier et al., 2013), it may not be the most efficient or effective in quieting physical responses to trauma, let alone the limbic reactions associated with PTSD discussed in Chapter 1. A specific concern from the client's point of view is the need to repeatedly re-experience the situation that caused the initial disturbance.

Cognitive behavioral therapies using SD principles normally supplement exposure with cognitive restructuring techniques. Cognitive Processing Therapy (CPT), for example, cited prominently as an effective treatment by the National Center for PTSD (Galovski et al., 2020), stimulates exposure by having clients repeatedly talk about trauma-related thoughts and then examine them for factual accuracy. In this way, cognitive restructuring is used to alter maladaptive thinking the clients formed after the trauma into adaptive thinking. A *reduction* in PTSD symptoms is sought through retellings of the trauma story as clients repeatedly confront the feared trauma-related event from the past. This is believed to activate the fear structures and provide an opportunity for PTSD symptoms to diminish. And this is believed to be another mechanism of recovery from PTSD (Gallagher & Resick, 2012; Resick et al., 2014).

Prolonged Exposure Therapy (PE), another approach using SD in its process, is also endorsed by the U.S. Department of Veterans Affairs (2020d). Key components of PE include education about the therapy, breathing instruction, and repeated first-person, out loud retellings of the trauma story with eyes closed. Here's how PE's use of graduated exposure via verbal retellings of trauma-related events is described on the Center's PTSD website: "PE works by helping you face your fears. By talking about the details of the trauma, and by confronting safe situations that you have been avoiding, you can decrease your symptoms of PTSD and regain more control of your life."

Although exposure therapies like these generally espouse a concern for client safety, in practice they tend to emphasize exposure over client comfort. This may be one cause of higher dropout rates, which are evident in the PTSD effectiveness studies discussed in the next section. Advocates of exposure therapies sometimes claim treatment will be more effective and durable if clients re-experience the full extent of the trauma's formation through deep, first-person reactivations. However, the extent to which this client distress is justified by the results is questionable and warrants further investigation.

van der Kolk et al. (2007) caution that "uncontrolled exposure" may cause adverse client effects. Survivors, who already demonstrate elevated levels of symptom avoidance, will naturally resist re-experiencing what happened to them. This also delays potential therapeutic benefits. The authors argue for a staged process instead, one respecting a victim's level of tolerance to exposure.

Rather than one standardized approach, these authors also recommend the use of different therapeutic techniques in combination, due to the multidimensional nature of PTSD. In suggesting this, they are essentially agreeing with the NIMH recommendation regarding the use of a variety of treatment options. Most therapists, they report, use an eclectic approach anyway, during which they regularly assess which interventions are most effective at reducing symptoms. Although cognitive behavioral therapies with exposure are recommended by the American Psychological Association and the PTSD Center as preferred trauma treatments, in this case, "most recommended" does not translate into easiest on the client or even most effective.

A CLOSER LOOK AT COGNITIVE BEHAVIORAL THERAPIES FOR PTSD

In order to evaluate claims of EBP effectiveness and cognitive behavioral therapy superiority, investigators have been looking beneath the surface of these pronouncements. In contrast to the findings of the National Center for PTSD, other researchers have reached very different conclusions concerning the publicized effectiveness claims about cognitive behavioral therapies.

A team of investigators at NYU's Langone Medical Center conducted a review of nine RCTs of the PTSD treatment of military subjects (Steenkamp et al., 2015). Five of the studies had investigated the efficacy of CPT and four the effects of PE. The NYU team's findings contrast sharply with reports from the APA and the National Center, due in part to different premises about what constitutes treatment effectiveness. Essentially, the NYU team questions whether modest but statistically significant improvements (*reductions*) in symptoms alone should be accepted as evidence of treatment effectiveness. Stated in the form of a question: When a group of subjects demonstrates symptom improvement, but the majority of them still have PTSD following treatment, how can this information justify superior effectiveness claims? This is the same efficacy versus effectiveness distinction raised by Tanenbaum in her 2005 article.

Although the NYU team confirmed the randomized controlled studies of PE and CPT with military personnel and vets did show "clinically meaningful" improvements for many, they argue subject nonresponse rates were high and, more importantly, approximately two-thirds of the subjects still had a PTSD diagnosis following treatment. Based on these findings, CPT and PE were judged only "marginally superior" when compared with nontrauma psychotherapies. In a separate commentary, the study's lead author added: "Our findings showed that PE and CPT are not as broadly effective as we might have once thought or hoped... As many as two-thirds of veterans receiving PE or CPT keep their diagnosis after treatment, even if their symptoms improve" (Steenkamp, 2015).

Because CPT and PE were deemed less effective than previously claimed, the NYU team called for improvements in current PTSD treatments, and the development and evaluation of new trauma and nontrauma related therapies. When coupled with the fact that the NIMH and van der Kolk also recommend avoiding a one-size-fits-all approach, this evidence calls into question the judiciousness of labeling any therapy an "intervention of choice" or recommending EBP use until and unless new findings are reported in the literature.

van der Kolk (2015), considered a leader in the research and treatment of PTSD, continues to argue for a more flexible approach to trauma treatment in a more recent book. In a review of multiple research studies, he presents unfavorable information about cognitive behavioral therapy dropout rates and short- and long-term treatment effectiveness. In two studies, only about one-third of the subjects who completed treatment had improved (Ford & Kidd, 1998; Bradley et al., 2005). A large meta-analysis of 38 separate studies found that although subjects who completed cognitive behavioral treatment had fewer PTSD symptoms, complete recovery was rare (Bisson et al., 2007). Bisson and her colleagues recommend that future research include well-designed, comparative studies of one type of treatment versus another, along with different treatments used in combination. This is what Bisson and her colleagues wrote about intense exposure during treatment:

> *Future trials should consider adverse events and tolerability of treatments in more detail. Our results suggest that several of the currently available treatments might benefit from modifications that would make them more acceptable to people with chronic PTSD and possibly also more effective (pp.102-3).*

In a large Veterans Administration study (Seal et al., 2010), less than 10% of 49,425 subjects with PTSD attended all nine recommended exposure therapy sessions over a 15-week period, evidence of an extremely high noncompletion rate. An inadequate level of safety during exposure may have been one reason. Exposure therapy patients are expected to talk about their traumatic experiences in detail, over and over, session after session, until symptoms are *reduced*. This requirement triggers arousal reactions in need of greater regulation during treatment. The danger of overexposure continues to be a concern, with evidence showing elevated attrition rates are one result.

A large study of CBT use with PTSD patients conducted by Schnurr et al. (2007) reported 38% of the subjects in the study dropped out, only 15% were symptom-free after treatment, and three months later most of the subjects still had full-blown PTSD. In commenting on these and other results, van der Kolk concludes CBT is only as effective as a supportive therapeutic relationship, corroborating the finding of Steenkamp and her colleagues.

The cited study by Bisson et al. (2007) and another by Benish et al. (2007) found no single PTSD approach performs better than any other, and that trauma and nontrauma therapies are equally effective. Even though the nontrauma therapies did not use exposure techniques and did not directly target traumas, they were nevertheless judged just as effective! These findings bolster the conclusions reached by van der Kolk (2015), Steenkamp et al. (2015), and Miller, Hubble, et al. (2013) that all therapies are equally effective treatments for PTSD.

The 1992 APA decision to recommend the use of RCTs in all mental health studies greatly influenced the conduct of PTSD research and spurred the EBP movement. While these actions were intended to instill greater scientific rigor and less bias in mental health research, they appear to have made matters worse. Explicit claims of superior treatment outcomes for cognitive behavioral therapies are based primarily on RCT results. However, meta-analyses of years of RCT studies have now determined these therapies are no more effective than nontrauma approaches.

PSYCHOTHERAPEUTIC FACTORS AND TREATMENT EFFECTIVENESS

So, if the choice of therapy does not significantly contribute to treatment outcomes, what does? In two studies, investigators found variables called common factors, not the choice of therapy, were more strongly related to treatment outcomes than the method used. Secure therapeutic alliances, treatment planning, psychoeducation about a disorder, empathy, and high expectations were among the factors accounting for greater symptom improvement (Wampold et al., 2010; Miller, Hubble, et al., 2013).

Wampold and Imel (2015) reported treatments tested in clinical settings are also just as effective as those using procedures derived from randomized controlled trials. This finding presents even more evidence that RCTs should not be called the gold standard for PTSD. The same study confirms the manner in which treatments are conveyed—client-therapist factors—contribute much more to outcomes than the method used. Given these results, Wampold and Imel conclude that efforts to mandate the use of particular PTSD therapies are both "illogical and unwise."

THE PATH FORWARD

Considering the sum of evidence, as well as the contradictions apparent in the research literature, statements that cognitive behavioral therapies are the treatments of choice for PTSD should be withdrawn. There is mounting evidence the effectiveness claims about these therapies are distorted and exaggerated. Reductions in symptoms are modest at best, repeated exposures to traumatic events turn survivors away, and the recovery trajectory of many is painfully slow. The best practice therapies for trauma are turning out to be no better than nontrauma methods.

The evidence used to endorse these approaches is no longer defensible. Given recent meta-analyses of years of RCT research, the claims may even be misleading. At the least, the superiority claims of cognitive behavioral therapies and the very concept of EBPs should be investigated. Can the mental health profession continue to endorse EBP methods resulting in elevated dropout rates, low remission rates, and marginally superior reductions in PTSD symptoms when compared to other therapies? I think not.

On a policy level, reviews should be conducted to determine whether the APA's definition of treatment efficacy is objectively flawed and in need of revision. By defining efficacy merely as symptom relief, studies of PTSD therapeutic effectiveness are ignoring other critical effectiveness indicators, like completion of treatment, client satisfaction, and symptom remission. Future research should pay careful attention to: a.) dropout rates; b.) the percentage of subjects achieving symptom *remission* versus symptom *reduction* in the short and long term; c.) differences in treatment effectiveness between cognitive behavioral methods and emerging therapies; and d.) the long-term effectiveness of all trauma therapies used on their own or in combination with other approaches.

Finally, as recommended by several researchers referenced in this chapter, it's time to study and advance safer, more effective, short-term PTSD treatment approaches, especially ones that can address the limbic anomalies associated with trauma. It's time for the profession to re-examine its assumptions about trauma treatment and to promote more honest discussions of current and emerging methods. To build on Tanenbaum's metaphor, it's also time to call the train back to the station; it's time to approach the study of PTSD with greater integrity.

This is not the settled science many have claimed. Cognitive behavioral therapies are not the most effective treatments for PTSD. The contradictions evident in the research literature are what cause practitioners to reject the legitimacy of EBP superiority claims. And these discrepancies will only enflame the controversy going forward, until and unless the questions are resolved with data as opposed to rhetoric. For reasons which will become clear in Part II of this book, MEMI is one of those promising options.

PART II

MEMI History and Development

"Traumatized people chronically feel unsafe inside their bodies: The past is alive in the form of gnawing interior discomfort. Their bodies are constantly bombarded by visceral warning signs, and, in an attempt to control these processes, they often become expert at ignoring their gut feelings and in numbing awareness of what is played out inside. They learn to hide from their selves." (p.97)

—Bessel A. van der Kolk
*The Body Keeps the Score: Brain, Mind,
and Body in the Healing of Trauma*

CHAPTER 4

The First Two Eye Movement Therapies

According to Shapiro (1989), the inspiration for the first eye movement therapy was as serendipitous as the 1928 discovery by Alexander Flemings that penicillin was growing in his lab's untended petri dishes. However, a review of research conducted during the 1970s reveals the creation of eye movement therapies was, in all likelihood, more than happenstance. The genesis of these revolutionary techniques can best be understood when viewed through the lens of two endeavors—eye movement research and groundbreaking developments in the Neuro-Linguistic Programming (NLP) field.

BRAIN RESEARCH – SPRINGBOARD FOR EYE MOVEMENT THERAPIES

A century before the creation of eye movement therapies, the relationship between ocular movements and human experience had already become a subject of speculation. In the late 19th century, William James (1890), known as the father of psychology, proposed that eye movements were associated with thoughts and the processing of sensory information. It's a wonder his observations were not examined more thoroughly before the relationship between eye movements and brain hemisphere activation was investigated in the 1970s. Studies of the eye's anatomy and function had been conducted, but the relationship between eye movements and brain processing had not been meaningfully explored.

In a cluster of studies in the 1970s, subjects were asked questions designed to activate the right or left hemisphere of the brain. Of interest was whether activation of either hemisphere would be accompanied by observable eye movements. Taken as a whole, three related studies confirmed eyes move in the opposite direction of (contralateral to) the brain hemisphere processing the information. When the left hemisphere is processing tasks, the studies report, the eyes move to the right. When the right brain is doing the processing, the eyes move to the left (Kinsbourne, 1972; Kocel et al., 1972; Galin & Ornstein, 1974).

The study by Kocel and her colleagues was conducted at Langley Porter Neuropsychiatric Institute in San Francisco. While the results did confirm the eyes of subjects moved contralaterally to the brain hemisphere processing the information, the study was interesting for another reason. Diagonal eye movements (a combination of horizontal and vertical) were also accepted as valid indicators of contralateral hemisphere activation, based on whether they moved left or right. A diagonal eye movement from a subject's lower right to the upper left, for example, would only be recorded as a left-directed lateral eye movement. Any differences that might exist between diagonal and vertical eye movements were not investigated.

Kinsbourne (1972), in addition to confirming opposite hemisphere activation, concluded right-handed subjects usually turn their eyes and head to the right when processing verbal problems. When solving numerical and spatial problems, subjects look up and left. However, left-handed subjects performed differently "in all these respects" (p. 539).

The Galin and Ornstein study (1974) was interesting in yet another respect. The eye movements of subjects were scored in vertical *and* horizontal directions. When subjects were asked hemisphere specific questions, verbal questions elicited more downward eye movements and more right-directed movements than spatial questions.

The cumulative results of these studies of left and right eye movements and brain hemisphere activation yielded preliminary evidence that eye movements might play a more dynamic role in information processing than just contralateral hemispheric activation. And that is what James was contemplating in 1890.

NEURO-LINGUISTIC PROGRAMMING EYE MOVEMENT MODEL

In 1976, Robert Dilts was enrolled in a Syntax 100 class taught by John Grinder, one of the cofounders of Neuro-Linguistic Programming (NLP). Grinder gave the class an assignment to select a behavior of their own that they had not paid much attention to in the past, create a name for it, and decide how their experience of it then changed. It seems that the purpose of Grinder's assignment was to move his students' perception of their behaviors from unconscious to conscious awareness. Giving an unconscious behavior a name draws conscious attention to it.

Dilts asked his instructor for clarification about the assignment. Here is how Grinder replied: "What about that? Your eyes just moved to the side." Dilts (2006) later explained his reaction to Grinder's suggestion in the following way:

> *As soon as I became aware of the movement, I remember being cognizant that I had "gone inside" and had been thinking about something that was just below my conscious awareness. I gave this phenomenon the name of something like "unconscious cuing." From that moment it was as if scales fell from my eyes and I suddenly became aware of all the things people did unconsciously to cue themselves: blinking their eyes, touching their faces, looking to different locations, making little gestures, noises, and facial expressions, etc.*

That conversation must have triggered something in Dilts, because the following year he conducted a seminal eye movement study of his own at Langley Porter Institute. He was most likely familiar with Kocel's eye movement study, as her investigation was also conducted at Langley Porter. However, the research Dilts undertook was broader in scope than the three brain hemisphere investigations described in this chapter.

Whereas previous studies were primarily interested in hemisphere lateralization, Dilts hypothesized that eye movements are not random but purposeful, and movements to specific locations in one's visual field (e.g., upper left or lower right) correlate with the type of neurosensory information being processed internally. Subjects were asked questions designed to stimulate the processing of visual, auditory, or kinesthetic information and electrodes were used to track subjects' eye movements and brain hemisphere activations. One can understand how the topics under investigation in this study were logical extensions of the earlier research. For example, Dilts and his NLP cohort must have been intrigued by the Galin and Ornstein finding that verbal questions elicited more downward and right-directed eye movements.

Results from the Dilts study confirmed that eye movements to the left and right occur in tandem with contralateral brain hemisphere activation. But more importantly, the results also confirmed that eye movements to particular locations in the visual field correlate with the simultaneous mental processing of individual sensory modalities (visual, auditory, and kinesthetic). Eye movements up and to a corner, for instance, correlate with the mental processing of visual information. Eye movements out to either side on the horizon are an indication of auditory information processing. These findings led to the development of the NLP eye movement model (Bandler & Grinder, 1979; Dilts et al., 1980) depicted in *Figure 4.1*. Although Dilts is often credited with discovering the eye accessing positions depicted in the model, he credits Grinder and Bandler with the initial coding of the eye movements in relation to the neurosensory information being processed by the brain (Dilts, 2006).

NLP Eye Movement Model

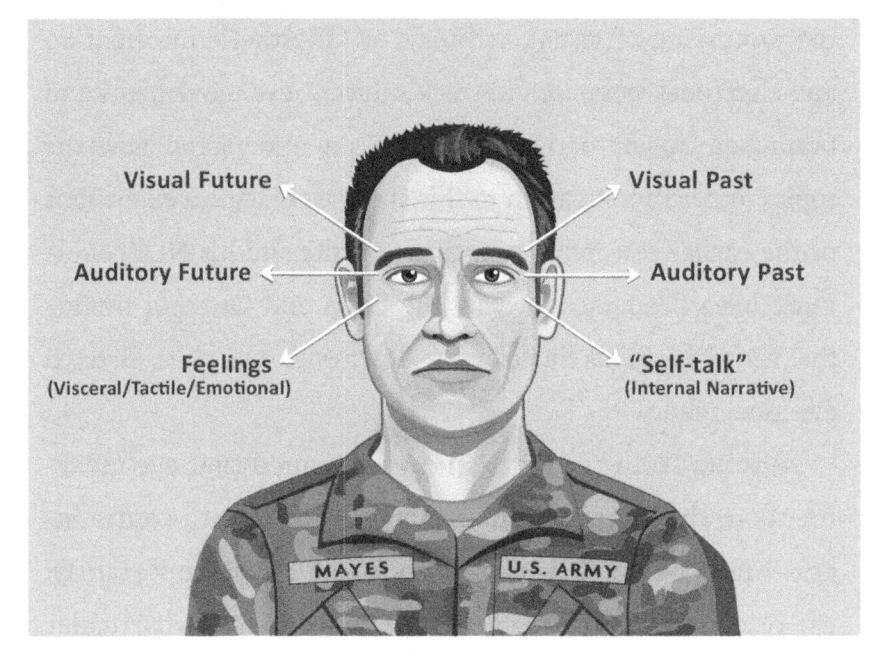

Figure 4.1

The model specifies that eyes moving up and to a subject's left, above the horizon, indicate visual information from the past is being processed (an image of a recent car accident or a mathematics problem). This result appears consistent with the Kinsbourne (1972) finding confirming eyes move up and left when solving numerical problems. Eyes moving up and to the right indicate the processing of future or imagined visual information (an image of an upcoming sailing trip, or envisioning a yellow dinosaur with purple stripes).

In a similar left-right orientation, if eyes move left on the horizon, past auditory information is likely being processed (recalling the sound of a gunshot during a recent home invasion). Eyes moving to the right on the horizon indicate imagining or mentally constructing auditory information one has not yet heard (anticipating the sounds of an upcoming rock concert or constructing what one will say next). This may be consistent with Galin and Ornstein's (1974) finding confirming verbal questions result in more right-directed eye movements. When thinking about (constructing) what to say next, eyes frequently dart to the right and back again. The eyes of individuals being interviewed on television will often move quickly to the right and back to center when they are formulating what to say next, especially if they're responding to an unanticipated question.

When eyes move down to the left, it's an indication a person is talking to themselves, also known as internal narrative or *self-talk*. Because a downward glance was reported by Galin and Ornstein in response to verbal questions, the respondents in that study could have been engaging in self-talk. Eyes traveling down to the right indicate the processing of *Feelings*: emotions (sadness, anger, or fear), tactile feelings (a touch on the cheek), or visceral feelings (a pain in one's side).

Dilts and DeLozier (2000) report these patterns are consistent for right-handed people. Left-handers sometimes have the left-right orientations for visual and auditory processing reversed. Further, a small number of ambidextrous or right-handed people will reverse some, but not all, of the individual patterns. Kinsbourne (1972) also reports a difference in habitual eye movements for right- and left-handed subjects.

Springer and Deutsch (1993) reported similar patterns for hemispheric language dominance. Right-handers have left-hemisphere dominance for language processing in 95% of the cases. Left-handers have left hemisphere dominance in 61% of the cases, right-hemisphere dominance 19% of the time, and another 20% process language in both hemispheres. They also reported language dominance in ambidextrous people is generally similar to left-handed people. No direct comparisons can be made between this study and the Dilts investigation. However, when the findings of all these studies are considered as a whole, results for handedness, language dominance, and eye movements show noteworthy similarities.

The NLP eye movement model was tested in a study by Tomason, Arbuckle, and Cady (1980), who reported the model's hypothesis was not supported by the results. Although they did find the eye movements in response to sensory specific questions are not random, they were unable to validate the eye locations depicted in the NLP model. Perhaps in response, Dilts (1983) suggested future studies of the NLP model should videotape subjects and seek to determine the specific sensory modality activated at the time of the eye movements.

In a commentary rebutting the findings of Tomason and his colleagues, Beck and Beck (1984) recommended a "proper" test of the NLP model that would include modality specific stimulus questions, videotaped observations of the eye movements, and follow-up process questions to determine the sensory modality in use at the time. Beck and Beck also discounted the rejection of the NLP model by Tomason's research team, arguing that they misunderstood the model.

The suggestions for future research proposed by Dilts and Beck and Beck were incorporated into a study conducted by Buckner (Buckner et al., 1987). The results strongly confirmed the existence of four observable eye movements—those associated with the auditory and visual modalities. However, trained observers were unable to correctly identify kinesthetic processing from subjects' eye movements. The inability to identify the kinesthetic modality could suggest a shortcoming in the model. It's also possible the kinesthetic process is more complex than originally thought, as Bandler has contended (1985a). The internal narrative location of the model was not tested.

Eye movements to the kinesthetic (Feelings) location usually indicate the processing of only two of the three modalities anyway—visceral, and emotional feelings. Tactile sensations are also categorized as feelings, even though they are most often considered a sensory modality and not a feeling. In my clinical experience, tactile feelings during trauma recall occur very infrequently when compared to the other two feeling modalities.

In the NLP model, the eye location for feelings in right-handers is down and to a person's right. Identifying potentially three different Feelings-related modalities at the same location creates complications not found with eye movements to the visual or auditory locations. I agree with Bandler that this eye location and its functions are more complex than the others. The inability of trained observers to identify the specific modality (visceral, emotional, or tactile) from eye movements reported by Buckner and his colleagues may be due to these complications. Additional research is needed to understand the role of eye movements in accessing the kinesthetic modalities.

Even though the NLP model was only partially corroborated by Buckner's research, this does not diminish the pivotal importance of the Dilts study. First, the occurrence of observable eye movements in tandem with auditory and visual processing was confirmed. Second, despite incomplete validation of the model, the research established a functional eye movement and sensory processing paradigm with continuing relevance. This is the important conclusion to be drawn from the studies described in this section.

THE INTRODUCTION OF EMDR

According to Shapiro (1989), the inspiration for eye movement desensitization and reprocessing (EMDR) came while she was visiting a park in 1987. She noticed distressing thoughts she was having were "suddenly disappearing and not returning." After self-reflection and experimentation, she concluded this effect was the result of automatic and multisaccadic eye movements occurring simultaneously. This brief description left a lot to the imagination. In a retelling of the story, Marich (2011) described Shapiro's eyes that day as "moving in a rapid, diagonal fashion" (p. 41).

After experiencing the multisaccadic eye movements, and how her negative reactions associated with her thoughts had diminished, experiments Shapiro later conducted led her to conclude others shared her experience, and that rapid, saccadic eye movements while thinking about distressing memories had a desensitizing effect (Shapiro, 1989; EMDR Institute, 2020a). Following this experience, she created the eye movement desensitization (EMD) procedure, the precursor to EMDR.

I was curious about Shapiro's actual eyes movements on that day in the park. Were they truly automatic, as in unconscious? Or was she intentionally testing what effect they might have? Did they go back and forth between the same two points, or travel to and from multiple points? If they rotated between the same two points repeatedly, how many times? Was there a sequence or pattern to the movements? Was the speed faster than usual, or did her eyes move normally, like when you're just thinking about something? Did they approximate the patterns in the NLP eye movement model? Diagonal means in a direction from corner to corner. Which corners? I had a lot of questions. To my knowledge, Shapiro never gave a full account of the eye movement directions, locations, or patterns from that day, so there is no way to analyze what actually happened. You would think so profound an event would be recalled and documented in greater detail.

Given her experience in the park, I also wondered how and why Shapiro chose the two bilateral eye movements she later used in her experimental procedure. As reported in her first journal article, subjects were instructed to follow the therapist's finger as it moved rapidly back and forth once each second. The first pattern was a horizontal movement at about eye level. The second pattern was a diagonal movement from the subject's lower right (beginning at about chin level) to the upper left (rising to eyebrow level). Each pattern was repeated 10-20 times and performed 12-18 inches from the subject's face (Shapiro, 1989).

It's also interesting to note the relationship between EMD's diagonal saccades and the NLP eye movement model, particularly the beginning and end points of the saccades. In the NLP model, a subject's lower right is where visceral and emotional feelings are accessed. A subject's upper left is where past visual information is accessed. Again, in my experience, the three variables (visual imagery, and emotional and visceral feelings) accessed at these locations are the most active correlates in the persistence of traumatic memories. When strategically targeted with eye movements, they are also the most successful avenues to desensitization. So, choosing these locations as the bilateral end points for EMDR's two saccades was advantageous, whether by chance or intention.

EMDR CONTROVERSIES

Because Shapiro's method was unrelated to previous models or lines of research, the psychological community reacted unfavorably to EMDR following its introduction. When Shapiro also theorized that trauma symptoms were caused by imbalances in the neural networks of the brain, critics dismissed the suggestion as fanciful, uninformed, and unsubstantiated. The neuronal imbalance claim could have related, in some sense, to prior studies of hemisphere activation and contralateral eye movements, if Shapiro had made that connection. However, even though she claimed bilateral stimulation was the principal mechanism restoring neuronal balance in the brain, no hemisphere lateralization eye movement studies were referenced in her first research article. In response to her supposition that EMDR's saccadic eye movements were the vehicle achieving bilateral stimulation, researchers leveled pointed criticisms in presentations and psychological journals (Herbert et al., 2000; Tavris, 2003).

Several years before Shapiro's epiphany in the park about rapid eye movements and distressing memories, the role of eye positions in diminishing reactions to negative experiences was a topic being explored in NLP seminars. Workshops in the early 1980s featured exercises involving the visualization of troublesome personal memories and the use of eye movements to alter reactions to them. Participants were instructed to use their eyes to move an image of a memory from directly in front of them to different locations in their visual field—upper left, lower right, etc., and to hold the image there. When asked to observe how moving the image to a new location altered their perceptions of and responses to the memory, participants reported the change resulted in less intense reactions (R. Klein, personal communication, March 16, 2016). Andreas and Andreas (2015) also confirmed this technique had been part of NLP trainings long before EMDR's introduction.

This training activity—using one's eyes to move an image of a memory—foreshadowed the eye movement therapies yet to come. Although the eye movement exercises in NLP trainings were self-directed and did not follow the movement of an object, one can easily see the relationship between that eye movement exercise in NLP trainings and the standardized eye movement techniques that followed.

Unknown to many, Shapiro had worked as an assistant to NLP cofounder John Grinder years prior to developing EMDR. As an associate of Grinder, she would have received information about NLP's founding presuppositions, the usefulness of pattern interruptions, and test-retest procedures. She also would have been exposed to the NLP eye movement model, as well as emerging NLP strategies for resolving phobias and traumatic experiences, like visual kinesthetic dissociation (S. Andreas & C. Andreas, personal communication, March 6, 2016). Because the NLP eye movement model was published in 1979, its introduction preceded Shapiro's 1987 inspiration in the park by almost a decade. Shapiro must also have learned

NLP's principal theory that all human experience has a structure composed of thoughts, feelings (emotional, visceral, and tactile), and sensory information (visual and auditory). And she probably learned that reactions to difficult memories can be tempered simply by moving an image of the experience from one location to another. Many in the NLP community were infuriated when Shapiro (2001) later added emotions and associated physical symptoms—two basic components of the NLP theoretical model—to EMDR procedures without crediting the model's developers.

This controversy rose to a new level in 2002, when in an online forum about his recently published book, Grinder recounted a conversation he'd had with Shapiro while she was working in his office in the early 1980s. His exact written comments in that forum were later reported by Fredericks (2011) on her professional website and reposted recently by Carroll (2020) on John Grinder's Facebook page:

> *Francine Shapiro worked (administration and sales) in the Santa Cruz offices of Grinder, DeLozier and Associates in the '80s. She approached me one day and told me that a friend of hers from New York has [sic] been raped and she wanted to help her through this trauma and ensure that she exited cleanly and without scars. I told Francine to put her in a resourceful state (anchored) and have her systematically move her eyes through the various accessing positions typical of the major representational systems (with the exception of the kinesthetic*

access). I suggested that she see, hear (but not feel) the events in question—obviously the kinesthetic were to remain resourceful (the anchored state) while she processed the event. She later reported that the work had been successful. You may imagine my surprise when I later learned that she had apparently turned these suggestions into a pattern presented in an extended training, with no reference to source, with a copyright and a rather rigorous set of documents essentially restricting anyone trained in this from offering it to the rest of the world.
John Grinder

It appears Shapiro did not respond to Grinder's accusation at the time. However, the controversy did resurface when Grimley (2014), in response to an EMDR article by Logie (2014a) published in *The Psychologist*, questioned the ethical integrity of the EMDR community, given the therapy's use of NLP strategies without appropriate sourcing. In his letter to the editor of the journal, Grimley also referenced Grinder's account of the instructions he gave Shapiro about how to help her friend as further evidence. This time, however, there was a response. In the next issue of the periodical, Logie (2014b) refuted Grinder's claim and reported that in a personal communication Shapiro insisted "no such conversation ever took place." I leave the reader to decide what transpired between Grinder and Shapiro. It's unlikely there will be further clarification. Francine Shapiro passed away in 2019.

Nevertheless, Shapiro insisted the development of her new procedure was unrelated to any knowledge she acquired while associated with the NLP working group. This generated a strong reaction from the NLP training community at the time of EMDR's introduction; her actions were considered unethical. At least one NLP trainer challenged her publicly at a conference, accusing her of not referencing the NLP model for techniques used in EMDR (R. Klein, personal communication, March 16, 2017).

These criticisms from the NLP and psychological communities were probably what prompted Shapiro to later develop a complex information processing system in defense of the therapy, essentially retrofitting a new theoretical model onto an unsubstantiated practice. The adaptive information processing (AIP) model began as a working hypothesis to explain her discovery, but was later developed into a full-fledged theory with the same name. Among the weighty topics included in Shapiro's model were personality development, the genesis of psychological abnormalities, the nature of psychotherapy, and EMDR's role in treatment (Shapiro, 1995; Shapiro & Forrest, 1997; Shapiro, 2001; Shapiro, 2002). The assertion that this theory was added in response to the controversy over EMDR's introduction was confirmed by Marich (2011):

One of the early criticisms of EMDR is that it was atheoretical. Shapiro proposed the AIP model, which evolved into the adaptive information processing model, as foundational support for her discovery (p. 48).

The EMDR Institute website (2020b) carries a simpler characterization of the theory. It describes a system composed of interconnected neurological networks of associated thoughts, emotions, images, and sensory information. Except for the contention that trauma-related sensory information is lodged in maladaptive neurological networks, the website's description is strikingly similar to those found in NLP models more than a decade before EMDR was introduced.

Several years after Shapiro developed this information processing system, Lilienfeld and Arkowitz (2020) further derided the therapy in a commentary. Based on evidence available at the time, they contended EMDR's mechanism of change was not the eye movements as claimed, but the technique's repeated exposure to disturbing events. This, they charged, was the same mechanism used in cognitive behavioral trauma therapies. Therefore, there was "nothing new with EMDR, and what was new did not work" (p. 81). They also ridiculed the theories circulated by EMDR proponents as reasons for the therapy's success, referring to them as "explanations in search of a phenomenon" (p. 81).

Ironically, however, the authors also paid EMDR an unwitting compliment when they wrote: "Yet not a shred of good evidence exists that EMDR is superior to exposure-based treatments that behavioral and cognitive-behavioral therapists have been administering routinely for decades" (p. 81). While this statement was meant to denigrate EMDR for not performing any better than exposure therapies, performing just as well was quite an accomplishment! A more objective and fair-minded analysis would have described the therapies as equally effective. In deriding EMDR, they were undoubtedly defending the decades-old and extensively researched exposure therapy industry. But they were also being forced to acknowledge the effectiveness of this new therapy, in spite of its perceived flaws.

One year earlier, a meta-analysis of the comparative effects of EMDR and cognitive behavioral therapy (CBT) in the treatment of PTSD had found the therapies were equally efficacious (Seidler & Wagner, 2006). These authors cautioned that future research should be conducted using randomized controlled trials, a signal the studies in the meta-analysis were considered inferior because they were not "evidence-based." Over time, however, EMDR would be proven effective whenever comparisons with other therapies were investigated.

In a systematic review of all research from the therapy's inception, including 87 studies and several meta-analyses, Landin-Romero et al. (2018) found that EMDR demonstrated equal or higher PTSD efficacy when compared to medication and other trauma approaches. They conclude that the evidence for EMDR's effectiveness is strong, even though descriptions of how it works remain controversial. Cognitive and behavioral enthusiasts are now forced to reckon with these findings showing EMDR on par with exposure therapies. As proof of this assertion, in 2018 the National Center for PTSD listed

EMDR, prolonged exposure (PE), and cognitive processing therapy (CPT) as the three "most effective" trauma-focused psychotherapies for PTSD (Norman et al., 2020).

EMDR has achieved commercial success in spite of its dubious theoretical foundation and steep learning curve. Despite its demonstrated effectiveness, even prominent advocates of the therapy have criticized its complexity. Marich (2011) states that EMDR is ". . . still largely regarded as too complicated to understand." In her how-to publication, *EMDR Made Simple: 4 Approaches to Using EMDR with Every Client*, she attempts to remedy the therapy's confusing protocol and procedures. It appears, however, that in an effort to make EMDR simple, the author may have added new complications of her own.

In my own training and experience, I have learned EMDR's complexities have caused a significant subset of trained practitioners to abandon the use of the therapy, or to only use EMDR's eye movements and other aspects of the methodology but ignore several parts of its protocol. As a respected EMDR colleague of mine once observed, "There's the standardized eight-phase EMDR model and its many adaptations, and then there's real life!" As a practitioner of EMDR and a trainer of MEMI, in my professional opinion, EMDR's success can be attributed to the eye movements themselves and several other techniques drawn from NLP and its eye movement model.

At the same time that EMDR was introduced, a pair of NLP innovators created a second eye movement therapy, one true to NLP principles, procedures, and its eye movement model. My goal, some three decades after the introduction of these two therapies, is to bring forward a new, easy-to-learn, but even more effective eye movement therapy based on an uncomplicated, NLP-based theoretical model.

EYE MOVEMENT INTEGRATION (EMI)
— AN NLP-BASED MODEL

The same year the EMD article was published, Connirae Andreas heard of Shapiro's work with back and forth eye movements to help diminish trauma symptoms. Although it made sense from an NLP perspective, she believed EMDR was flawed because it did not direct eye movements to all the accessing positions in the NLP model. Encouraged by her husband, Steve, to explore this theory, Connirae found her first willing subject in the person of their house cleaner that same day. In her words:

> *I asked him to think of a situation where he was unresourceful.*
>
> *"That's easy," he said, and he immediately looked unresourceful to me, too.*
>
> *Then I asked him to think of this situation as he allowed his gaze to follow my index finger, and to notice what happened in his experience. I started with the left-right on the horizon eye movement that Shapiro was using.*
>
> *When I asked for a report, he said, "Mild change, but not much."*

Then I began including all the other eye directions (e.g., I guided him in moving his eyes back and forth; up left to up right; up right to down left; up left to down left; straight left to up right, etc.). After each set of movements, I paused to ask what, if anything, had shifted in his experience. What happened was that with each new direction of eye movements, he appeared to be more resourceful.

Some directions seemed to make much more of a difference than others, but for him, each direction added at least a little something. I don't remember his exact comments any longer, but they were generally statements like, "When I think of the image, it's more in color now," or "Now I feel more relaxed," or "This time some ideas started to come to me for what to do." The changes had to do with how he literally saw things, how he felt, and his ability to access creative ideas.

So, this quickly confirmed my guess that systematically guiding a client through each combination of eye directions would increase resourcefulness. My "theory" about what was happening was that since each direction of eye gaze was associated with a different kind of brain processing, these different ways of processing were being "connected" or integrated. It is as if the whole brain could now become engaged to work out the "problem" situation.

Steve and Connirae Andreas worked together to develop a procedure for what would be called Eye Movement Integration (EMI). It was first taught by Connirae as a part of her Core Transformation training program in 1990 (C. Andreas, personal communication, March 6, 2016). At its inception, the therapist's finger in EMI moved from point to point across the entire visual field. A client's eyes even followed the tracing of geometric and pictorial figures while they held representations (auditory, visual, and kinesthetic) of an experience in consciousness.

More than 20 separate eye movements were developed for use with EMI, versus only two movements for EMDR. The disparity in that number was one of several distinct differences between the two therapies when they were introduced. Another was EMI's focus on all internal representations of an experience (cognitive, visual, auditory, visceral, and emotional). EMDR's initial focus was only on a visual image and a cognitive characterization of the experience, although several years after its introduction more attention was being paid to the emotional and physical reactions to traumatic events. Several other differences between the two therapies will be reviewed later in this chapter. What made EMI superior to EMDR was the comprehensiveness of its eye movements, its adherence to the NLP model, its attention to all sensory modalities of an experience, and the simplicity of its procedures.

EYE MOVEMENTS ARE PURPOSEFUL AND UNCONSCIOUS

To demonstrate the relationship between eye movements and mental processes in trainings, I sometimes ask participants to silently spell words that are spelled and spoken differently—words like Aeschylus, ophthalmologist, phlegm, or pterodactyl.

Because spelling is aided by visual recall, according to the NLP model, this mental task triggers naturally occurring, unconscious eye movements. I then ask participants to report to which accessing positions their eyes moved when they were attempting to spell the words. For many individuals, their eyes move up to the *visual past* location.

Occasionally, a participant will circumvent the task, such as by purposefully staring straight ahead and overriding what would have been normal, involuntary eye movements. During one seminar, I observed a participant staring at me while others attempted the task. He later insisted his eyes did not move when he performed the exercise. I quickly asked him again how the word was spelled, catching him off guard. This time, with others watching, his eyes moved up and to his left. Participants close by were quick to comment on his eye movements. To be clear, eye movements *can* be consciously overridden, but this is not what is instinctive, unconscious, and natural.

The salient takeaway from the Dilts research is not that the eye locations in *Figure 4.1* are *foolproof*, but that they do have merit. Eye movements, in general, are *discernible*, and they do correspond to distinct mental processes for each individual, whatever the patterns might be. Even detractors of the NLP model have reported that eye movements are not random (Tomason et al., 1980). The role of eye movements in sensory processing is one reason—likely the major reason—why reactions to traumatic memories are desensitized when habitual eye movement patterns are manipulated. The fact that eyes *do* move systematically, not randomly, appears to be gaining acceptance, but the belief that eye movements are virtually the same across populations has never been asserted by EMI developers.

The two Andreases (1993) referred to the eye accessing cues in *Figure 4.1* as "crude indicators of basic, general categories of different processing" (p. 3). On the other hand, they believe the real significance of eye movements is their relationship to the processing of neurosensory information. "They are the *means* by which these brain functions are activated," they argue (p. 3). And, most relevantly, the following statement establishes why this is critical to understanding the success of EMI: "By deliberately moving the eyes in specific directions, one can alter the way a subject's brain processes a given piece of content" (p. 3). This guide will demonstrate exactly how that appears to happen.

Although the validity of the Dilts eye movement study has been challenged, the fact that this research spurred the creation of eye movement therapies is an underreported and underappreciated event. Rather than rejecting the NLP eye movement model outright, researchers and practitioners would do well to explore which findings are valid and useful. Stevens et al. (2017), called for the development of new therapies to address limbic system reactivity shortly after traumatic injuries occur to prevent the development of PTSD. MEMI is uniquely designed for that task. Studies to determine whether limbic reactivity can be reversed during and after MEMI treatment could answer that question.

Whether directed eye movements yield beneficial results while a person thinks about a negative experience should no longer be in question. However, how that occurs and which variables in that process are instrumental in stimulating symptom resolution should be examined. Researchers take note: If eye movements, internal representations, and behavioral responses to our environment are related, as research and clinical experience indicate, there is much to be gained by understanding this phenomenon. Instead of pouring more resources into the proliferation of pharmaceuticals and ad nauseum evaluations of traditional trauma therapies, perhaps now is the time to promote techniques that more closely address current brain science.

EMI AND EMDR — SIMILARITIES AND DIFFERENCES

During the early days of their development, EMI and EMDR had several features in common, which is not surprising considering the assertion they emerged from the same source. At first glance, one might have assumed they were indistinguishable. This was hardly the case; there were also significant differences. One was built on a foundation of collaborative inquiry and development, the other reportedly triggered by a stroll through a park. What makes clarification of the differences between these two therapies so difficult is their common ancestry.

EMI and EMDR Similarities

When first developed, both EMI and EMDR clients followed the movement of a finger with their eyes while thinking about a problem or experience. In each method, the therapist assessed the intensity of client reactions to memories after conducting eye movements, using the subjective units of distress (SUD) Scale (Wolpe, 1969). This is a self-report measure used routinely in all branches of medicine to assess client perceptions of pain intensity or psychological distress. A score of zero indicates no pain or distress at all, and a score of 10 the worst possible distress or pain.

In another similarity, neither technique utilized a graduated approach when exposing clients to disturbing experiences, like in systematic desensitization (SD) and most exposure therapies. This particular feature in each therapy rocked the scientific world; it was heresy. Mainstream trauma researchers were incensed about this challenge to PTSD treatment orthodoxy from cockamamie techniques involving eye movements.

Both EMI and EMDR employed an NLP strategy requiring clients to actively visualize a representation of the negative experience while they followed a finger or an object moving back and forth in front of their eyes. Visualizing a traumatic experience from a distance was an NLP technique derived from the hypnotic work of Milton Erickson (Dilts & DeLozier, 2000). Using the eyes to move an image of a problem state from one location to another in order to alter reactions to a negative experience was also a well-established NLP strategy. Requiring clients to track the movement of a finger or pen while visualizing a negative experience was Shapiro's unique contribution.

To be more precise, although having clients project an image of a problem state in front of them or onto a surface some distance away was common to both therapies, this strategy was actually part of a more intricate NLP technique for PTSD and phobias called *visual kinesthetic dissociation* (V/K/D). It was first reported by Bandler and Grinder (1979) and later formalized by Bandler (1985b). Creating greater physical distance from a problem state offered two beneficial possibilities: 1.) because it was farther away, the image could be perceived as less threatening; and 2.) the image could be viewed by an observer-self, as if it were happening to someone else, and therefore be less of a concern.

Another aspect of the V/K/D procedure employed both by EMI and EMDR was a technique called *breaking state*, which is used in between exposures to a problem state. Following the eye movements, and prior to retesting the problem state, a client's attention would be diverted away from the image of concern. In EMI, a client might be asked what day it is, what they had for breakfast, or simply be instructed to look at the therapist—anything to interrupt the connection to the problem state. The purpose was to reset the client's awareness following an intervention and prior to a retest of the traumatic event. EMI used this strategy just as it had been employed for years in NLP.

Although the use of the breaking state strategy was evident in EMDR procedures as well, it was not labeled as such, and NLP was not referenced as the source. Subjects were asked to blank the picture out and take a deep breath before the retest (Shapiro, 1989). In fact, the exact phrase "blank the screen" is language commonly used as part of the V/K/D procedure in NLP (Andreas & Andreas, 1989; O'Connor & Seymour, 1990).

EMI also used a test-retest model originally developed by behaviorists Miller, Galanter et al. (2013) and later adopted by NLP developers. Called the TOTE Model (Test, Operate, Test, Exit), it requires testing the differences between a problem state and some desired state following treatments until the desired state has been achieved. In the case of EMI, a pretest of the reactions to a trauma was conducted and the qualities of the problem state noted (Test), therapist-guided eye movements were performed (Operate), a retest of the reactions was conducted after each eye movement set (Test), and the procedure ended when reactions to the memory had been desensitized to the client's satisfaction (Exit).

EMDR therapists elicited client descriptions of both irrational beliefs (problem states) about traumatic memories and desired replacements (desired states), but only with regard to cognitions. EMI, on the other hand, elicited cognitive, kinesthetic, visual, and emotional problem states as per NLP principles. Positive outcomes (desired states) were sought in all of these areas. As discussed in this chapter, when Shapiro (2001) later developed EMDR procedures, the therapy began addressing all of the modalities found in NLP.

Although the use of the test-retest procedure was evident in EMDR's original process, for some reason Shapiro did not reference the TOTE Model or NLP's application of it. Evidence that Shapiro had appropriated NLP knowledge and strategies without crediting sources infuriated NLP developers. On the other hand, Shapiro was apparently also upset with the NLP community for creating a second procedure, EMI, using therapist-directed eye movements. At a luncheon meeting with Steve Andreas during an Ericksonian Foundation Conference, Shapiro asked Steve to stop teaching and promoting EMI, viewing it as an infringement on her work. During a video call with me, Steve said he politely declined and they never discussed the topic again (S. Andreas, personal communication, March 6, 2016).

EMI and EMDR Differences
While EMI and EMDR had a great deal in common when they were introduced, it's also clear there were significant differences between the two approaches. At its outset, EMDR used only two back and forth eye movements—one horizontal and one slightly diagonal. EMI used multiple eye movements that crisscrossed the entire field of vision. EMI's horizontal, vertical, diagonal, and pictorial movements were designed to stimulate all the accessing positions in the NLP eye movement model.

The stated theoretical models on which the therapies were based also differed. Shapiro (1989) hypothesized an "imbalance of neural elements" in the brain resulted in persistent, negative reactions to recalled trauma, but the therapy lacked a theoretical foundation at its outset. EMDR's bilateral saccades were thought to alternately stimulate neural pathways, thereby restoring balance and desensitizing memories. However, after that claim was criticized as unsubstantiated, Shapiro developed increasingly more complex models to justify her procedure.

EMI, on the other hand, was rooted in the theory, presuppositions, and methodology of NLP. Instead of a focus on bilateral brain stimulation, as in EMDR, the Andreases theorized memory integration would be achieved more efficiently if eye movements associated with all the sensory modalities were stimulated. Using the NLP eye movement model as a basis, they developed 20 separate eye movements intersecting all of the accessing positions (visual, auditory, kinesthetic, and internal narrative).

In another difference, EMDR's eye movements were very rapid. In contrast, EMI therapists were taught to vary both the eye movement speed and the distance of the pen or finger from the face, based on verbal and nonverbal feedback from clients. Interestingly enough, the speed of the eye movements used in EMDR are now much more like those originally used in EMI. In another difference, if a subject's eyes repeatedly blinked whenever passing over a particular location, Steve Andreas recommended that small, rhythmic circles be traced over that spot until the blinking ceased, as if erasing some problem. These adjustments to the speed and form of the eye movements made EMI more client-friendly, in my opinion. EMI clients were also offered more protection from intense exposure.

In one very significant difference, EMDR strongly encouraged clients to re-experience the full intensity of a trauma's formation during the eye movements, as if they were back in the situation. This is also a characteristic of prolonged exposure therapy (PE). EMDR practitioners were cautioned to expect very strong reactions from clients. Not to establish that deep connection was thought to jeopardize the success of the therapy.

A lot has changed in that regard since the early days of EMDR. Currently, EMDR practitioners are more aware of the need to blunt the harsh reactions caused by deep exposure with grounding techniques and more powerful reciprocal inhibition during trauma exposures. This is particularly true of those therapists who do not adhere to the entire 8-phase EMDR model and provides more evidence that EMDR has borrowed certain EMI practices over time. From the outset, EMI discouraged deep exposure and instead fostered a "kinder and gentler" approach during treatment. EMI was designed to avoid reactivating the severe, first-person thoughts, feelings, and sensations associated with traumatic memories. According to Connirae Andreas, when EMI is used, "a strong, unpleasant emotional reaction is *extremely* unusual" (C. Andreas, personal communication, March 6, 2016).

In my experience, severely distressed PTSD clients are often unable to talk about what happened without decompensating. Some simply refuse to proceed. Ironically, even some therapists, who are themselves ill at ease when clients present with severe symptoms, intentionally delay or avoid addressing the symptoms associated with PTSD. When specific safety mechanisms were subsequently added to EMI by Klein (2015), it became clear deep exposure to traumatic experiences was completely unnecessary for PTSD symptom desensitization.

In his rational emotive behavioral therapy (REBT), Ellis (2008) proposed all maladaptive emotions and behaviors are the result of faulty cognitions (irrational thinking). His solution was to challenge the irrational beliefs of patients and assist them in adopting more realistic perspectives (cognitive restructuring). Both EMI and EMDR identified cognitions associated with traumatic experiences, but they differed in the extent to which cognitive restructuring should be used. An EMI therapist would straightforwardly ask what thoughts occurred to clients while they were recalling traumatic experiences. When retesting reactions following eye movement sets, clients would be asked if the thoughts had changed. Were they the same or different? No special effort was made to challenge cognitions, imply they were irrational, or suggest they be changed.

In the original EMD experiment, if clients had difficulty identifying a belief statement about an experience, the therapist would explain what negative self-assessments were and give examples to stimulate a response (Shapiro, 1989). Shapiro also elicited statements from subjects expressing how they would like to characterize the experience (desired belief) at the end of treatment. Before and after treatment, a semantic differential scale assessed how strongly subjects agreed with a statement describing the desired outcome. With this level of emphasis on changing cognitions, EMDR's original procedure demonstrated an affinity for cognitive restructuring unlike what was found in EMI. This is still a difference between the two therapies.

After using MEMI with hundreds of clients, I made an interesting discovery: cognitive restructuring is unnecessary. I found belief statements about traumatic experiences are automatically reorganized, along with—or more likely as a result of—improvements in kinesthetic and sensory reactions to recalled trauma. Inevitably, when clients become less physically and emotionally reactive, and the visual representation loses potency, thoughts about the experience become less negative and more benign. One only needs to ask, "What are your thoughts now?" Cognitive restructuring is used infrequently with MEMI, usually only when a client is unsure about whether to agree to treatment.

Finally, EMI was much easier to learn. The complexity of EMDR's theoretical model and protocol required more instructional time and a costly period of supervision before certification.

While there were other differences between the therapies when they were introduced, these were the most distinctive. The manner in which EMDR was created—devoid of a sound foundation until a theoretical model was later appended—probably weakened its appeal. It definitely raised suspicions about its actual origins. It seems, like *Occam's razor*, the number of assumptions required to develop a plausible theory for EMDR, distinct from its NLP roots, created a model much too cumbersome for the cure. All the while a simpler rationale, anchored in NLP principles, pedagogy, and practice, with a coherent path from theory to application, was available in EMI. Comparative studies could further clarify the similarities, differences, and the relative effectiveness of the two therapies as they are used today.

Evidence suggests that eye movements interact with the brain during the formation and recall of traumatic memories. New research should investigate whether habitual eye movements contribute to the persistence of PTSD symptoms, and whether their strategic manipulation helps reset the limbic reactions reported by Stevens et al. (2017). Disagreement still exists about whether MEMI or EMDR is more successful. Both are effective treatments for PTSD, undoubtedly because they each use eye movements as the principal agents of change.

CHAPTER 5

The Creation of Multichannel Eye Movement Integration

This chapter summarizes my initial experiences in using eye movement integration and the actions I then took to reconceptualize the approach as a cohesive and fully-documented therapy. Multichannel Eye Movement Integration (MEMI) is descended directly from the original Eye Movement Integration (EMI) methodology developed by Connirae and Steve Andreas (1993) and a later adaption by Klein (2015), which he called Eye Movement Integration™ (EMI™). These two techniques are so similar in form and content that I use the phrase "eye movement integration" in this book when referring to the techniques, unless there is a particular reason to specify either EMI or EMI™.

Whereas EMDR has been heavily criticized for its complex procedures and esoteric theories, eye movement integration has been faulted for inadequate documentation and systematic evaluations of its effectiveness. Without a clear protocol and written procedures, formal testing of the technique was not even feasible. To my knowledge, no randomized controlled trials of eye movement integration have been conducted. Unfortunately, the technique's trajectory has been stalled for years at the modeling stage. Recognizing this as the case, I resolved to redevelop this solution-focused intervention with the goal of bringing it to a much larger audience.

My ensuing development work produced an uncomplicated theoretical model featuring five relevant NLP presuppositions and a supporting rationale—a foundation on which this new, multichannel therapy could be constructed. After expanding eye movement integration's brief steps into a detailed 10-step protocol with written procedures, several innovative therapeutic interventions were added to the protocol and new assessments for measuring treatment outcomes were determined.

Because other trauma therapies, including EMDR, had been criticized for not assuring client safety and stability during treatment, Klein appended two strategies to the original EMI for use in EMI™. The purpose of each was to forestall severe client reactions during exposure—and for a good reason. It was suspected, and later confirmed, that inadequate protections during trauma treatment were linked to higher dropout rates in exposure therapy studies. This continues to be a significant cause for concern (Bisson et al., 2007; Schnurr et al., 2007; Seal et al., 2010; van der Kolk, 2015).

The first protection Klein added was the *anchoring* of positive resource states in clients before accessing traumatic reactions, a robust form of reciprocal inhibition. With origins in behavioral psychology, reciprocal inhibition is an intervention designed to reduce anxiety in a person by introducing a stimulus with the opposite effect (Wolpe, 1954). When a relaxing, invigorating, or uplifting state is instilled in an anxious individual prior to exposure, the link between the fear-causing stimulus and the reaction is weakened. Klein uses an NLP anchoring procedure to achieve this result. An experience conveying confidence or competence from a client's past is revived, anchored, and held in consciousness during the eye movements and exposure to the traumatic experience.

Klein's second enhancement, called therapeutic dissociation, was designed to visually interrupt the connection between clients and their traumas by having them project an image of the experience on a surface some distance away. This variation of NLP's V/K/D procedure described previously allows a client to view the traumatic experience as an external observer, rather than reliving it as a first-person participant. Anchoring and therapeutic dissociation are both used in MEMI because they afford clients more protection during exposure than the safeguards found in other therapies. Instructions for their use will be covered in Chapter 7.

Because eye movement integration's processes and procedures were derived from NLP, successful use of the therapy originally required an understanding of NLP principles. After I had used the approach with dozens of clients, it became clear the technique, as it stood, would be difficult for practitioners unfamiliar with NLP to master. The results achieved with my clients were remarkable, but I had to rely on my NLP experience to fill in missing information. So I had an advantage: I was already a certified NLP practitioner when I took my first EMI™ training in 2002.

At the time, the approach was taught in one-day seminars with no significant follow-up, except for a few available videos. Comprehension of the NLP theoretical model, on which the technique was based, required attendance at additional seminars. Practitioners not familiar with NLP methodology were left with many unanswered questions after completing EMI™ training. Learning the technique was also hampered by insufficient documentation of its procedures, as has been discussed. There were no operations manuals to take home following a training and no recommended assessment techniques, other than the subjective units of distress (SUD) Scale developed by Wolpe.

When I began training practitioners in the use of EMI™, I found attendees shared the same concerns I had about the technique's limitations. Many who completed trainings confessed a reluctance to use what they had learned with clients until they felt more confident. They also expressed a desire for step-by-step written information and instructional videos on the use of the technique. I was convinced the technique would need to be reorganized so it could become accessible to a wider range of practitioners. For individuals unfamiliar with NLP principles, it would have to be to be re-envisioned as a fully-formed therapy with its own theoretical model, protocol, procedures, and instructions.

To respond to the lack of written information, I began documenting the procedures I was using and compiling supplementary materials for distribution at the trainings I was conducting. This led to a multiyear development effort culminating in the publication of this book. In the course of that work, I reconceptualized eye movement integration and added a concise theoretical model distilled from NLP principles. To bring this new model to life, I developed a comprehensive protocol with clinician instructions, procedures, therapist scripts, and a worksheet for recording results following eye movement sets. These additions, along with the adoption of a standardized PTSD assessment instrument, allowed for systematic evaluations of MEMI as a treatment option. However, the foundations of the therapy, the theory, presuppositions, and beliefs framing its operations are true to those referenced by Steve and Connirae Andreas when they created EMI in 1989.

MEMI PRESUPPOSITIONS AND THEORETICAL MODEL

Presuppositions are defined as assertions or propositions accepted as true in order to pursue a line of discussion or a desired outcome. Called useful fictions in NLP, they are beliefs considered valuable, even in the absence of scientific evidence. NLP presuppositions were based on an assumption that the most successful therapists share similar views about life and learning. It followed that, if those views could be identified, organized, and condensed into counseling strategies, they could also be *modeled* and taught to others. From the masterful techniques and linguistic patterns of Fritz Perls, Virginia Satir, Milton Erickson, and others, a set of overarching beliefs was shaped into NLP principles, the presuppositions, and used to support the development of all NLP products.

According to one source, there are more than 20 NLP presuppositions (Hoobyar et al., 2013), although Dilts and DeLozier (2000) list 17 in a more comprehensive treatment of the topic. Andreas and Faulkner (1996) list only 10. The precise number has varied in NLP writings over time. Regardless of the exact number, incorporating all of the most frequently cited presuppositions into this guide would have made the task of learning MEMI too cumbersome, and it wasn't really necessary. Although *all* NLP presuppositions would apply in some fashion to this new therapy, the five featured in this chapter will adequately convey the NLP beliefs sustaining MEMI, while also establishing a framework for describing how it works.

Before explaining the five MEMI presuppositions, the following hypothetical scenario about one man's efforts to stop smoking with the help of MEMI will illustrate how they guided the development of this therapy:

> *Kurt had been a smoker for 27 years when he decided to seek help in stopping the habit. His therapist asked him to think of a recent time when he was smoking that was particularly troubling to him, one that stood out in his mind. He explained his cravings were really bad after leaving work that afternoon, and he re-enacted a ritual he always performed when he got behind the wheel: He patted his left breast pocket with his right hand, pulled the cigarette pack out, flipped up the box top, and took a cigarette from the pack. He looked down at the cigarette and said to himself, "This is disgusting! Why am I doing this?"*

But he dismissed the thought. He placed the cigarette between his lips, pushed in the lighter, and waited for the lighter to pop out. Then he lit the cigarette and replaced the lighter. He started the car, cracked the power window to his left, took a long drag, inhaled deeply, and blew the smoke sideways out the window. He said he did this every day, the same way each time.

He remarked that he could see himself sitting in the parked car and the view through the windshield. He could feel the texture of the stitched, leather-wrapped steering wheel. He could hear the click of the lighter as it popped out. He could see the lighter's red coils moving toward him and feel its heat as it approached his face. He could even feel a tickle at the back of his throat, which he recognized as a craving.

The five MEMI presuppositions are as follows:

1. **Human experience is organized and systematic.**
   We, as humans, organize what we do. Generally speaking, there's a beginning, a middle, and an end to our experiences, unless they are interrupted. Cakes have recipes. Books have tables of contents, introductions, and chapters. And appliances have instruction manuals. In our personal lives, whenever we take a shower, fry an egg, or eat a slice of pizza, we tend to follow the same routines. We are constantly learning, systematically experimenting with new behaviors, and adopting patterns that suit us. The ones that work for

us become habitual; the ones that don't, we abandon. If this were not the case, we'd never settle on just one way to apply lipstick or shave our stubble! Kurt's smoking ritual was organized and systematic. The components of his experience were what he thought, saw, heard, and felt.

2. **All experiences have a structure.**
This presupposition suggests the structure of an experience is comprised of four basic elements: its associated *context, thoughts, sensory information,* and *feelings.* These elements provide dimension to all human states of being—whether positive, neutral, or negative. It's how we comprehend an experience and are able to communicate it to others. Because human experiences have a structure, past experiences can be *activated, observed,* and *described* in the present, allowing us to monitor changes in reactions to distressing memories following therapeutic interventions.

When a person is recalling an event, they are retrieving a mental representation of the experience from memory and bringing it into consciousness. This reactivation allows a therapist to observe a client's behavioral reactions to it, and ask about and record related thoughts, feelings, and sensations. Recording this information allows us to describe the way the client is recalling an experience at that time. This information also becomes a baseline against which we can assess future changes to the experience.

Following each set of MEMI eye movements, a *retest* is conducted to detect changes in the experience to determine whether its associated context, thoughts, feelings, and sensations are the same or different. We are evaluating whether the experience has been *reorganized* and, if so, how the structure has changed following MEMI pattern interruptions.

Structure of Experience Theoretical Model

[Figure: Four quadrants labeled Context, Thoughts, Feelings, Sensory Information surrounding a central box labeled Structure of Experience]

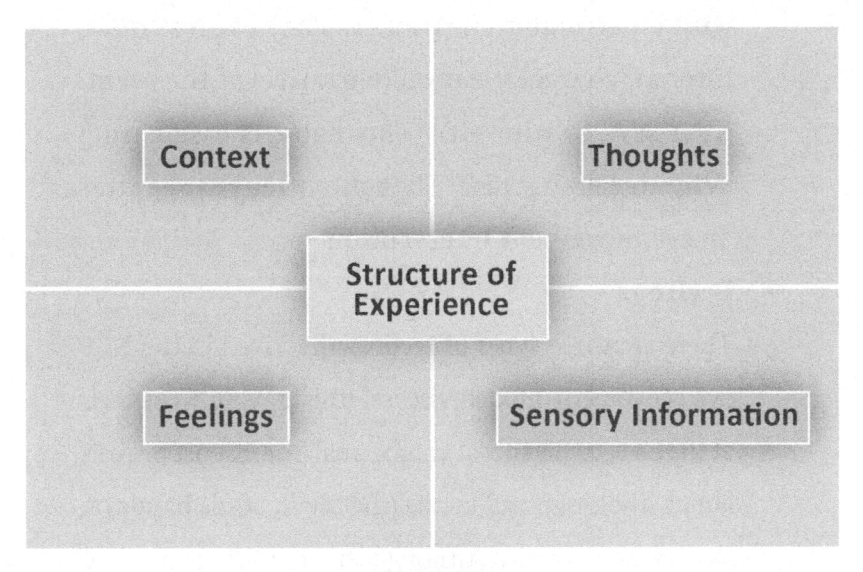

Figure 5.1

Figure 5.1 illustrates the four elements of the Structure of Experience theoretical model used in MEMI, which were derived from a more intricate casting of NLP's theoretical model and presuppositions. The MEMI protocol, procedures, step-by-step instructions, therapist scripts, and assessment strategies are designed to assess changes in these four elements:

- **Context**

  Context is the who, what, when, and where of an experience. (Kurt is alone in his car after work, about to have a cigarette.) Although the context sometimes changes after eye movement interventions, this does not occur frequently.

- **Thoughts**

  The thoughts, or cognitions, are those associated with a particular experience. They express one's internal characterization (narrative) of the event. Kurt says to himself, "This habit is disgusting! Why am I doing this?" Thoughts often change after an eye movement intervention.

- **Feelings**

  There are three types of feelings described in the NLP eye movement model: visceral (the craving Kurt feels at the back of his throat), emotional (the disgust he feels about smoking), and tactile (the touch of his hands on the steering wheel). Although tactile feelings are also considered sensory information and could be grouped with other sensory modalities, they have more in common with visceral and emotional feelings than sounds, images, smells, or tastes. All three types of feelings are reportedly *accessed* from the same location in the eye movement model (lower right).

  The feelings and sensory information elements also have descriptive *subelements* (called submodalities in NLP) that amplify the features of each element. Examples of submodalities for feelings would be pressure or pain (for visceral feelings); sadness, anger, or fear (for emotional feelings); and texture or location on the body (for tactile feelings). One could also describe submodalities as the components that make up a modality.

The concept of submodalities can be difficult to grasp, so here's a brief example: If an individual feels *pain* in their lower abdomen (a visceral submodality) when thinking of a traumatic memory, you could ask (as you would in MEMI) how intense the pain is on a scale from 0 (no intensity) to 4 (highest intensity). The question is part of the pretest and the score becomes baseline information for comparison following an eye movement intervention. If your client reports a score of 4 in the pretest (highest intensity), and following an eye movement set it goes down to 1 (low intensity), this is an indication that one aspect of the memory has been *reorganized.*

- **Sensory Information**

    Sensory information reveals the qualities of an experience through its related images, sounds, smells, and tastes. Examples from Kurt's experience were the *sound* of the lighter clicking out and the *visual image* of the lighter's red coils. Possible submodalities for the image of the lighter could be distance (near or far), movement (movie or still photo), or clarity (clear or unclear). If your client says it's very clear in the pretest, you could ask if it's still very clear following eye movement sets. Again, the questions are part of the pretest and the answers become baseline data.

3. **Experiences are stored and retrieved using sensory data.**
Sensory information—the images, sounds, smells, and tastes of an experience—provides the medium through which memories and ideas are mentally represented when stored and later retrieved. Sensory data also allow us to describe a recalled experience. If I think about what I had for breakfast today, I *see* myself sitting at my desk in front of my laptop. From a brass lamp on my right, I *see* light reflecting down on the desktop and up into my eyes. To my left is a round bowl of blueberries and raspberries. When I think about how they *taste*, my mouth waters. To my right is a steaming hot cup of vanilla chai tea. I can *smell* its spices.

In the sensory information category, the visual modality undoubtedly plays the most significant role in trauma memory storage and retrieval, with the auditory modality occupying a less important and less frequently occurring second place. This is why visual imagery is central to trauma work, and why it must be given thoughtful attention. As already noted, the most reactive of the modalities during trauma re-experiencing are visual imagery and visceral and emotional feelings.

4. **When patterns are interrupted, experiences reorganize.**

Habitual patterns of behavior are an enduring human attribute. Kids who learn to tie single knots in their sneakers are thrilled to adopt that pattern of behavior until it doesn't work anymore—like when the laces come undone from running around. Enter the need for a double knot solution! Think of the laces coming undone as the *pattern interruption* that creates the need for a pattern adjustment. Adopting a double-knot strategy reorganizes the experience and establishes a new habitual set.

In Kurt's scenario, the structure of his experience (the smoking ritual) is known through its elements—context, thoughts, feelings, and sensory information, and elaborated on via feeling and sensory submodalities. He's *disgusted* (emotional feeling) when he thinks about smoking, he can *feel* the tickle craving at the back of his throat (visceral feeling), and he *sees* the lighter's coils approaching his face (visual sensory information). Now, suppose Kurt's therapist suggests they do a set of eye movements focused on the structure of that experience to see if it might reorganize. For your information, a listing of many submodalities for each sensory information category is included in Chapter 9.

5. **When an experience is reorganized, the results tend to be beneficial.**

According to the NLP model, eye movements to particular locations in a person's visual field are associated with the processing of cognitive, kinesthetic, and sensory information. With that in mind, Connirae Andreas theorized that guiding a client's eyes to all the locations in the model, while a client thinks about a traumatic event, would reorganize the structure of an experience in beneficial ways.

To test out this presupposition, Kurt and his therapist agree to use MEMI and focus on the structure of his smoking experience. Here's an abbreviated baseline of information: His thought about the experience was to question his behavior: "Why am I doing this?" When asked about the intensity of the tickle craving at the back of his throat, he said, "Very intense." When asked how clear the image of the lighter's red coils approaching his face was, he said, "Very clear."

After a round of eye movements, Kurt is asked to think about the experience again and decide whether it's the same or different. Without prompting, he says, "It's different. The craving is less intense." He also says, "The image of the lighter is fuzzier now, not as clear." When asked if those changes make the experience better or worse, he says, "Better, it's not as real." When asked what his thought is about the experience, in light of those changes, Kurt says, "I have to stop." His thought before the eye movements was *Why am I doing this?* After the intervention, he's thinking he must quit, a positive shift in his cognitive response. Although this scenario is fictitious, it does accurately depict how an experience might be reorganized in a beneficial way following the use of MEMI.

The MEMI protocol—the processes, strategies, and procedures—contained in this guide are rooted in these five NLP presuppositions. They were chosen because they sufficiently convey the NLP assumptions underlying the MEMI theoretical model. The only other book about eye movement integration, published by Beaulieu (2003), combined the eye movements of EMI with several strategies she adopted from the EMDR protocol. The book was a disappointment to eye movement integration practitioners. Although it was billed as a "comprehensive clinical guide," its procedures were confusing, it contained extraneous material, its depictions of key NLP models were misconstrued, and it lacked cohesion. The approach also required clients to re-experience traumas without adequate protection. In a true sense, *Multichannel Eye Movement Integration* is the first easy to use but complete guide to this type of eye movement therapy.

MEMI INNOVATIONS

The MEMI theoretical model, protocol, and procedures are strengthened by several innovations involving the use of strategic comments spoken by the therapist during the eye movements—in the form of direct commands, embedded commands, and visual, spatial, and temporal reframing statements. In eye movement integration and EMDR, therapists rarely speak while the eye movements are being performed. When I began using the technique, I noticed how frequently, due to my silence, a client's thoughts would wander to topics other than the aspect of the trauma receiving focus. And there was no way for me to know how their internal attention was focused unless a client self-reported that information. I found myself periodically reminding clients of the task at hand with verbal comments, such as, **"You're still thinking about that experience as you watch my finger move."**

After discovering how helpful comments like this are in maintaining a client's focus, it occurred to me that other direct or subliminal verbal suggestions could be incorporated into the therapy to augment its effects. I began experimenting with hypnotic suggestions meant to appeal to a client's deeper thought structures and desire for change. This made sense on many levels. Visual, emotional, and visceral reactions to a memory could be targeted; cognitive shifts could be stimulated; metaphors prompting change could be inserted; and assurances could be given that a client's well-being would be safeguarded.

These statements spoken by the therapist during exposure have three intended outcomes:

1. To verbally reinforce the resource anchor during exposure to the trauma and the eye movements.
2. To remind clients to keep their eyes focused on the finger or pen moving in the foreground while they continue to think

about the image of the problem state (traumatic experience) across the room.

3. To help transition a client's thoughts, feelings, and sensory reactions from problem state to problem-free state using visual, temporal, and spatial reframes, and direct and embedded commands.

Visual Reframe

A *visual reframe* alters the perception of an event by suggesting different ways of "seeing" or envisioning an experience. In NLP theory, when the perception of an experience changes, it is believed the reaction to it will also change. If a person "sees" a larger-than-life movie of their attacker a few feet away when recalling an assault, that is what "frames" their perception of the event. After conducting a set of eye movements, your client's perception of the event and reaction to it often improve. There's no guarantee it will, but this is what usually happens. This result reflects MEMI's fifth presupposition: *When an experience is reorganized, the results tend to be beneficial.*

The visual reframe is also useful when working with a client who does not have a defined trauma, but has anxiety related to a particular event or situation. If your client is angry about a spat with a sibling, you could suggest they "reframe" its related image by using their imagination to change it from color to black and white, make it smaller, or move it farther away. In many cases, the reaction to the image will become less severe.

This strategy imbues a sense of control over the experience and fosters an atmosphere in which a change in perception is likely to occur. Again, you can never be sure that it will, but it frequently does.

Temporal Reframe

A *temporal reframe* alters a client's perception of an experience by moving it forward or backward in time. By telling your client they are sitting in your office in the present, and the image of the negative experience is "across the room in the past," you are linguistically *reframing* the perception of the experience in relation to when it occurred. Where they are sitting in their chair is *now* and across the room is the *past*. This reinforces the reality that your client is not *in* the past and need not experience those thoughts, feelings, and sensations *from* the past as if they are reliving it. This explicit demarcation of time appeals to both the conscious and unconscious minds, allowing perceptual shifts in a recalled trauma to more readily occur.

Spatial Reframe

Similarly, a spatial reframe alters the perception of an event by modifying the physical distance between a client and the negative experience. By telling your client they are seated "here in your chair," and the image (and everything related to it) is in the "distant background way across the room," you are reframing the perception of distance between your client and the problem state.

All three of these reframing techniques help to create and reinforce therapeutic dissociation, the second protective mechanism promoted by Klein and now an integral part of MEMI procedures. No other current therapy affords the same level of protection during exposure as that provided by anchoring and therapeutic dissociation.

Direct and Embedded Commands

Direct and *embedded commands* are hypnotic techniques designed to stimulate changes in cognitions, sensory responses, and somatic reactions. For instance, while your client is both thinking about a traumatic event and watching the pen move, you might voice a *direct command* for change, like: **"You can let your feelings diminish now,"** spoken in a normal, conversational tone. Another option would be to deliver an indirect or *embedded command*, one encapsulated within a larger statement and spoken in a manner appealing to the unconscious mind. In this statement—**"You may find that... your thoughts about this will change"**—the underlined words are the *embedded command*. They are intoned in a manner different from the first part of the statement. Shifting from a conversational tone to a monotonic, robotlike voice, you utter the command part of the statement with more emphasis and volume. This is an appeal to your client's unconscious mind to change their thoughts about the problem state. Specific instructions for executing these types of commands are discussed in Chapter 8.

When a client is asked to envision a traumatic experience, watch a pen move around, and listen to unusual vocalizations all at the same time, a brief state of confusion often follows. Although purposefully creating confusion like this is paradoxical and illogical, it has a purpose—to allow the brain an opportunity to reorganize the experience. I contend that this disruption in the habitual response, this state of confusion related to a problem state, is what stimulates the brain to recalibrate its PTSD neurological correlates. And this is one reason I refer to MEMI as a limbic therapy. For a fleeting moment, your client's eyes might dart around, blink or squint inquisitively, as if searching for elements of their habitual response. They may even look bewildered. This provides evidence the traumatic experience has been reorganized, resulting in beneficial shifts in cognitive, sensory, and kinesthetic reactions to the event. Signs of a memory's reorganization will be evident: facial and skeletal muscles relax; the size, shape, and clarity of images are altered, making them less intimidating; anxious feelings diminish; and thoughts about the experience become more benign.

Research investigating whether these cognitive, sensory, and kinesthetic changes occur in concert with neurological adjustments could confirm what has been theorized for years—that eye movements and limbic system reactivity are linked. Considered as a whole, the additions described in this guide to MEMI have transformed the 30-year-old eye movement integration approach into a *limbic*, multichannel therapy.

MEMI CLINICAL OBSERVATIONS

Although formal evaluations of MEMI have yet to be undertaken, I did complete a small pilot study with subjects from my private practice. Those results, showing dramatic improvements in PTSD symptoms after only two to four sessions, are included in Appendix D. Clinical experience with more than 1,000 clients has also provided me ample insight into the power of MEMI, as well as its limitations—when it's most effective, when it's not—and how to apply the therapy with certain disorders. A number of these insights are reported in Chapter 10.

In my process of testing the efficacy of various eye movements, as well as the protocol and procedures of MEMI, a number of assumptions consistently supported by client behavioral responses were confirmed:

- It's unnecessary to connect *all* the NLP accessing positions with one another in order to desensitize a problem state.
- The different eye movements used by therapists (e.g., left to right, corner to corner, or up and down) are not equally effective in alleviating trauma symptoms—some work much better than others.
- A random approach to the eye movements is less effective than a strategic one targeting the visual, kinesthetic, and internal narrative accessing positions in the NLP eye movement model.

- Eye movements are indeed interlinked with the mental processing of cognitive, somatic, and sensory information. I cannot conceive of any other reason why MEMI therapy consistently results in less threatening and more benign thoughts, feelings, and sensory information following eye movement interventions.
- The mere interruption of a client's habitual eye movements when recalling a trauma appears to be marginally helpful in resolving symptoms.
- Reversing the direction of eye movements during a pattern's execution is especially effective in reorganizing memories.
- The center of the field of vision (straight ahead on the horizon, or just above or below it) is a location where clients frequently visualize experiences, also confirmed by Dilts (2000) and Andreas and Andreas (1993).
- The use of strategic, verbal suggestions (reframes, direct and embedded commands) in tandem with eye movements to the targeted accessing positions increases treatment efficiency and effectiveness.
- When clients describe traumatic experiences, the internal representations most frequently cited—and the most troublesome and symptomatic—are visual imagery and the feeling (visceral and emotional) states.
- Insufficient attention was previously given to the thoughts (cognitions) associated with traumatic memories when using eye movement integration. Clients may report being unaware of related thoughts, even say they have none. However,

they do exist, and it's important for therapists to elicit the thoughts during pretests in order to allow comparisons following eye movement interventions.
- Changing irrational thoughts related to traumatic experiences to rational narratives with cognitive restructuring is unnecessary when using this therapy. Cognitions are spontaneously altered when somatic and sensory reactions to problem states are desensitized.

These assumptions guided the development of several new and innovative MEMI techniques. As discussed, fixed eye movements replaced the random and arbitrary patterns of eye movement integration. Furthermore, the new patterns strategically targeted the most reactive feeling and sensory modalities associated with trauma recall in a gradually escalating exposure sequence, which is described in Chapter 8. Verbal reframes and subliminal commands added live, linguistic features to the therapy where none had existed before. All of these enhancements, coupled with new formative and summative assessments, transformed MEMI into a full-bodied, multisensory, limbic eye movement therapy for PTSD. And in spite of all these changes, the total number of eye movements used in MEMI versus in eye movement integration was significantly reduced, making MEMI easier to learn.

PART III

MEMI Protocol, Procedures, and Results

"A whole life can be shaped by an old trauma, remembered or not."

—Lenore Terr
Unchained Memories: True Stories of Traumatic Memories Lost and Found

Multichannel Eye Movement Integration

CHAPTER 6

MEMI Basic Eye Movements

In this book's introduction, I drew a distinction between *basic eye movements* in MEMI and the more intricate eye movement combinations called *sets*. This chapter depicts and describes the five basic eye movements used in the therapy. I ask practitioners to master these first because it later makes the task of learning the *sets* much easier. It's like developing basic vocabulary in a foreign language before trying to put sentences together. To continue with the analogy, the basic eye movements are actually the "building blocks" of the more complicated *sets*. The four eye movement *sets* will be introduced in Chapter 8, where Step 6 of the MEMI protocol is explained.

Therapists often ask why MEMI features only five basic eye movements, whereas eye movement integration recommended the use of between 10-20 patterns. I'm also asked whether the number was limited for any particular reason. It was not my intention to restrict the number. Instead, my goal was to create a unified system of eye movements that satisfied three requirements:

1. The basic eye movements had to target the sensory modalities from the NLP eye movement model that were most frequently occurring and the most reactive in response to traumas (the visual, emotional, and visceral modalities).
2. The movements, taken as a whole, had to be more effective at desensitizing reactions to traumas than the random approaches used in eye movement integration and EMDR.
3. The movements, to the extent possible, had to assure client safety and security.

Eye movement integration offered little guidance as to which eye movements to use and when. None were recommended for use over others, nor were suggestions made about which modalities (visual, auditory, visceral, emotional, or internal narratives) from the NLP model should be targeted more frequently or in what order. There was no particular system or rationale for making those decisions. Instead, therapists were encouraged to experiment with the patterns and decide which ones worked best for them. There was only one specific recommendation—that all six accessing positions (the same as eye movement locations) in the NLP model should be linked with one another during treatment. How to accomplish this was left up to the therapist's discretion.

As discussed in Chapter 5, practitioners completing eye movement integration training were reluctant to use the therapy without a prescribed approach to the eye movements. EMDR trained practitioners have also hesitated to use that therapy, but for different reasons: its excessively complex theories and procedures. Undoubtedly, some therapists are uncomfortable working with trauma clients to begin with; treating PTSD is a weighty responsibility. Being uncertain about how and when to use particular eye movements adds to practitioner discomfort. Their caution is understandable and their uneasiness is most likely driven by a desire to do no harm, a therapist's number one ethical obligation.

This lack of direction in eye movement integration also led to widely varying application of the technique among trained practitioners, particularly with regard to the choice and sequence of the eye movements. Without an explicit standard, replication and formal evaluation of the therapy's outcomes were precluded, unless and until the therapy could demonstrate greater procedural uniformity.

With all of this is mind, I began conducting eye movement experiments with my clients. During that process, I found myself questioning the soundness of eye movement integration's recommendation that all the accessing positions in the NLP model should be connected with one another during treatment. Although six different locations had been identified in the model—with cognitive, sensory, and kinesthetic relevance to mental processing—there was no evidence they were equally effective in desensitizing trauma symptoms. In addition, when creating eye movement integration, the Andreases suggested the use of elliptical and geometric patterns could also be helpful in desensitizing reactions. How or why they might be useful was not adequately explained.

In my experiments, I was interested in identifying eye movements that were reliable, fast acting, and effective in desensitizing visceral and emotional feelings and visual imagery—the locations associated with the most severe reactions during trauma recall. It followed that strategically targeting these modalities might be a more efficient, possibly even a more effective means of reorganizing traumatic memories. In the end, the five basic eye movements of MEMI emerged organically, after trial and error, and informed by clinical tests with hundreds of subjects. Four of the five basic movements had existed in some fashion in eye movement integration. Only one pattern is unique to MEMI. However, there was logic behind their selection, and the order in which they were presented was carefully considered.

I began by experimenting with preset movements involving the locations I had determined were most reactive. I found my assumptions were warranted. The eye movements that focused on those modalities produced more rapid and predictable improvements in symptoms. As indicated in Chapter 5, the use of random eye movements will produce some beneficial changes, but the testing I did confirmed a preset approach was more effective in reducing PTSD symptoms.

In eye movement therapies, the movement of a therapist's finger (or some object, like a pen) to one or more points in the visual field is called a *sweep*. It may help if you visualize the basic movements before the illustrations are introduced. Imagine you are looking at a glass building. You see a person board an elevator on one floor and go up to the next. That represents a vertical sweep from one point to another. If another person steps onto an escalator and travels from left to right, down to the floor below, that represents a diagonal sweep. These are each two-point sweeps because they connect just two locations.

Three-point sweeps connect three accessing positions. If a person rides an elevator up one floor, takes the escalator back down to the floor below, and walks back to where they first boarded the elevator (a triangle), that represents a three-point sweep.

After years of experimentation, five basic eye movements were designated for use in MEMI. Names were assigned to the patterns simply for the sake of learning:

1. **Above the Horizon** (a horizontal, 2-point sweep)
2. **Standing Triangle** (a 3-point sweep)
3. **Sitting Triangle** (a 3-point sweep)
4. **Figure 8** (a pictorial pattern)
5. **Shrinking Circles** (a pictorial pattern)

EYE MOVEMENT 1 — "ABOVE THE HORIZON"

The first basic eye movement is a 2-point sweep called "Above the Horizon." You draw it in the air horizontally about two inches above your client's head. Your pen or finger moves horizontally back and forth as many as 20 times, connecting the *visual past* and *visual future* accessing positions as depicted in *Figure 6.1*.

The speed of these sweeps is roughly one-two seconds across and the same back.

This back and forth movement is performed prior to each of the other four eye movements because the location is less reactive (safer) than other areas of a client's visual field. Your clients will quickly learn how this horizontal sweep marks the start and finish of all eye movements. The Above the Horizon sweep is also used to facilitate a smooth transition from one basic movement to another. This eye movement is almost the same as the horizontal eye movement used in EMDR, but the sweeps are generally wider, slower, and above eye level.

Above the Horizon Eye Movement

→ Back and forth from START

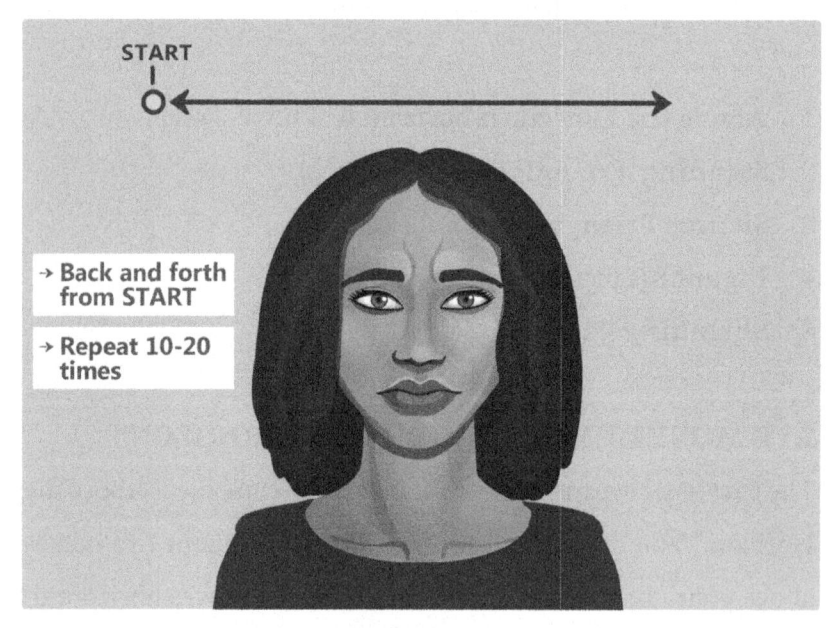

→ Repeat 10-20 times

Figure 6.1

MEMI *Basic Eye Movements*

EYE MOVEMENT 2 — "STANDING TRIANGLE"

The second basic movement is a 3-point sweep called the "Standing Triangle," drawn on the left side of your client's visual field and beginning at your upper left (client's upper right). As shown in *Figure 6.2*, it's called the Standing Triangle because, if the motions were drawn as lines on a wall, the triangle would look like it's standing on one of its points.

Standing Triangle Eye Movement

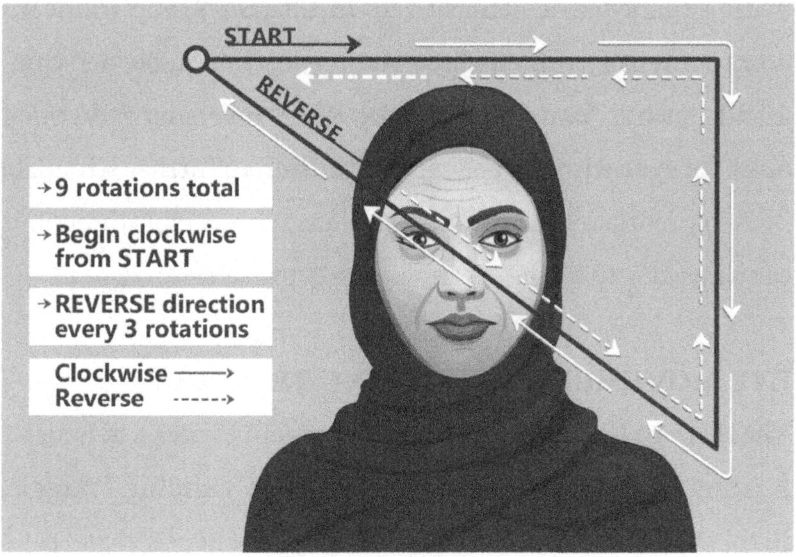

Figure 6.2

This eye movement can be drawn either clockwise or counterclockwise. I suggest you begin all the sweeps in a clockwise direction for uniformity. Although I'm not certain it will make a difference in the outcome, beginning in the same direction each time will facilitate your learning and help you avoid confusion later on. The direction is often reversed during the eye movement sweeps, yet always from the START position.

The benefits of reversing eye movement direction became evident to me the more I employed this strategy. Visually reversing the direction serves as a subliminal metaphor for changing course or undoing or "reversing" traumatic reactions. Just as the visual movement is stopped and reversed, so can the constellation of physical, emotional, and cognitive reactions to the traumatic experience be desensitized. In Chapter 8, you will learn how to intensify this effect by adding *direct* or embedded commands, such as **"and now reversing it"** or **"reversing everything now"** in sync with the change in direction to further stimulate memory reorganization. This technique for reversing directions can be used with all the eye movements and sets.

EYE MOVEMENT 3 — "SITTING TRIANGLE"

The third basic eye movement, depicted in Figure 6.3, is also a 3-point sweep. It's the complement of the Standing Triangle, in that you draw it on the right side of your client's visual field (your left side). It's called the "Sitting Triangle" because it appears to be sitting on one of its sides. The words sitting and standing have no other significance. Like its counterpart, this basic movement is drawn both clockwise and counterclockwise, and its direction is always reversed beginning from the START position.

Sitting Triangle Eye Movement

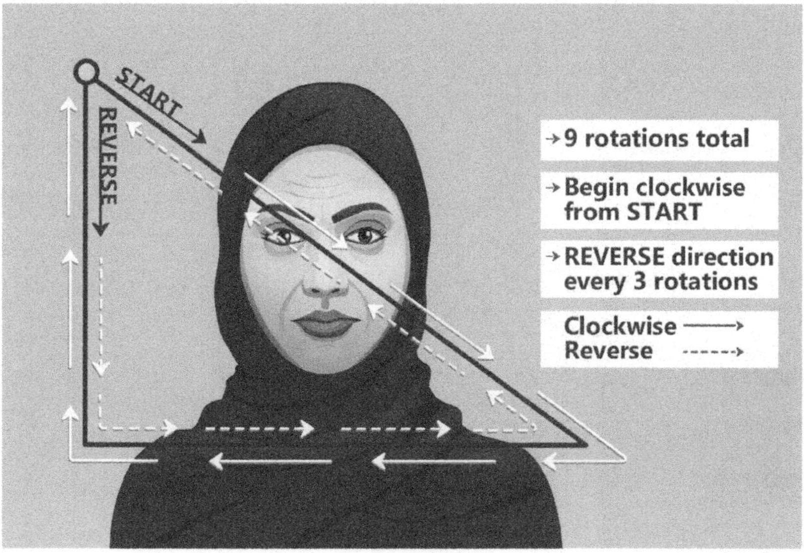

Figure 6.3

EYE MOVEMENT 4 — "FIGURE 8"

The fourth basic eye movement, depicted in *Figure 6.4*, is called the "Figure 8." You begin this pattern at the top-center of your client's visual field and at the same height as the Above the Horizon pattern. It's always preceded by a few Above the Horizon movements that eventually stop at the top-center and pause for a second or two before you begin to trace the figure. This pattern is also drawn in both directions (clockwise and counterclockwise), reversing at the top-center START position.

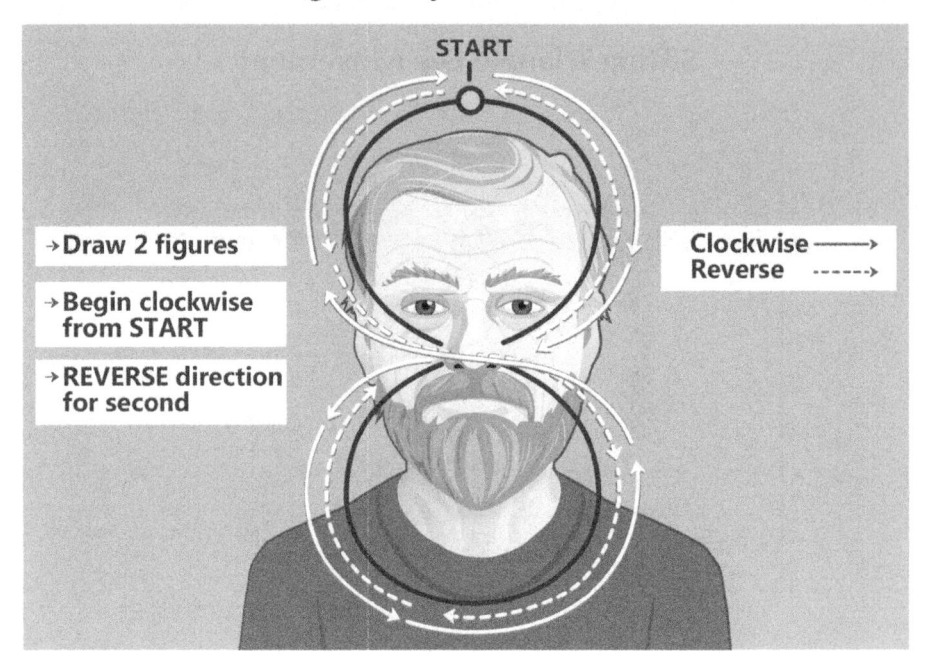

Figure 8 Eye Movement

- Draw 2 figures
- Begin clockwise from START
- REVERSE direction for second

Clockwise ⟶
Reverse ----->

Figure 6.4

EYE MOVEMENT 5 — "SHRINKING CIRCLES"

The last basic eye movement is called "Shrinking Circles." As illustrated in *Figure 6.5*, this movement also begins at the top-center of the visual field. After 2-4 Above the Horizon sweeps, pause your pen or finger at the center START position for a second or two before beginning to trace the outermost circle. Again, I recommend you begin in a clockwise direction for uniformity. The first and largest circle is drawn clockwise from the START position. Once you complete the circle and arrive back at the START position, pause for 1-2 seconds before tracing the next circle. The direction is reversed with the second circle from the START position, and all subsequent circles are drawn in that counterclockwise direction. Each successive circle is drawn smaller, and as they reduce in size they naturally appear to shrink upward.

Figure 6.5 shows a total of 8 circles. This is the recommendation, but if you draw 6 or 10, it will not affect the results. The pattern ends when you circumscribe the last circle (no larger than a pea) before moving into a few Above the Horizon sweeps.

Shrinking Circles Eye Movement

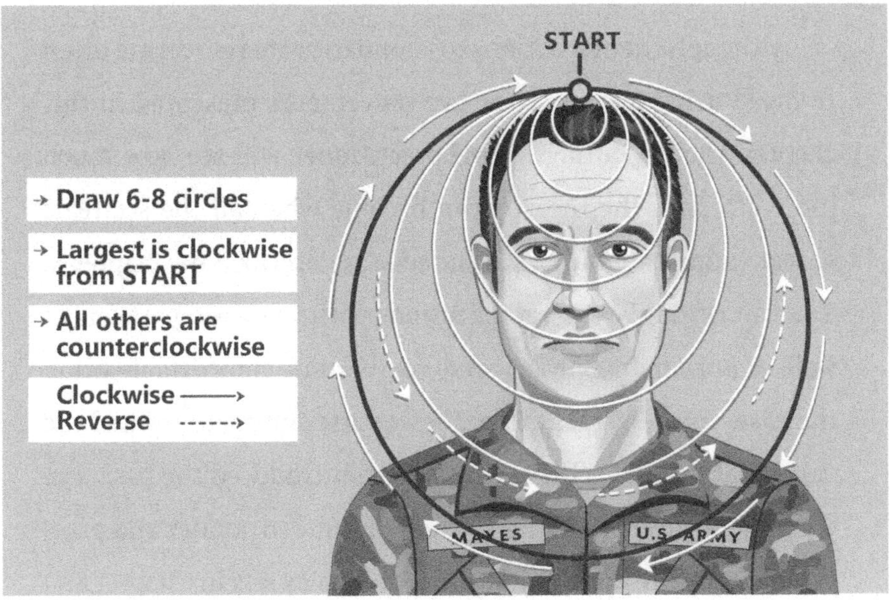

- → Draw 6-8 circles
- → Largest is clockwise from START
- → All others are counterclockwise

Clockwise ——→
Reverse -----→

Figure 6.5

The Shrinking Circles movement is unique to MEMI. After adding the "reversing" verbalization to the Figure 8 pattern while changing the direction of the sweeps, I realized a similar metaphor could be created for this pattern. The "shrinking" of the circles became a metaphor for reducing the size of the reactions to the problem state (a spatial metaphor). A verbal intervention was later added to suggest a reduction in problem state symptoms as the circle sizes decreased in size: *"And now a circle... encompassing everything, John... and shrinking it down now... smaller... and smaller."* At this point, however, I suggest you focus only on the mechanics of performing the circles—it's a little tricky—and not worry about the verbal intervention. The verbalizations will be addressed in Chapter 8.

Although client reactions to traumatic experiences are often resolved using just the basic eye movements presented in this chapter, the beginning MEMI practitioner will see how much more effective the therapy can become when all the strategic verbalizations are built into the sets, as described in Chapter 8. You can certainly use verbalizations with the basic patterns as well, as I often do, but I suggest you become comfortable using the basic eye movements first, before attempting to the add the verbalizations. To achieve that, I have introduced the basic eye movements in this chapter to give you time to ponder and practice them before taking on the more complex *sets* in Chapter 8.

CHAPTER 7

MEMI Protocol Steps 1–5

The MEMI protocol represents a paradigm shift away from cognitive behavioral therapies and toward an approach that more immediately targets the brain's reactions to traumatic experiences. Given recent developments in neuroscience referenced in Chapter 1, and mounting evidence of the inadequacies of contemporary exposure therapies cited in Chapter 3, trauma researchers are recommending a shift in focus to therapies that more directly target limbic abnormalities during trauma recall (Stevens et al., 2017). MEMI is a therapy that promotes such a shift.

The MEMI protocol is based on the therapy's theoretical model described in Chapter 5. The model is put into practice via specific procedures, therapist instructions, sample scripts, three assessment techniques, and a worksheet for recording changes in the elements of a memory's structure. Whereas eye movement integration had no formal tracking procedures, the MEMI Worksheet provides a mechanism for observing and recording progress following each eye movement set. Neurophysiological responses, cognitive shifts, and changes in a traumatic event's context are all documented.

A new assessment designed specifically for this therapy, called the *Intensity Scale* (I-Scale), measures microchanges in the strength of client reactions to feelings and images associated with traumatic events. The *Subjective Units of Distress Scale* (SUD Scale), used commonly in medical and mental health practice, provides a global, in session measure of perceived distress or disturbance in relation to the entire problem state.

PTSD CHECKLIST

The PTSD Checklist for DSM-5 (PCL-5) is a standardized, pre and post treatment measure designed to diagnose PTSD and measure progress in relation to the DSM-5 PTSD diagnostic criteria. I have been using the PCL to assess MEMI outcomes for over a decade. In 2010, while experimenting with the earlier version of this instrument designed for use with the DSM-IV diagnostic criteria, I conducted a pilot study to determine the instrument's compatibility with the MEMI protocol. Not only was it a good fit, comparisons of pre and post MEMI outcomes were extremely positive. Although there were only five subjects in the experiment, precluding generalization of the results, the PCL was retained as one measure in the MEMI protocol. (For informational purposes, a summary of that study is contained in Appendix D.)

When the PCL was revised to align with the DSM-5 PTSD diagnostic criteria in 2013, I noticed an even closer fit with MEMI's two other assessments. The PCL-5 shared several characteristics with the new I-Scale, particularly in the way they both assess

PTSD sensory information and feeling reactions. In addition, the response options for the PCL-5 and the I-Scale were structured similarly. Each used a Likert-type scale with five possible responses, yielding scores from 0-4 and representing either the intensity of client reactions to PTSD symptoms (I-Scale), or how bothered clients were by the symptoms (PCL-5). The SUD Scale also measures a client's level of distress, but in relation to the entire problem state and not individual symptoms as the PCL-5 and the I-Scale do. Correlation studies of these three instruments could determine whether they measure similar constructs and further validate the MEMI protocol. Instructions for using all three of these assessments will be described in detail in Chapter 8.

DESIGNING THE THERAPY SPACE

Before explaining the steps, I would like to recommend at this point that you give consideration to the physical space you will use for MEMI client sessions. The room should be large enough for your client's chair to face a blank wall, curtain, or screen from a distance of 7 to 10 feet. This is not always possible, but it should be a goal. These are the surfaces upon which your client will project images of the problem state in order to achieve therapeutic dissociation. If the room is very small, selecting another location is advisable. The wall or other "viewing" surface should be devoid of framed pictures or complex designs, as they may create a visual distraction. If there are windows in the room, they should be covered with solid curtains or blinds to prevent natural light from flooding your client's visual field.

Chairs or stools with no arms or low-profile arms are best, because arms on a chair will interfere with your hand movements during the sweeps. The two chairs should face each other, but be slightly offset, as depicted in *Figure 7.1*. If you are right-handed, place your chair to your client's right. If left-handed, place your chair to your client's left. This will allow you to extend your dominant hand in front of your client during the eye movements but not obstruct their view of the problem state behind you.

MEMI PROTOCOL STEPS 1-5

This chapter introduces the first five steps in the protocol—essentially, all the groundwork necessary to prepare your client for the eye movement interventions and data collection in Steps 6-10. During this first half of the protocol, you will be: confirming or ruling out a PTSD diagnosis by administering the PCL-5; creating a working alliance with your client; securing an agreement to change the problem state; gathering baseline data; establishing client protections prior to exposure; and explaining the procedures to come.

More specifically, these are the first five steps in the protocol:

1. Administer the PCL-5 and establish rapport
2. Secure agreement to change
3. Pretest elements of structure
4. Anchor a resource state
5. Introduce therapeutic dissociation

MEMI Protocol Steps 1-5

Chair Positions for the Eye Movements

Figure 7.1

STEP 1. ADMINISTER THE PCL-5 AND ESTABLISH RAPPORT

In this first step, you will be seeking two outcomes. One is to determine whether or not your client qualifies for a PTSD diagnosis using the PCL-5. The other is the establishment of an interactive rhythm with your client, otherwise known as *rapport*.

Administer the PCL-5

If you suspect your new client has been exposed to one or more traumatizing events, based on your interactions prior to or at the initial appointment, you should administer the PCL-5 before beginning treatment. Developed by the PTSD Center of the U.S. Department of Veterans Affairs (Weathers et al., 2013), the checklist is aligned with the DSM-5's PTSD diagnostic criteria and offers a validated pre and post measure of treatment outcomes. With only 20 multiple-choice questions, the checklist can be completed in about 10 minutes. The checklist is normally readministered from two to eight weeks after treatment has been completed, making pre and post comparison of results possible. A copy of the PCL-5 can be found in Appendix A.

Even if your client does not qualify for a PTSD diagnosis, PCL-5 data might still be helpful as a practical measure of symptom reduction. For example, if your client does not meet all the requirements for a PTSD diagnosis, but they have very high re-experiencing scores on the checklist, the items measuring those symptoms could still be compared pre and post treatment.

Establish Rapport

Rapport is a basic NLP strategy designed to create a communication connection between you and your client, or to place the two of you in sync at the beginning of a session. The technique is designed to make your client feel comfortable with you and follow your lead during treatment. According to Dilts and DeLozier (2000), rapport is established when a therapist "mirrors" a client's posture, breathing, facial expressions, and gestures and repeats a client's language patterns and key words when conversing. Once established, rapport makes it easier for you to guide your client through the steps that follow. Here are some behaviors you could mirror with a client:

- Breathing (rapid, slow, deep, or shallow)
- Arm and leg positions (crossed or uncrossed)
- Posture (relaxed or rigid)
- Head tilt (down, up, cocked, or straight)
- Rhythm, speed, and tone of speech (loud, soft, fast, slow, smooth, or choppy)
- Key words (those emphasized or repeated)
- Gestures
- Facial expressions

Practically speaking, you unobtrusively match the actions of your client by breathing in unison, casually reflecting body language and gestures, using the same tone of voice, and copying their temperament, all with the goal of building trust and assuring that a communication loop is established. Milton Erickson, known as the father of modern hypnotherapy, called this technique "going to school on your client."

This is not as difficult as it might seem, although putting it all together does require some practice. If you are new to the technique, begin by mirroring your client's most obvious behaviors—hand and leg positions, posture, and head tilt—before adding the rest. And you don't have to match all the behaviors listed here, just three or four will suffice. This technique can be seen in practice in video demonstrations of MEMI at **www.deninger.com** or **www.multichanneleyemovementintegration.com**.

Mastering how to establish rapport with your client is like learning to drive a car. You can only read the manual for so long before you have to get behind the wheel and work the pedals. You can also practice establishing rapport with friends or non-MEMI clients, because the technique is helpful in all communication situations.

STEP 2. SECURE AGREEMENT TO CHANGE

When your client expresses an unwavering commitment to change the negative responses associated with a traumatic experience, the probability of achieving those changes increases. If your client agrees to a change, but their tone of voice or nonverbal behaviors are not congruent with that response, the potential for success is diminished. For example, if your client answers, "I think so" when you ask if they want the image of their attacker to appear less threatening, those words convey uncertainty. Similarly, if they respond, "That would be nice," but their head is shaking from side to side, nonverbally saying no, the agreement to change is inadequate. In cases like these, you should explore that incongruence and seek a firmer commitment before proceeding.

Client agreement is usually clear and obtained easily. Pursuit of this agreement is more important in situations in which an individual is unsure about the need to change their response, under pressure from others not to change, doubtful that change is possible, or even afraid a change might make matters worse.

The way to seek a commitment to change is typically straightforward, as in the following script:

> *"Before we begin, I have a question for you. We want to make sure there's no part of you that would object to making this change. If any part of you is reluctant to make the change, your success might be hampered. So, given the fact that your memory of this event has caused you difficulty with intrusive thoughts, flashbacks, and anxiety, do you agree that you would like to change how you react to it?"*
>
> Your client answers yes.
>
> *"And is there any part of you that's not sure about wanting this change? Any part?"*

Your client answers no, with congruent behavioral responses. If your client, for any reason, is reluctant to make the change, you should explore the reasons for the uncertainty. A client who would like to change, but does not think it's possible, can be asked:

"If the experience were less disturbing, would that be better for you?" and/or *"Even if you're not sure changing the experience is possible, are you open to that possibility? Would you accept a change if it happened?"*

Once the agreement to change has been secured, you move on to the pretest.

STEP 3. PRETEST ELEMENTS OF STRUCTURE

The first pretest task is to assist your client in selecting the memory (or portion of it) to be the focus during the eye movement sweeps. Traumatic memories can be unidimensional or complex, rooted in a single event in one moment in time (witnessing a murder) or linked to several events together and forming a complex, interrelated mass (multiple instances of intrafamilial abuse). In the latter case, a client may be flooded with intrusive images and somatic reactions from several offenses—all intense—that compete for attention. So, where do you start?

Focusing on just one aspect of an event—one moment in time—and its symptom structure, especially if there were multiple offenses, is advisable for two reasons:

1. A single focus will facilitate before and after testing.
2. Instead of being flooded with multiple images and feelings associated with different events, a single focus will be more manageable, tolerable, and imbue a sense of control in your client.

MEMI Does Not Use Systematic Desensitization

You will not develop a graduated hierarchy of distressing events with your client when using MEMI, nor will you work from the least disturbing event to the most difficult. Instead, you and your client will identify the most troubling aspect of an event or situation as the focus of treatment, *but only if that selection will not compromise client safety.* The chosen experience might be the one occurring most frequently in thoughts, the one causing the most distress, or the most difficult to dismiss when thoughts about it do occur. Selecting the most threatening aspect may seem counterintuitive, but this is usually desirable. First, when the most extreme manifestations (visual, emotional, and visceral) of a memory are desensitized or integrated, less provocative aspects of a traumatic experience are usually reorganized and become less menacing as well. Second, the protections afforded by anchoring and therapeutic dissociation in MEMI almost always provide adequate protection, even when addressing the most troublesome aspect of a memory.

The following are the major differences between MEMI and systematic desensitization, in both theory and practice.

MEMI	**Systematic Desensitization**
1. No graduated hierarchy	1. Uses graduated hierarchy
2. Begins with most distressing aspect	2. Begins with least distressing aspect
3. Uses therapeutic dissociation	3. No therapeutic dissociation
4. Uses resource anchoring	4. Uses breathing/relaxation techniques
5. Repeated exposure unnecessary for desensitization	5. Repeated exposure deemed necessary for desensitization
6. Deep exposure unnecessary	6. Deep exposure to all aspects required
7. Verbalizing the trauma story is optional	7. Frequent retellings of trauma stories are required

When to Avoid the Most Distressing Memory

Although infrequent, there are times when beginning with the most disturbing aspect of a memory is not advised. The case of a rape victim, "Rebecca," described in Chapter 11, is one example. Rebecca had been to three different therapists before her first appointment with me. She had refused to address her PTSD memories with any of them; she was too frightened. She canceled our first appointment, and her husband had to accompany her to my office when she finally decided to attempt another appointment. At the beginning of our first session, she insisted she would not discuss what had happened to her in any way.

I agreed to that. Instead, I asked her to tell me what her days were like. She disclosed that when home alone, she sat on the floor in a dark closet and rocked back and forth. We never discussed why she chose to be in the closet or the fact that she had been raped. Instead, I asked if she would like to be more comfortable at home and not have to hide in the closet. She said yes. This was her *agreement to change*, but only in relation to the closet behavior.

Rebecca's habit of creating a safe place for herself is what I call a surrogate response—a behavior and state of being closely associated with the problem state, yet detached enough from it to avoid severe distress, a coping mechanism. There was no reason for me to probe her intentions related to that safety zone she had created for herself and risk a more severe reaction. For these reasons, beginning by addressing the surrogate response, rather than the more threatening problem state at the core of her distress, made more sense. In essence, the purpose was to calm her arousal symptoms by starting at the edges of her response repertoire, and then move closer to the center. I was also hopeful that addressing the closet behavior would help desensitize the central problem state—the rape itself. We began eye movement sweeps focused on a recent time when Rebecca was in distress in the closet.

At her second appointment, Rebecca reported she had stopped retreating to the closet, and she expressed a desire to work on the sexual assault. It appeared the gains she had achieved during our initial session had instilled enough confidence in her to cross that threshold. After the third eye movements set, and without being asked, she described the rape in some detail without decompensating. This need to begin more cautiously, with an indirect approach, is rare but sometimes advisable.

Selecting the Problem State

The following script is a guide to use when helping your client select the problem state for focus:

> *"Before we begin, it's best if we select just one part of your experience to focus on. Jumping around from one part to another may interfere with your success. If you <u>do</u> find yourself jumping around while we're doing the eye movements, that's OK. Just tell me, and we'll work around it.*
>
> *"Now, the aspect of your experience that we are most interested in is the part you would say causes you the most difficulty. It may be the part you think about most often, the one that's hardest to ignore when you do think about it, or the one that causes you the most anxiety. If you have more than one, just decide which one you think is worse. Do you have one in mind?"*

Most clients have little difficulty deciding which aspect of their traumatic memory is the most distressing. For later comparisons, you will want to observe the intensity of your client's verbal and nonverbal reactions as they briefly access (think about) that part of the memory. You can make a mental note of the facial expressions, posture, muscle tension, and voice quality you observe. These are the behaviors you will expect to be improved or extinguished after the memory has been desensitized. The language your client uses to describe the traumatic experience (their thoughts) should also change, becoming less negative.

If your client has difficulty choosing which aspect of a trauma is the most distressing, you can ask questions, such as:

"Which one is the most pressing for you?"

"Which one, if resolved, would give you the most relief?"

"Which aspect do you have flashbacks or dreams about?"

Once the problem state has been selected, even if your client has not divulged details about the memory they have chosen, there is one task remaining before conducting the pretest. You will explain the two measures that will be used to assess changes in perceptions following each eye movement set.

Intensity Scale (I-Scale)

Again, this scale measures your client's perceptions of the three representational systems I believe are the most frequent, threatening, and symptomatic during trauma recall—visceral feelings, emotional feelings, and visual images. You will explain how the I-Scale assesses the intensity of these variables during the pretest and following each eye movement set, using these five response options:

0 = no intensity at all
 1 = low intensity
 2 = moderate intensity
 3 = high intensity
 4 = the highest intensity

An Intensity Scale value from 0-4 is called an I-Score.

Subjective Units of Distress Scale (SUD Scale)
When describing the SUD Scale, you will explain that it's a cumulative measure of overall symptom changes. It is administered after each eye movement set and at the end of a session. Both I-Scale and SUD Scale responses are recorded on the MEMI Worksheet (Appendix B) in order to track progress.

You can use the following script to introduce the I-Scale and the SUD Scale to your client:

> *"After each eye movement set, I will ask you for two different scores. The first will be a score from 0-4 that expresses how intense your reactions are to the visual images and feelings associated with this memory. Zero equals no intensity at all and 4 is the highest intensity. I'll explain how that works as we go along.*
>
> *"The second score will measure how distressful or troubling the whole memory is following each eye movement set. This is a percentage from 0-100%, with 0% representing no distress at all and 100% the worst*

possible distress. Before we begin, this overall score is arbitrarily set at 100%, meaning the memory as a whole is as distressful as you usually recall it. After each eye movement set, I'll ask you if the memory is the same or different, what changed, and if the changes make it better or worse. If it's better, your score will go down to 90%, 80%, or 70%. If worse, it will go up. We will take intensity and overall score readings after each set."

Note: The terms *SUD Scale* and *I-Scale* are not included in the instructions to your client, although you can mention them by name if you believe it will be helpful. Also, some clinicians prefer to use a 10-point SUD Scale, with 0 representing no discomfort at all and 10 the worst possible distress. The 100% scale seems preferable, primarily because it allows a client to be more discriminating than a 10-point scale does.

Once these tests have been explained to your client, you can proceed with the actual pretest of the structural elements. However, in rare situations, a pretest might not be conducted at all, like in my work with Rebecca. In her case, attempting a pretest, when she would have to divulge specific reactions she had during the assault, would have violated our agreement to not discuss the rape. There was also a strong possibility she would have terminated our session, as she had with previous therapists. Instead, we began with a pretest of her reactions while she was in the closet. In addition, as you shall see in this chapter and the next, the MEMI protocol allows for conducting the pretest without asking your client to tell their trauma story.

Pretesting the Elements

The pretest is normally conducted before anchoring a resource state in your client. If you establish a resource anchor before the pretest, the protection afforded by the anchor could distort or mask your client's habitual response to the trauma. It's important that you observe as unfiltered a client response as possible, while also taking care to avoid too strong a reaction. For this reason, when performing a pretest you will ask your client to very briefly project an image of the event onto a surface across the room. Although this physical separation (dissociated view) will usually prevent your client from "collapsing" into the experience and triggering undue distress, if your client should begin to decompensate, you can quickly interrupt the regression by saying, **"OK, come back here. Don't go there yet. Stay here with me now"** or **"Look at me, Bill. We don't want you to go there yet."**

Some may argue that even using a dissociated view when gathering pretest data will restrict the true expression of the problem state. On the contrary, a dissociated view will often help your client more calmly and accurately recollect their habitual response, because any anxiety caused by a first-person, associated view is diminished. Compelling clients to recall their reactions during elevated emotional distress, like some exposure therapies do, is neither necessary nor advised. Furthermore, deep and repetitive exposure to the raw images and sensations from the initiation of one's trauma is not required for symptom amelioration.

It seems, almost by nature, exposure therapies place much more emphasis on reliving traumatic experiences than on shielding clients from the harsh neurosensory reactions to recalled traumas. This results in the dramatically high dropout rates and questions about exposure therapy effectiveness discussed in Chapter 3. As van der Kolk (2015) wrote, "We can only 'process' horrendous experiences if they do not overwhelm us" (p. 225).

You will use the MEMI Worksheet to record pretest information as well as the changes that occur after eye movement sets. Instructions for how to do this are explained in Chapter 9.

The following script describes how to introduce the pretest to your client:

"In a minute, I'm going to ask you to project an image of that experience out there on the wall across the room, but don't look out there yet. Look at me now. When you do look out there, I want you to take a brief snapshot of the event and come right back here. We don't want you to be back IN that experience again, but very briefly viewing it from a distance instead. I will then ask you questions about the experience that will help us make comparisons later. Now, if describing the details of your experience will be too difficult for you, we'll skip questions about the 'who, what, where, and when' for now. Would you be willing to describe what happened, or not? It's completely optional. You can always describe the event at a later time, when you feel more confident."

Clients are not required to describe traumatic experiences during MEMI treatment unless they choose to. Giving your client a choice about whether to reveal the details of what happened is a unique feature of the MEMI protocol that further enhances client safety and security. When using MEMI, you will be able to resolve PTSD symptoms without even knowing what happened during the original event, which is very reassuring to survivors. With this being the case, why would anyone want to risk triggering re-experiencing or arousal symptoms? Yet most exposure therapies require clients to describe what happened over and over. In any case, clients who initially refuse to "tell their stories" in MEMI often volunteer the information after memory desensitization has been achieved, when they are composed, and the desire to divulge what happened becomes important to *them*—just like Rebecca did.

MEMI clients are never prevented from describing their traumas, because repetition may build resilience. But here is a caution that challenges the principal assumption underlying exposure therapies: Multiple retellings do not guarantee symptom reduction. Some individuals get stuck in trigger/anxiety loops—caused by continuous, distress-generating retellings of the tragedy. Others drop out of treatment due to the pain.

The belief fostered by some EMDR and exposure proponents that deep exposure to the formation of a trauma during treatment is a requirement for desensitization must be challenged. I believe the use of repetitive exposure to neutralize the brain anomalies associated with trauma is not the most expedient or effective approach. Research is beginning to support this view (Stevens et al., 2017).

Following a demonstration of EMI at the 5th International Congress on Ericksonian Approaches to Hypnosis and Psychotherapy, Steve Andreas (1993) explained why it's ill-advised to pressure clients to repeat their trauma stories. A retelling requires a person to linguistically associate into the experience as the first-person narrator, in that time and place when the memory was formed. There are times when clients will insist on explaining their trauma story to you as the therapist, even though the telling is emotionally difficult for them. But they only need to tell it once, and only if it's important to *them*.

In my experience, even the most difficult memories can be resolved without undue distress using MEMI. The brain is a flexible mechanism with many paths to resetting its programs, not just one. A MEMI demonstration at the 2012 National Conference of the American Mental Health Counseling Association, conducted with a volunteer who did not tell her story, can be viewed at **www.deninger.com** or **www.multichanneleyemovementintegration.com**.When I contacted the volunteer several months later, she reported the memory was still desensitized.

STEP 4. ANCHOR A RESOURCE STATE

Resource state anchoring is an NLP strategy designed to counterbalance or neutralize the reactions clients have during exposure to traumatic events. Again, this is the equivalent of Wolpe's reciprocal inhibition. Resource state anchoring in NLP is best understood by first defining its component parts: state, resource state, and anchor.

Andreas and Faulkner (1996) define a *state* in NLP as "the physiology and neurology of a particular mindset or skill, positive or negative" (p. 335). A state is given shape (one could also say structure) by its context, thoughts, feelings, and sensory information associated with a particular experience. A negative state, characterized by self-limiting thoughts, troublesome images, sad feelings, or anxiety can arise whenever an individual is reminded of a disturbing event. Conversely, recalling a triumphant personal experience can stimulate a positive state, with uplifting thoughts, pleasant images, and gratifying feelings.

The authors describe a *resource state* as a "typically positive, action-oriented, potential-filled experience in a person's life" (p. 334). In MEMI, a positive state from an individual's past (e.g., one associated with a personal accomplishment) becomes a resource state when it's brought to life to counteract the reactions triggered by exposure to a traumatic memory. It serves a similar purpose as the relaxation training used in exposure therapies, but is more relevant, potent, and effective.

Andreas and Faulkner describe an *anchor* as "a particular stimulus; sight, sound, word, or touch that automatically brings up a particular memory and state of body and mind" (p. 331). When anchoring a resource state in your client, you will use a two-step process. After selecting an empowering client memory, you will elicit the thoughts, feelings, and sensory information associated with the memory. Then you will attach a verbal anchor (link) to the positive experience, that when fired (invoked) in the future, will restimulate those positive responses in your client. In MEMI, clients are anchored in resource states before exposing them to traumatic memories, except when an anchor is deemed unnecessary. Anchored resource states are then maintained throughout exposure.

There are three types of anchors: auditory, visual, and kinesthetic. The word **Powerful** is used as an anchor in the scripts throughout this book. This an example of an auditory (in this case, vocalized) anchor. Auditory anchors are by far the type most commonly used. Although kinesthetic (tactile) anchors are considered stronger in their capacity to establish and maintain resource states, they are rarely used. A therapist touching the arm of a client to install an anchor might compromise the integrity of a trauma survivor. Visual anchors are the least effective type and the most infrequently used, for hearing people, that is. In my work with deaf and hard of hearing clients, however, visual anchors are almost always used. Because auditory anchors are obviously out of the question, American Sign Language signs or gestures are the primary way to install a resource state in deaf clients.

When selecting an experience to anchor, begin by asking your client to recall a personal experience when they felt the opposite of their response to the traumatic event. For example, if recalling the event makes your client feel "weak," you would ask them to select a personal experience when they felt extremely strong; if fearful, then fearless. Klein refers to these as competent states. The nature and severity of your client's traumatic experience will help determine the characteristics of an appropriate anchor. In other words, the *power* of the resource anchor is important, because both you and your client must have confidence the anchored state will be robust enough to counterbalance reactions to the traumatic experience. The obvious purpose is to keep your client as resourceful (secure) as possible when accessing the traumatic content. Once you and your client have agreed on an experience to be anchored, you will ask questions designed to elicit the images, sounds, thoughts, and feelings associated with the experience.

Anchoring Instructions

With soothing, melodic vocalizations, like those used in hypnosis or guided imagery, you will ask your client to close their eyes, move back through time, and re-enter the uplifting experience you are about to anchor. In the following script, the anchor selected is the word powerful, based on "Carlene's" report that she felt powerless at the time of her trauma. The capitalized, underlined, and unitalicized word **<u>Powerful</u>** in the text denotes times when the anchor is fired (spoken with greater emphasis and volume), causing the powerful thoughts and feelings to be rekindled in your client. Notice that the italicized and uncapitalized word ***powerful*** appears in several other places in the script as well, but these are times the word is spoken without emphasis and the anchor is not fired.

"So now, Carlene, take a nice, long, slow, deep breath in, and as you exhale, let your eyelids gently drop down and rest comfortably. Breathe in very slowly and exhale just... as... slowly. That's good. As you relax every part of you... every part, from the top of your head down to the tips of your toes, begin to recall that powerful feeling just as you experienced it then, as if you're reliving that moment all over again.

"And if you will... now, recall that day, that very moment, and settle into that powerful experience. Remember what it was like to be there."

Repeat details the client has shared.

"See everything you saw then, all the images. Hear everything you heard then, all the sounds. See yourself as powerful as you were then. See everything in your surroundings—the faces, the objects, the actions. Feel all the powerful feelings you felt at that time. Notice the exact location in your body where those feelings are the most powerful. Feel them growing in intensity, just as they did then. Embrace that experience. Make those feelings just as powerful now as they were then. Allow them to spread throughout your body, into every nook and cranny. And now, allow all those feelings, sensations, and images to rise to the very top! Feel them at their fullest."

> When your client is observed to be at the top or peak of that experience—and just before they are about to descend—you confirm the experience, fire the anchor, and then repeat it.

"That's right, Carlene. __Powerful__... __Powerful__. And now, you can hold onto those feelings throughout our time together today. And anytime you hear me say that word... __Powerful__... __Powerful__... those strong feelings will intensify inside you, no matter what is happening. You will feel just as powerful now as you did then. Good... Good... Very good. Now, as you slowly open your eyes and come back here, bring all those powerful resources with you."

To test that the anchor has actually been established, you will change the topic of conversation in order to "break state." You might admire what your client is wearing or comment about the weather. You might simply say, *"Wow, you're very good at this!"* or ask, *"How do you think you're doing so far?"* Then you refire the anchor by asking, *"And if I were to say the word __Powerful__ Carlene, what happens?"* If the anchoring was successful, you will observe an immediate, resourceful response in your client—a deep breath, rising shoulders, or a grin. Your client will likely also report the (somatic or emotional) feelings associated with the anchored state are stirring inside again. If the anchor is unsuccessful, meaning the resource state is not re-triggered after the refiring, you may have to consider selecting another experience to anchor. Following a successful refiring of the anchor, you will periodically reinforce it throughout the session with firing comments, such as, *"And remember, Carlene, __Powerful__!"*

Further information about anchoring resource states can be read in basic NLP texts or found online at **www.nlpu.com**

or **www.nlp.com**. Demonstrations of the anchoring technique are also included in MEMI videos at **www.deninger.com** or **www.multichanneleyemovementintegration.com**.

STEP 5. INTRODUCE THERAPEUTIC DISSOCIATION

Therapeutic dissociation creates an imagined visual separation between your client and their traumatic memory during treatment. When asked to project a distressing image of the experience on a surface across the room, a beneficial physical distance is created between your client and the traumatic image. In mental health nomenclature, the term *dissociation* signifies a break of some sort from conscious awareness. These states range from the relatively harmless (missing your bus stop) to the seriously pathological (as in dissociative identity disorder). Coupling the term therapeutic with dissociation to describe this procedure in MEMI indicates the technique is beneficial—not pathological—which turns the term *dissociation* on its head and demonstrates how negative constructs can also be viewed as having value in NLP.

Associated versus Dissociated View

In NLP, a helpful distinction is drawn between two ways of recalling visual experiences. A person is either associated into an experience (as if re-experiencing it and looking out through their own eyes at the scene around them) or dissociated from it (viewing it from some other vantage point). With an associated view, the person sees, hears, and feels the event as they did when it was occurring. An individual might say, "I'm staring down at my trembling hands, and I feel my palms sweating; I'm reliving it again!" This perception of the event locates the person's awareness inside the body, as opposed to observing themself going through the experience from some external perspective (Young, 2004).

In a dissociated view, a person might say, "I'm watching myself from across the room. It looks like my hands are trembling in my lap." While a person using an associated view is described as "in the experience," in a dissociated view a person is "outside of it." O'Conner (2001) went so far as to describe association and dissociation as two different ways of experiencing the world.

More importantly, shifting a client's visual perspective from associated to dissociated (or vice versa) can change their perception of and reaction to the experience itself. Consider Rodney, an urban police officer who was sitting in his cruiser on a dark street when shots were fired at his vehicle. He felt trapped and panicked. Later, every time he thought of the experience, his physical and emotional reactions were severe. When asked from what perspective he recalled the experience, he responded that he felt as if he were seated in his patrol car again and he was looking around frantically. I asked him to replay the experience, but view it from outside the car and some distance away. When he did, the severity of his physical and emotional reactions diminished.

Visual Kinesthetic Dissociation

An understanding of associated and dissociated views led to the development of a standardized NLP technique called visual kinesthetic dissociation, or V/K/D. The V signifies the visual representation of a particular memory and the K the kinesthetic representation, or its associated feelings. According to Dilts and DeLozier (2000), V/K/D is a combination of the hypnotic techniques of Milton Erickson and the spatial sorting strategies of Fritz Perls. The approach was introduced by Bandler and Grinder (1979) and used as a treatment for trauma and phobias.

To separate your client from their negative reactions to a disturbing memory while using V/K/D, you use a movie metaphor to create a new way of viewing the experience. You verbally guide your client into an imaginary movie theater and have them take a seat near the stage and movie screen. Then you ask them to imagine they can "float" their awareness (and another pair of eyes) out from their body in the seat and up into the balcony's projection booth. From there, they can see themself seated down in the theater, watching the stage, as well as anything portrayed on the movie screen. You then ask your client to "run" a movie of the problem state from the projection booth, while simultaneously observing themself in the first-floor seat, and the re-enactment of the problem state on the screen.

This strategy creates what is called a *double dissociation* in NLP. Twice removed from the re-enactment of the traumatic experience on the screen, your client is no longer a participant but an observer. This separator state created by V/K/D impedes the harsh, habitual reactions to the memory. Running a movie of the experience from start to finish and viewing it from the projection booth also serves as a pattern interruption that desensitizes the memory and calms its neurosensory reactions.

V/K/D can become even more complex, involving imagined interactions between the person seated in the theater and their younger self in the movie. A complicated but remarkably effective strategy, V/K/D can be used on its own as a "cure" for PTSD and phobias, or in combination with MEMI. This is but a brief description of the technique.

Therapeutic Dissociation Instructions

A parallel concept used to describe this separator state is therapeutic dissociation. And as you shall see, this is another way of creating a visual, temporal, and spatial separation between clients and their negative experiences. As its name implies, therapeutic dissociation is a beneficial means of disconnecting your client from their habitual reaction to a trauma during exposure. You remind your client that the experience took place in the *past* (across the room on the wall), but they are in the *present*, in their chair (temporal separation). Likewise, the physical space between your client and the memory is reinforced. They are watching a visual representation of their younger self going through the experience on a surface across the room (visual and temporal separation). They are not associated into the experience but separated from it, and in the role of an observer. They are also a distance away from the experience across the room (spatial separation). Thus, therapeutic dissociation and V/K/D are essentially two different ways of rendering the same phenomenon.

In this final step before beginning the eye movement sweeps, it's important to carefully explain to your client how therapeutic dissociation works, because it's an effective safeguard when used as designed. I prefer to employ elements of V/K/D without going into the entire procedure, and I have found the protections afforded by therapeutic dissociation are sufficient *for most clients*. However, you should remember that V/K/D is an option, particularly when clients are unable to maintain a dissociated view of an experience.

Adding Gestures and Vocalizations

As a means of reinforcing the separation in time and space between your client and their problem state, you will also use specialized vocalizations and gestures along with therapeutic dissociation. After reminding your client that they are safely anchored in their resource state, you will introduce therapeutic dissociation with the following script:

> *"When it's time to begin the eye movements, Mary Ellen, you will project the image of your experience out there on the wall...*
>
> Gesture toward the wall with your dominant hand.

... across the room. Not now, but when I tell you. As soon as you project the image, I will raise my pen to this position."

Raise your finger or pen to your client's visual future accessing position.

"That will be your cue to put your eyes on the pen and follow it wherever it goes, while trying not to blink."

Demonstrate how the eyes should move by following your finger or pen with your own eyes as you move it.

"You will move just your eyes, and not your head. I will move the pen slowly, but if it becomes uncomfortable for any reason, just let me know, and we will make adjustments. OK?"

Seek a yes answer.

"Remember, you are seated here in the present... "

Gesture with two open hands toward your client in the chair, then "fire" the anchor.

*"... and feeling **Powerful**."*

Again, gesture with your dominant hand toward the wall, turn your head, and "throw your voice" in that direction.

"You will be observing a younger version of yourself way over there, going through that past experience."

Continue to look in that direction, gesture, and vocalize toward the wall, while also keeping an eye on your client for any break in their composure.

"You are free to alter the image in any way you like to make it more comfortable... by putting it out of focus, by changing it from color to black and white... If it's a movie, you can run it in slow-motion... you can make it smaller... lower the volume... or you can move the image farther away.

"When we're finished with the eye movements, you will look back at me and we'll take a short break. I'll then ask you to look out there again and tell me if what you see is the same or different. I won't guide or coach you in any way. OK? Ready to begin?"

Examples of therapeutic dissociation with gestures and vocalizations can be viewed in demonstration videos at **www.deninger.com** or **www.multichanneleyemovementintegration.com**.

The first five steps in the protocol have set the stage for the curative eye movement sets to come in Steps 6-10. Obtaining an unequivocal agreement to change the problem state and grounding your client in safety and security are of paramount importance. A client who commits to this healing process and is at ease in your care has already begun to recover. They are stepping forward with intention and moving away from the problem state's habitual response pattern. Likewise, in order for your client to embrace change in the face of the neurophysiological roadblocks to trauma resolution, it's important for you to exude confidence, energy, and hopefulness. If you are at all uneasy about working with survivors or, worse yet, have your own unresolved trauma, take steps to address your own history, misgivings, and fears.

CHAPTER 8

MEMI Protocol Step 6

The first five steps in the MEMI protocol have prepared you and your client for the eye movement sets described in this chapter. While it's important for you to exude confidence and hopefulness, remember how terrified your client is likely to feel. Be patient if you have to repeat information you explained in Steps 1-5. Your client is about to confront disturbing memories they have been avoiding for a long time, perhaps decades. And take a deep breath of your own. You are about to embark on the most consequential part of this therapy.

To place where you are in the MEMI process into context, the remaining five steps in the protocol are:

6. Conduct eye movements
7. Test Structure of Experience elements
8. Take I-Score and SUD Score readings
9. Record results on MEMI Worksheet
10. Conduct future rehearsal and self-appreciation exercises

(Loop back)

Here is a summary of the remaining steps in the MEMI protocol. The first eye movement set is performed at the beginning of Step 6. It will be followed by retesting the traumatic memory's elements (context, thoughts, feelings, and sensory information) in Step 7. This is when you will ask your client if the problem state has changed and if so, how. I-Scores of trauma-related feelings and imagery and a SUD Score are then requested in Step 8. The responses from Steps 7 and 8 are recorded on the MEMI Worksheet in Step 9. The process then loops back and Steps 6 through 9 are repeated during Sets 2, 3, and 4. After the last set, a final SUD Score assesses whether the overall problem state has been sufficiently desensitized and the eye movements can be discontinued. The protocol culminates in Step 10 with a future rehearsal of the problem state and an exercise in self-appreciation.

STEP 6. CONDUCT EYE MOVEMENTS

The four eye movement *sets* described in this chapter are made up of combinations of the five *basic eye movements* presented in Chapter 6. The sets have been carefully sequenced to create a unified whole, and they include strategic verbalizations designed to enhance the efficiency and effectiveness of the therapy. Unlike the random use of eye movement sweeps in eye movement integration, MEMI eye movement sets are fixed and sequenced. The structure of the sets and the other innovations are the result of years of testing.

Explaining in print how the eye movement sweeps and therapist vocalizations are performed in tandem is complicated, to say the least. Putting it all together requires the acquisition of two contrasting skills—one requiring verbal memory and one manual dexterity. You will then have to practice performing both skills simultaneously. Viewing the video demonstrations conducted with volunteers at an AMHCA Conference and at a Northern Virginia Counselor's presentation at **www.deninger.com** or **www.multichanneleyemovementintegration.com** will allow you to see the therapy in action. The sample scripts and written instructions found in this chapter will also make mastery of the sets less complicated.

Eye movement integration was proven effective in reducing the symptoms associated with negative experiences long before the fixed eye movement sequences and verbalizations were added in MEMI. But standardization of the eye movements established consistency and uniformity in the therapy, while also enhancing its effectiveness. Further, adding strategic vocalizations created a dynamic, multisensory approach to trauma unlike any other.

EMI developers theorized that the eye movements would be more effective if they linked all of the accessing positions in the NLP eye movement model with each other in order to stimulate the greatest number of neurological connections. However, clinical experience with MEMI has confirmed that an approach strategically and systematically targeting key accessing positions (internal narratives, visualizations, and feelings) streamlines the therapy without compromising results; linking *all* accessing positions is unnecessary. And adding strategic verbalizations in a multichannel format further improves the outcomes.

Again, it's important for you to first master the basic eye movements and practice them with clients or friends before attempting the eye movement *sets* presented in this chapter. If you haven't yet done so, take the time now to learn the basic movements before attempting to master the more intricate sets. This will also later confirm how much more effective the multisensory sets are with verbal comments added to them. Descriptions of the four sets in this chapter include graphic depictions, step-by-step instructions for physically performing the sweeps, and sections offering scripts and tips.

Set 1 Eye Movement Sweeps

Each eye movement set begins with the Above the Horizon pattern. You will quickly note that Set 1 is the same as basic Eye Movement 1. Hold a finger or a pen up to your client's visual future accessing position located next to the START button in *Figure 8.1*. (Step 5 in the protocol has already prepared your client for this starting point.) As soon as your client's eyes are focused on the pen, begin moving the pen in horizontal, back and forth, *smooth pursuit* movements, about two inches above your client's head and from 8 to 15 inches in front of your client's face.

If the movements are too fast, you might not detect meaningful behavioral shifts in your client's body language or facial

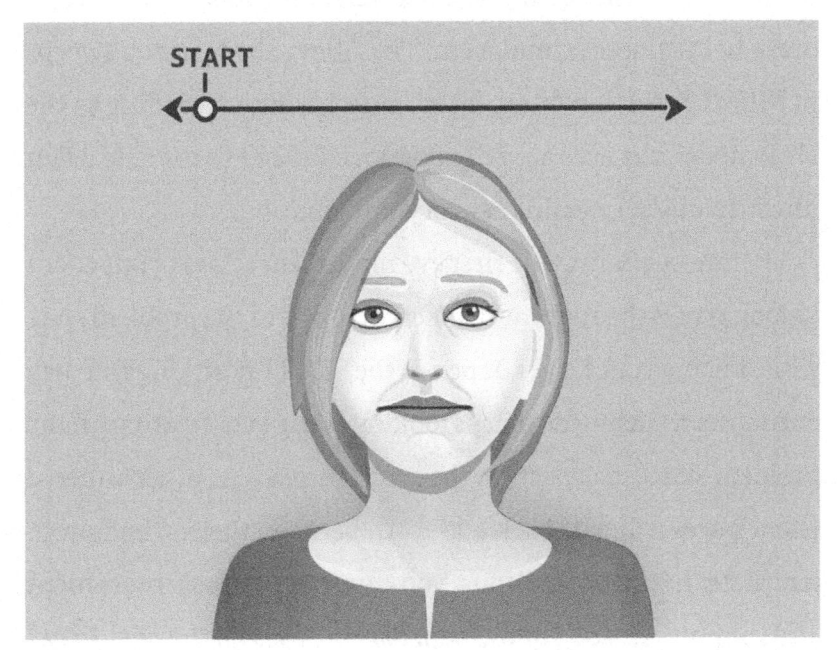

Set 1 — Above the Horizon

Figure 8.1

expressions that are important to track. A comfortable pace would be about two seconds across and two seconds back. This 2-point sweep (connecting only two locations) is repeated 10-20 times and should take about 20 to 35 seconds to complete. The movements should glide as far out to each side as your client's eyes can comfortably track without their head moving–roughly 12-15 inches from either side of your client's head. Of course, the distance to either side will vary, based on how close to your client's face you are performing the movements.

In EMDR, comparable horizontal eye movements are sometimes more restricted, traversing just a few inches on either side of the nose, because it's believed that having the eyes cross the midline of the face is sufficient to achieve bilateral brain hemisphere stimulation. The Above the Horizon sweeps in MEMI go farther out to either side, because according to the NLP model, the eyes actually do move farther to the side when unconsciously accessing sensory information.

Before beginning the first eye movement set, ask your client to look across the room at the mental image of the problem state while raising your finger or pen to the START position. You may encounter a client who delays looking at the pen, fixating on the problem state image across the room instead. At other times, a client's eyes will dart back and forth between the pen and problem state. In these situations, you can stall the pen's movement and simply say, *"Look at the pen, Bill"* or *"Eyes on the pen, Sally."* You might wiggle your finger or tap the pen with a finger from the hand holding it to add a visual cue. The goal is to keep your client's eyes focused on the pen throughout the sweeps.

Sometimes a client will be drawn by curiosity to see if the problem state is actually changing and will look directly at the image instead of the pen in the middle of a sweep. If your client is not focusing on the pen, you can call a time-out and comment that they appear to be having difficulty. After a simple explanation about the importance of following the pen's movements, clients are usually able to do as requested. If your client is still unable to do so, you can ask them to disregard the problem state for a moment and practice following the pen's movement before resuming.

Eyeglasses sometimes interfere with the smooth tracking of the pen. You can ask your client if their glasses are required to follow the pen, and if not, suggest they be removed. Lack of visual acuity while tracking the pen does not interfere with symptom resolution; it may even add protection, if it inhibits your client's association into the problem state.

Some eye movement integration practitioners have cautioned against using the technique with clients prone to seizures. Beaulieu (2003) found no evidence this was a problem. In any case, you should ask your client if, for any reason, they would have difficulty following the pen's movement. Some clients have problems smoothly tracking objects, as when their eye movements stall, and then have to catch up to the pen. If this occurs, you can slow down the movements. As long as their eyes reach the targeted accessing positions, any difficulty in smoothly tracking the pen should not interfere with the results. If your client does have a seizure disorder, erring on the side of caution by consulting with a medical specialist is advised.

Clients often visualize traumatic events straight in front of them and at horizon level. If your client accesses the image of their trauma above the horizon, you can ask them to move the image down, so the first sweep is positioned just above the visualization. Of course, by firing the anchor, you can also remind your client that they are **Powerful**, in the present, and the image is across the room in the past.

If your client repeatedly blinks as the sweeps are underway, while moving the pen you can verbally remind them to refrain from blinking, with a verbal statement like, ***"Try not to blink, Judy."*** Clients will sometimes blink—as if reacting to something—as their eyes move over a specific position in the visual field. Steve Andreas suggested these reactions to particular locations might represent "problem areas." He recommended moving the finger or pen slowly back and forth over the spot, as if erasing a mistake, until the client no longer blinks.

Joan was a MEMI volunteer at a training session, who was angry with a colleague following an altercation. She wanted to be free of the resentment she was holding. During the second eye movement set, she kept blinking each time the pen passed over the *auditory past* accessing position. When I moved the pen back and forth over that location several times as part of one sweep, Joan recalled an event when her abusive mother belittled her over a minor infraction. She realized she had also been belittled by her colleague and the two events might be related. We desensitized the experience with her mother by conducting a set of eye movements focused only on that problem state. Then we returned our focus to the resentment she had for her colleague with another eye movement set. Joan no longer blinked when her eyes moved over the auditory past location and her feelings about her colleague were resolved satisfactorily.

Set 1 Scripts and Tips

You are free to modify the sample scripts in this guide in order to make them your own. The scripts are presented in bold, italics, and within quotation marks. Of course, not all of your remarks can or should be prescribed. These scripts are meant as a guide.

You will be speaking intermittently, not constantly, during the eye movement sets. Pauses between verbalizations in the scripts are represented by an ellipsis (three periods). Instructions for therapists are depicted in nonbold and unitalicized print. Clients normally listen without talking. Other therapies encourage client-therapist dialog during the eye movements, but conversation distracts clients from the two tasks of watching the pen and thinking about the trauma.

The first eye movement set is an opportunity for your client to become adjusted to the procedure as much as it is to begin resolution of the problem state. This set of sweeps, with its location above the horizon, is less likely to trigger reactions in clients. In other words, the sweep is more resourceful, a safer place to start.

Here is a sample script for use during the first eye movement set:

"All right, Bill. Now it's time for you to project the image of that experience out there—and remember, still feeling <u>Powerful</u> here in your chair... Here we go..."

Raise your pen, wait for your client's eyes to focus on it, and begin the sweeps.

"This is kind of like splitting your awareness... For example, I could notice someone coming through the door over there without ever looking away from you ... In the same way, you can watch this pen in the

foreground and still think about that experience in the background... Good... Focusing your eyes on the pen here while thinking about that experience over there... That's right... Good."

> When the sweeps end, move the pen behind your back and out of sight. Then break state by asking your client to look at you while you briefly engage them in conversation.

The first posttest follows, in the form of Steps 7 and 8 in the protocol. Changes are recorded on the MEMI Worksheet (Step 9). The process then loops back to Step 6 and the second eye movement set is conducted. Instructions for conducting posttests and recording results on the MEMI Worksheet are explained in Chapter 9.

Set 2 Eye Movement Sweeps
Set 2 begins with a few of the Above the Horizon sweeps, as performed in Set 1, before smoothly transitioning into 6 to 9 repetitions of the 3-point Standing Triangle sweeps depicted in *Figure 8.2*. All sweeps are bidirectional and can be reversed at any time from the START position. I recommend reversing direction after every three rotations for uniformity. If you're performing 9 rotations altogether, you would reverse the movement twice. Reversing sweep direction is a potent metaphor for changing or undoing the entire problem state and can be reinforced with a comment like *"And reversing it."*

Set 2 — Standing Triangle and Self-talk Command

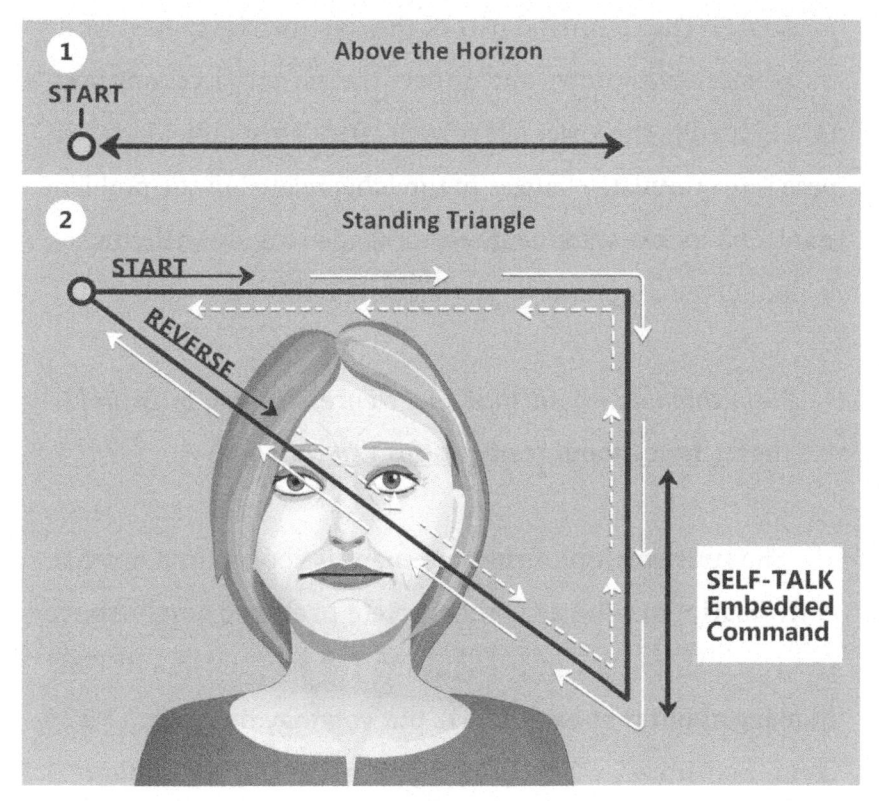

Figure 8.2

Near the end of the rotations, you will also verbalize the first embedded command. To reiterate, an embedded command is an intoned directive nested within a larger question, statement, or quotation. The command is vocalized differently than the rest of the sentence, drawing attention to the comment's imperative nature—not too forcefully, but the emphasis should be noticeable compared to the rest of the statement.

Notice the location of the self-talk embedded command in *Figure 8.2*. The command part of the statement is spoken while the pen is moving down and up over the self-talk accessing position located in the lower left of your client's visual field. Its purpose is to stimulate changes in thoughts related to the problem state. The spoken statement recommended for use with this set, including the command (underlined), is as follows:

*"Still thinking about that experience, but you may find that... **Your thoughts about this will change**."*

The first portion of the statement is spoken in a normal, conversational tone as you complete back and forth Above the Horizon sweeps in preparation for the command: **"Still thinking about that experience, but you may find that... "** The command, however—***"Your thoughts about this will change"***—is intoned with a slightly deeper pitch (lower timbre) and in a monotonic voice, while sweeping down and up two times over just the self-talk location. You begin stating the command when your pen reaches the top of that location shown in *Figure 8.2* (about 12 inches above the bottom of the vertical sweep). While speaking the command, you move your pen down and up twice, synchronizing the pen's movements with the rhythm of your speech. After the command is completed, from the bottom of the triangle you move the pen diagonally back to the START position and finish the set with one or two more Standing Triangle sweeps before moving the pen behind your back. All these actions will require some practice to appear seamless.

Immediately following the embedded command, revealing behavioral responses might be observed in your client. Their eyes might blink or slowly widen, or their head might tilt back slightly or cock to the side. Sometimes a client will take a deep breath, or their upper torso or facial muscles will noticeably relax. These reactions can be read as transformational. They may be a result of: the change in your vocal tone, timbre, and pace; the repeated movement of your client's eyes over the self-talk location while thinking about the problem state; or the linguistic content of the command appealing to the unconscious mind. The actual reason, or combination of reasons, can only be known if your client recalls their internal reaction during the eye movements (many cannot). You don't have to ask at this time about their thoughts. Any changes will be captured during the posttest following the eye movement set.

In brief, the rationale for this particular embedded command is rooted in the belief that the self-talk accessing position in the NLP eye movement model has merit and occurs frequently across the population. Even if an individual does not access thoughts via this position, changes in cognition might be sparked by the eye movements alone, or the linguistic content and hypnotic mediations of the embedded command. These possibilities are credible, given clinical evidence that multichannel sensory input, when adeptly synchronized and applied to a problem state, is more effective than single channel stimulation. In essence, with a variety of pattern interruptions occurring at the same time, the efficiency and effectiveness of the therapy improves—just like the performance of a computer program with multiple paths leading to a single solution. Think of the success of Microsoft Windows.

Set 2 Scripts and Tips

Here is a script with instructions for conducting Set 2:

> *"OK, Bill, look out at that experience in the distance..."*

Raise your pen to the START position when your client looks at the image across the room.

> *"and focus your eyes on the pen."*

Perform several back and forth Above the Horizon sweeps as in Set 1 before beginning clockwise Standing Triangle sweeps from the START position.

> *"That's right, Bill... still aware of that experience, but **Powerful** at the same time..."*

After three Standing Triangles, reverse the sweep direction to counterclockwise from the START position.

> *"Good so far..."*

After three more sweeps, reverse the direction once again from the START position.

"Good... Good."

The movement of your pen should be clockwise at this point. Finish the last of the triangle sweeps, then begin the back and forth Above the Horizon sweeps from START while beginning to speak the comments.

The spoken statement recommended for use with this set, including the command is as follows:

"Still thinking about that experience, but you may find that..."

From your client's visual past position, move the pen straight down to the top of the self-talk position, then move it down and up twice over just that area while you state the embedded command.

"Your thoughts about this will change."

Transition the pen diagonally back to the START position and trace two more Standing Triangles before lowering the pen. When the pen is behind your back and out of sight, you break state by saying, **"Look at me, Bill,"** and engage your client in conversation.

Another assessment follows as you direct your client to look over at the problem state again, ask the posttest questions about the structure of the experience, and request Intensity and SUD Scores. The information is recorded on the MEMI Worksheet and the cycle repeats, but with Set 3.

Set 3 Eye Movement Sweeps

The third eye movement set combines the Figure 8 pattern with the Standing Triangle pattern, as seen in *Figure 8.3*. Like before, the set begins with several Above the Horizon sweeps. Those are followed by 6 to 9 of the same Standing Triangle sweeps that were performed in Set 2. The sweeps are still bi-directional and reversed every three rotations from START. After these Standing Triangle sweeps, prepare to introduce a verbal reframe combined with an embedded command that is spoken at the same time a Figure 8 is traced in the center of your client's field of vision. Notice that the Figure 8 sweeps are traced in both directions because the figure is reversed twice.

The spoken statement recommended for use while the Figure 8 is being traced is as follows, with the embedded command underlined:

"And now a figure 8 right here in the foreground. That experience and everything related to it in the distant... background. And reversing it—reversing everything now."

Say the first sentence of the statement, **"And now a figure 8 right here in the foreground,"** as you make the Above the Horizon sweeps and prepare to trace the figure 8. The second sentence, **"That experience and everything related to it in the distant... background,"** is spoken as you trace the first revolution of the "8" and prepare to reverse direction. As your pen arrives at the center-top of the figure, hold it in place for a couple seconds while saying, **"... And reversing it"** as you reverse the movement

MEMI Protocol Step 6

Set 3 — Standing Triangle and Figure 8 Sweeps

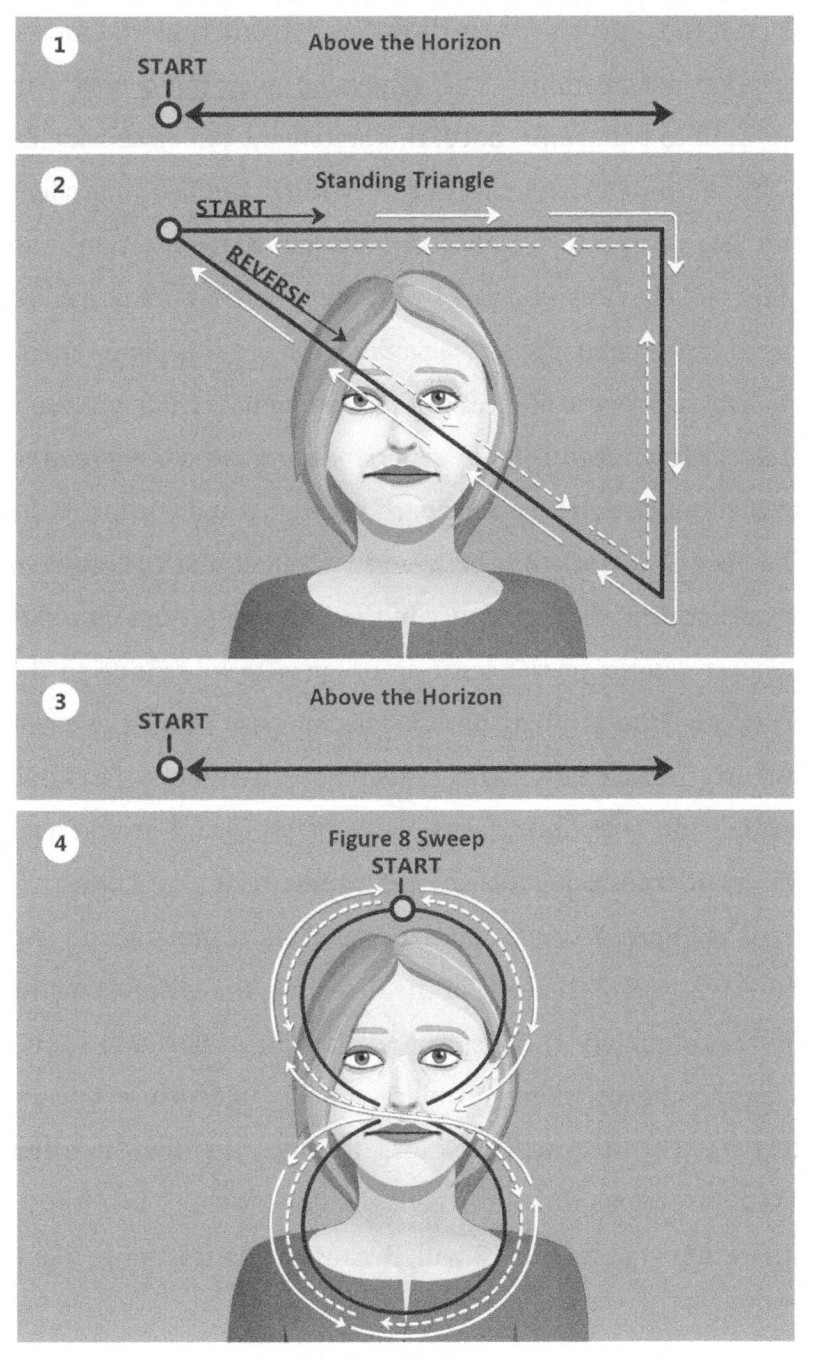

Figure 8.3

of the pen and trace the second "8" in the opposite direction. Back at the top, you reverse direction a second time and intone the embedded command *"... **Reversing everything now.**"* In addition to being embedded, this statement can be considered a direct command. The word "everything" implies your client can also reverse (or resolve) the internal representations and external behaviors associated with the problem state portrayed in the background, just as the pen's movement is being reversed.

The first two sentences of this statement include multifaceted reframes. Stating **"that experience and everything related to it in the distant... background"** highlights and reinforces the therapeutic dissociation between your client and the problem state. Locating the experience in the *"distant . . . background"* denotes greater spatial separation, but also hints (due to the pause and the familiar phrase "distant past") that the event might be farther back in time. The intent is to reframe the visual, spatial, and temporal aspects of the memory, and in so doing stimulate transitions that resolve trauma-related reactions.

The Figure 8 sweep and the embedded command add two more features to this set. For the first time, the eye movements more completely traverse the visualization position found straight ahead (where problem state images are often accessed). The diagonal linkages in the previous Standing Triangle sweeps did slice through that location, but not to the extent that a figure 8 will. Because a client is more likely to associate into a problem state when staring straight ahead, moving a client's eyes around in that position is delayed until this third set. By this time, the problem state should be partially desensitized, and the reframing procedure clearly reinforces therapeutic dissociation.

As complicated as this might seem, the set flows smoothly from start to finish and the results are routinely significant. Once again, clients often demonstrate subtle but meaningful behavioral shifts in the form of eye blinking, head tilts, muscle relaxation, or even an upturn at a corner of their mouth (indicating humor or satisfaction) after the embedded command is voiced. You should make note of these behaviors. You can ask at the end of the set if your client recalls doing them, and whether anything significant was occurring internally at the time. This set, and the Figure 8 sequence in particular, has proven to be a very powerful pattern interruption.

Set 3 Scripts and Tips

The spoken instructions recommended for use with this two-part set feature language used previously and new language to accompany the Figure 8 sweep.

"Ready again, Bill?"

> Raise your pen to the START position and commence several back and forth sweeps while saying...

*"Just like before, you can think about that experience out there in the past, remain **Powerful** here in the present, and focus your eyes on the pen. Good!"*

Begin the Standing Triangle sweeps clockwise from the START position. After 3 complete rotations, reverse direction.

"Good so far."

After 3 more rotations, reverse direction again. When these rotations are completed, move the pen into several back and forth sweeps while saying ...

"And now a figure 8 right here in the foreground."

Stop your pen at the top-center of your client's visual field, where START is located in *Figure 8.3*. Hold the pen there for a second or two. Very slowly trace an "8" in either direction, drawing it in the air as depicted. The pace is slowed to allow you enough time to say everything in the script below before the pen again reaches START at the top of the "8."

"That experience and everything related to it in the distant... background."

You again pause the pen at the top for a second before reversing direction and drawing another figure 8 while saying...

"... And reversing it."

Once back at the top of the "8" again, alter your voice and intone the embedded command while tracing the second reversed "8."

"Reversing everything now."

Once back at the top, glide your pen into a few Above the Horizon sweeps, do one Standing Triangle sweep, and move the pen behind your back.

Another posttest of the elements is then conducted, Intensity and SUD Scores are obtained, and the results are recorded on the MEMI Worksheet. Next, you move on to the fourth and final set.

Set 4 Eye Movement Sweeps
The eye movement sets are designed to build on one another. The first set's Above the Horizon sweeps begin with the resourceful visual future accessing position and avoid the locations where thoughts, feelings, and visualizations of past events are accessed. The second set stimulates the self-talk accessing position but avoids the areas where feeling states and visualizations are generally accessed. The third set more directly addresses the center of the visual field, where images are "seen," as well as the visual past location. The fourth set will address feeling states, often the most intense internal reactions clients experience.

Multichannel Eye Movement Integration

Set 4 — Both Triangle Sweeps, Circles and FEELINGS Command

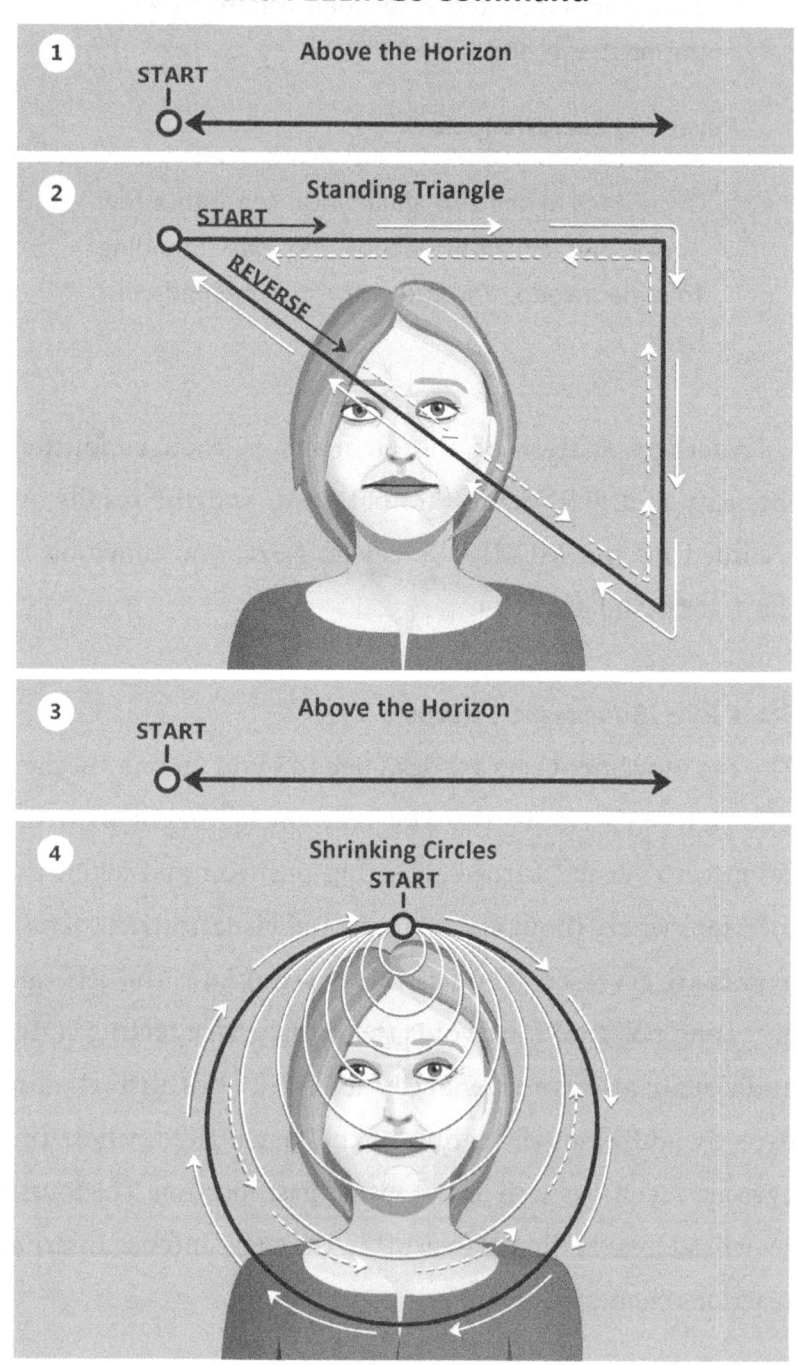

1 Above the Horizon
START

2 Standing Triangle
START
REVERSE

3 Above the Horizon
START

4 Shrinking Circles
START

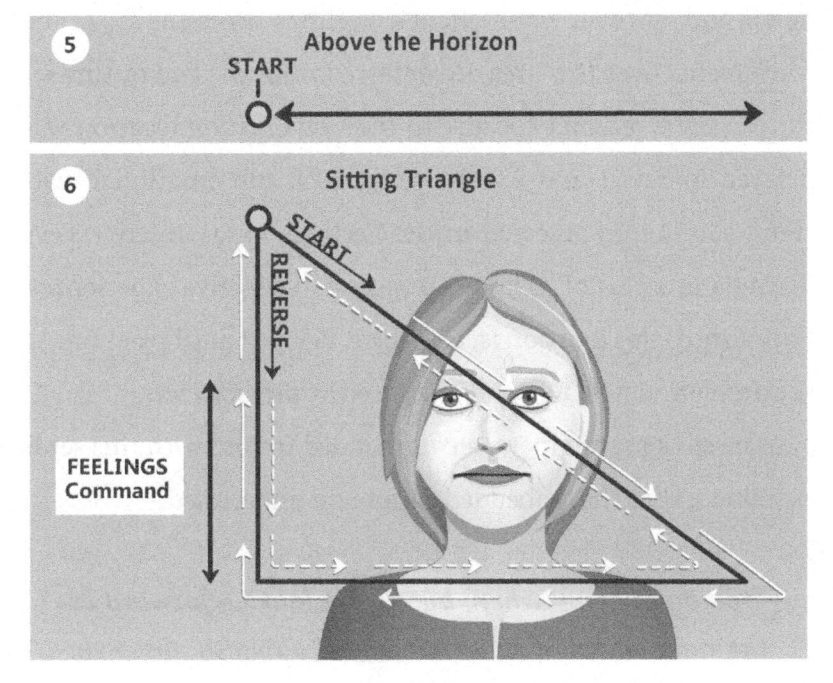

Figure 8.4

Figure 8.4 depicts the eye movement actions in Set 4:

- Above the Horizon sweeps
- Standing Triangle sweeps
- Shrinking Circle sweeps
- Sitting Triangle sweeps
- A verbal reframe while the circles are reducing in size (as part of Shrinking Circles)
- An embedded command near the end of the set (spoken as the pen moves down and up over the Feelings accessing position)

The embedded command is spoken while the pen is moving down and up over your client's Feelings accessing position. Movements over this area are deferred until the end of this set for the same reason exposure to the visualization location was delayed in Sets 1 and 2: Intense somatic and emotional reactions, sometimes accessed in the Feelings location, are a very distressing aspect of a client's response to negative experiences. Exposure to this location is, therefore, delayed until reactions to the problem state have been mitigated by previous sets.

The spoken statement recommended for use with this set is as follows, with the embedded command underlined:

"You don't know when, but you're looking forward to the time when... <u>your feelings will diminish, dissolve, defuse.</u>" (You could substitute the words disappear or decrease.)

This set is the most complicated of all, but will be experienced by your client as a unified whole when executed as intended. You can tell by now that the eye movement sets grow in complexity, as much to accustom your client to the form and rhythm of the therapy as to gradually add more intricate and stimulating pattern interruptions. In addition, the longer the eye movement repetitions continue, the more likely your client will relax into a quasi-hypnotic state, creating a heightened opportunity for memory reorganization.

MEMI Protocol Step 6

Sweep 4 Scripts and Tips

The initial eye movements and spoken instructions in Set 4 are similar to those in previous sets. But this set adds a 3-point sweep on your client's right side (Sitting Triangle) in order to traverse the feeling states' location at the end of the set.

"OK, Bill, here we go again."

> Raise your pen to the START position and trace several back and forth Above the Horizon sweeps.

"Still aware of that experience, but closely following the pen with your eyes."

> You may not need to fire the **Powerful** anchor at this point; the problem state may have been sufficiently desensitized by previous sets. The first Standing Triangle sweeps are traced clockwise from the START position, as in previous sets. After three complete rotations, the direction is reversed.

"Very good!"

> At the end of three rotations, you prepare to initiate the Shrinking Circles statements by moving from the START position into a few back and forth Above the Horizon sweeps. Move your pen to the top-center of the visual field where START is located in *Figure 8.4* and hold it there for a second or two. As you trace the largest (outermost) circle in either direction, say...

"And now a circle... encompassing** (or containing) **everything."

Trace the next smaller circle and each successive circle in the opposite direction. As you trace these circles, you synchronize the rhythm of the pen's movements with your spoken words.

"And reversing it. And it's getting smaller... and smaller... and smaller... and smaller... shrinking it down to the size of a pea."

Trace the last circle, literally the size of a pea, several times before transitioning into back and forth sweeps.

"That's right."

From the START position, begin tracing the Sitting Triangle sweeps clockwise. As before with the Standing Triangles, reverse direction from the START position every three rotations. As you complete the last rotation, move your pen into 2 or 3 Above the Horizon sweeps and say the first part of the spoken statement...

"You don't know when, but... you're looking forward to the time when..."

Move your pen in a downward sweep from the START position and intone the embedded command as the pen moves down and up three times over just the Feelings location. The words "diminish, dissolve, and defuse" are spoken in tandem with the downward strokes over the feelings location.

"... your feelings will diminish... dissolve... defuse."

Conclude with a couple of Sitting Triangle sweeps in either direction before moving the pen out of sight. Conduct another posttest of the elements, obtain final Intensity and SUD Scores, and record the results on the MEMI Worksheet.

The use of the Shrinking Circles pattern in the fourth set has a dual purpose. First, using the phrase "encompassing everything" when drawing the initial circle creates a visual-spatial metaphor intimating that all the elements of the problem state are encapsulated within that circle. Because they are contained, they can also be acted upon. Second, the language: *"And it's getting smaller... and smaller... and smaller... and smaller ... shrinking it down to the size of a pea"* as the circles shrink in size is another metaphor implying somatic and emotional reactions are also becoming smaller or being minimized.

Final Tips

This is usually the point at which the formal eye movement sets are concluded, but only if satisfactory results have been achieved—when a SUD Score of 50% or less is attained, and when your client confirms their reaction to the trauma in the future will be manageable. Performing all four sets may, in fact, be unnecessary, because satisfactory results are often achieved by the end of Sets 2 or 3. The negative aspects of individual memories have usually been resolved by this point. Although only four eye movement sets are presented in this guide, you can always perform additional eye movements by repeating previous sets, in whole or in part, or by improvising new sweeps to any of the accessing positions. But that's normally unnecessary.

Important note: Eye movement set sequences are sometimes altered due to anomalies that arise. For example, occasionally when you are doing sweeps with the selected problem state as the focus, a different visual image or aspect of the trauma will unexpectedly show up.

Marie developed severe anxiety when her fiancé called off their engagement. A year later, she was still unable to put that experience behind her or cease attempting to contact him. When asked for a memory to become the focus of treatment, she immediately described a painful image she could not get out of her mind: him gazing at her as he stood in a doorway. While we were conducting the eye movements, her head jerked, her eyes blinked twice, and she said, "I just remembered something." She described a more recent memory, when she saw her ex-fiancé through the window of a café having lunch with his new girlfriend. That image supplanted the one of him standing in the doorway, and was also more difficult for her to process. We began over again with this new image as the focus.

When different memories intervene in this fashion, they might also be accompanied by feelings or sensory information not previously reported. It's imperative, then, to make sure these new symptoms are desensitized as well. If a new memory arises, especially if it's more disturbing, it should be addressed before returning to the one originally selected for resolution. This may be the mind's way of forcing more troubling parts of an experience to the surface and marking the significance of those new aspects in perpetuating trauma symptoms.

Sometimes the different elements of a memory's structure do not resolve at the same pace. Occasionally, the image associated with a memory becomes less distinguishable, but the associated emotions or visceral feelings remain the same or even worsen. If this occurs, you can ask your client to be especially mindful of those unresolved feelings during the next eye movement set. You might even add an unscripted verbal statement that reflects the client's awareness of those feelings as the eye movements are performed. In other words, the somatic symptoms or emotions are given special attention during the next set.

When a client's memory of a negative experience is clouded or incomplete, eye movements may trigger the recall of details that had been repressed or forgotten. Chris had an active memory of being shuttled at night down a dark hallway to a nun's chamber in a boarding school when he was of primary school age. During the eye movements, he recalled what happened at the destination. The recall of additional details is unusual, but not rare. However, you should avoid going on "fishing expeditions" to retrieve missing information. Clients likewise should be discouraged from thinking that occluded memories will be recovered with MEMI. This therapy follows the path directed by a client's conscious and unconscious awareness, and verified by attendant thoughts, feelings, and sensory information. And as seasoned therapists know, a client's somatic and sensory records are often the harbingers of realizations yet to come.

CHAPTER 9

MEMI Protocol Steps 7 – 10

Although EMDR was popular with a small subset of mental health providers from its outset, eye movement integration did not garner the same recognition. Shapiro saw the need for procedures, data, and research validating EMDR's effectiveness and was an energetic promoter of her own approach. Eye movement integration was otherwise not marketed aggressively, and its brief seminars and lack of written procedures left participants without the confidence to begin using the technique. When I determined that eye movement integration was safer, more effective, and much easier to learn than EMDR, I began developing a fully constituted eye movement therapy derived from NLP principles, but with its own theoretical model, protocol, and procedures to support the therapy's replication. The last four steps in the MEMI protocol described in this chapter provide the procedures and data recording mechanisms necessary to track MEMI effectiveness and promote further research endeavors.

By now you should be comfortable executing each of the four eye movement sets and synchronizing the therapist comments with the movements. If not, take the time to review the instructions for the sets again and practice them until you can perform them comfortably. Then you can shift your attention to these last four steps in the MEMI protocol:

Step 7. Test Structure of Experience elements
Step 8. Take I-Score and SUD Score readings
Step 9. Record results on the MEMI Worksheet
Step 10. Conduct future rehearsal and self-appreciation exercises

STEP 7. TEST STRUCTURE OF EXPERIENCE ELEMENTS

The elements to be tested—Context, Thoughts, Feelings, and Sensory Information—are drawn from the Structure of Experience Model depicted in *Figure 5.1*, which was covered in Chapter 5. Changes in these elements following eye movement sets will naturally affect client I-Scores and SUD Scores, almost always in a positive direction. Instructions for recording changes to the problem state, I-Scores, and SUD Scores on the MEMI Worksheet following each eye movement set are provided later in this chapter. The MEMI Worksheet itself is included as Appendix B.

Context

Context refers to the details of a traumatic experience selected for focus during the eye movements—literally the "who, what, when, and where" of the problem state. At the time of the pretest, you ask your client to project a visual image of the event on a surface across the room, take a quick snapshot of it, and quickly return their focus to the present.

If your client is comfortable discussing the context (they often are), ask these four questions:

1. *"Who was there?"*
2. *"When was it?"*
3. *"Where did it occur?"*
4. *"What happened?"*

Divulging the particulars about the event is entirely optional. If your client chooses not to share specific information regarding the context, leave those questions unanswered on the MEMI Worksheet and move on to the next element. If your client agrees to share that information, questions about the context are asked after each eye movement set, because aspects of the context might have changed. For example, if the trauma involved your client being yelled at by another person, the other person might not be yelling after an eye movement set, but just standing there. Sometimes past actions like this will change or be dropped entirely from the scene. Changes in the context happen occasionally, but not frequently. Instead of asking all four questions after the second eye movement set and beyond, you can simply ask, *"Are there any changes in the context? Any changes in what happened or who was there?"*

Thoughts

The second element tested and retested is *Thoughts*, which is another word for cognitions. In the pretest you ask, **"What thoughts do you have about that experience?"** After eye movement sets, you can ask, **"What thoughts occur to you now?"** or **"What do you hear yourself saying about that experience now?"**

Clients are sometimes unaware of their thoughts, or even say they have none. They *do* have thoughts, but may not think they do. Sometimes clients only become aware of their original thoughts about an experience after their initial thoughts have changed. For example, if a client denies having any thoughts, but after an eye movement set says the whole experience "doesn't seem like a big deal anymore," that is a new thought. You can then ask, **"So, what were you thinking before we started?"**

Clients will sometimes respond with statements about feelings when asked about thoughts, particularly those individuals who process life's experiences more through feelings. If this occurs, you can comment that the response is actually a feeling and ask again for a thought. If your client is unable to identify a thought, you can provide an example from another situation—perhaps from a positive, hypothetical experience—to avoid feeding the client information. If your client still cannot come up with a thought, move on to the next element. However, it's important to return to the Thoughts element if your client later responds with a thought and not a feeling. For example, if they later say, "I'd like to react differently when that happens in the future," that is a new thought about the experience. So even when clients believe they have no thoughts about experiences, the thoughts are nevertheless there. It's your job to help elicit them.

Sensory Information

The next element tested and retested is *Sensory Information*. Client responses can be visual (an image), auditory (a sound), olfactory (a smell), or gustatory (a taste), although they are almost always visual or, infrequently, auditory. Just to reiterate, visual imagery and visceral and emotional reactions to traumatic memories occur more frequently than other response modalities, they are experienced by clients as more intense, and they play a larger role in memory desensitization. Therefore, it's important to identify the qualities of these reactions during the pretest. The following are examples of comments and questions you might ask your client regarding sensory information:

> *"Sensory information can be things you see, hear, smell, or taste. What sensations accompany the recall of your memory? Are the images you see close or far away? What are the sounds? Are they loud or soft? We will compare these responses to any changes that occur after each round of eye movements."*

Your client will almost always report a visual image associated with their problem state. You should specifically ask, *"What image is associated with your memory?"* not *"Are there any images?"* Asking the first question assumes sensory information actually exists and requires your client to be discerning, to probe internally for an answer. Asking the second question may cause your client to overlook the presence of sensory information. This is not leading your client but encouraging them to be more present at a time when they might be dissociating.

To elicit the characteristics of images or sounds, you will ask descriptive, predetermined, polar opposite questions about them. For instance, *"Is the image near or far away?"* This is not leading your client either, but asking them to specify the qualities of the image. If your client says the image is not near or far, but about 10 feet away, you simply accept and record that response. Eliciting the precise qualities of images and sounds is important for later comparisons. Clients may also use colorful descriptors, like fuzzy, vibrating, pulsating, shiny, or screeching. Recording these descriptors allows you to ask tailored questions after eye movement sets, such as, *"Is the pulsating of the image the same or different?"*

Although you will ask about both sounds and visual images, sounds are usually not reported. And it bears repeating that the images associated with traumatic memories are pivotal in the desensitization of traumatic memories.

Polar opposite pairs for smells and tastes are not included on the MEMI Worksheet because they are rarely reported. However, if a client does report one or more of them, you can write those in the Sensory Information section and formulate polar opposite questions from pairs, such as those you see here.

POLAR OPPOSITE SENSORY QUESTIONS

Images
Black & white or color
Close or far away?
Movie or still photo?
Bright or dim?
Life-size or bigger/smaller?
Framed or panoramic?
Clear or unclear?

Sounds
Soft or loud?
Near or at a distance?
High or low pitch?
Fast or slow?
Constant or intermittent?
Rhythmic or random?
Words or sounds?

Tastes
Sweet or salty?
Flavorful or flavorless?
Weak or strong?

Smells
Fragrant or foul?
Pleasant or unpleasant?
Faint or strong?

Feelings

The three types of *Feelings*—visceral, emotional, and tactile—should be explained to your client beforehand. The following is a sample script:

> *"Feelings related to difficult memories can be visceral (a stiff neck, shortness of breath, or a tight chest), tactile (a scratch or a burn) or emotional (anger or fear). What visceral, tactile, or emotional feelings do you associate with your memory?"*

Although the examples provided are meant to help clients understand the nature of the three types of feelings, you should avoid prompting, coaching, or second-guessing what their associated feelings might be. You could select a feeling you <u>do not</u> suspect your client is experiencing, just to serve as a prompt.

The definition of *visceral* chosen for this guide comes from *Merriam-Webster.com* (2020): *felt in or as if in the internal organs of the body.* You can explain that visceral feelings are experienced inside the body, subcutaneously (i.e., generated by the organs, nerves, bones, and muscles). With this explanation, clients are usually able to identify their own visceral responses. Emotional and tactile responses are normally much easier for clients to identify, although tactile responses are reported infrequently.

Sometimes a client believes the visceral or even emotional reactions to a trauma have a medical etiology. They may have been diagnosed with an illness by a physician or other medical professional. John, an adolescent client with PTSD, exhibited reactive agitation in his legs whenever he thought of a car accident in which he caused serious injuries to others. Although he'd been diagnosed with restless leg syndrome (RLS), that was not his problem. When we used the urge to wriggle his legs as the focus during the second eye movement set, not only did that movement subside, he also reported the disturbing image of the accident was less intense. The urge to move his lower limbs resolved after two MEMI sessions, when the memory of the accident had been desensitized. He then began sleeping through the night without difficulty.

Changes occurring after eye movement sets are almost always for the better, although clients may report no change at all after the first set. If that occurs, you can immediately reply, **"That happens sometimes. Let's do it again!"** There should be no hint of concern or apprehension in your voice, and this should not be viewed in any way as a setback—just something that occasionally happens for whatever reason.

Because clients usually describe only a few sensory qualities associated with a problem state, there's no need to ask about all the opposite pairs. However, you should at least ask about the visual-related qualities (i.e., close or far, bright or dim, etc.) printed on the **MEMI Worksheet**. If your client has difficulty identifying the qualities of an image, you can go through the entire list in this section, or ask about qualities not listed. But always use polar opposites, which will encourage a choice. The goal, of course, is to identify the prominent sensory reactions in the pretest so comparisons can be made following eye movement sets. Again, eliciting this information is generally not difficult because clients are quite familiar with their habitual responses to traumatic events.

On rare occasions, clients will report there is no image associated with the memory. There are two possible reasons for this. For one, some clients believe visual memories must be clearly discernible, or actually have the features of a lifelike picture before reporting them as authentic. Your client might say, "I see something, but it's not like a real image." In a situation like this, you might respond, **"Although you can't confirm it, act as if there is**

an image out there." This will encourage your client to hold the possibility of the visual image in their awareness, even though it may be considered incomplete. After an eye movement set, your client might report a much clearer and perhaps more threatening image of the problem state. Resolution of the clearer, more unpleasant image would then become the focus during the next set.

If a memory has been partially or fully repressed, clients may also report an incomplete image, or none at all. They may remember a time and place, sometimes with distressing somatic symptoms, or perhaps a foreboding sense about the individuals who were there, but no image of what happened. Like the client who does not believe an image is realistic, a set of eye movements may lead to a clearer recollection of the context, or it may not. While eye movements may facilitate recall, *this can never be predicted.* The accuracy of new information resulting from eye movements should always be substantiated by the cognitions, sensory information, and feelings associated with it.

Posttest Questions

Once the pretest has been completed, inform your client that you will be asking them three questions after each eye movement set.

1. ***"Is it the same or different?"***
2. ***"How is it different?"***
3. ***"Does that change make it better or worse?"***

You will also explain that, if the posttest response is better when compared to the pretest, this might result in improved Intensity and SUD Scores as well.

After the first eye movement set, briefly break state by making small talk with your client. Then say, *"OK, look out there now and tell me, is it the same or different?"* Clients sometimes ask what is meant by the question, perhaps seeking clarification about what is expected. Instead of leading your client (which is patently unnecessary), simply say, *"Different in any way that you perceive."* If your client says they are unsure, you can ask if any of the individual characteristics from the pretest have changed. For example, *"Is the pressure you felt in your chest the same or different?"*

If your client answers, "The same," move on to the next element. If your client responds, "Different," ask the second question: *"How is it different?"* Initial responses will usually be about changes in the images and feelings elicited as part of the pretest, not the context or thoughts. Clients may report the image is harder to see, less alive, or farther away; the sounds are muted; and/or the emotional or visceral symptoms have diminished.

The third basic question is asked after a stated difference has been recorded: *"Does that change make it better or worse?"* On the rare occasion when a client reports an aspect of a memory is worse, it may be a sign a particular reaction has become the center of focus, the images or feelings associated with the experience have become more intense, or that your client remembered new information about the same experience.

If they say it's worse, you should ask, *"How is it worse?"* or *"What makes it worse?"* The answer will dictate which aspect of the memory should receive focus during the next eye movement set. If, for example, your client says heart palpitations cited in the pretest are more pronounced, ask them to be especially aware of the palpitations during the next set. If a completely new symptom arises, you will want to make that a special focus during the next eye movement set. This focus on worsened or completely new symptoms almost always alleviates the symptom in question and usually improves your client's I-Score and SUD Score as well.

Most often, however, your client will answer "better" when asked if the change makes it better or worse. If better, you should first respond with surprise, such as, *"Oh! It's better!,"* spoken with a hint of wonder or excitement. It's a moment to be celebrated. Many clients have lived with symptoms for so long, they don't believe change is possible. Normally, what made the experience better is obvious, but you can expand on that by asking, *"How does that make it better?"*

Here are some typical responses from clients:

"The image isn't as threatening."
"It's changed the way I think about it."
"It's like a long time ago, not yesterday."
"I don't feel it as much."
"I'm not as bothered by it."

"I can't get it back."

"It's gone."

"It's changed how I remember it."

"How did you do that?" (a favorite)

After the second, third, and fourth eye movement sets, questions about changes in the problem state can be posed differently. Instead of asking if the experience is the same or different, you can say, ***"Look out there again and tell me what it's like now,"*** or ***"Look out there now and tell me if anything else has changed."***

STEP 8. TAKE I-SCORE AND SUD SCORE READINGS

When EMI was introduced in 1989, the primary assessment of treatment effectiveness (other than qualitative changes in feelings and sensory information) was the Subjective Units of Distress (SUD) Scale. Since then, a variety of other measures have been used with or incorporated into the therapy. MEMI determines treatment effectiveness through the use of formative and summative measures, both qualitative and quantitative.

Intensity Scale Score (I-Score)

The Intensity Scale is a formative measure I developed for use with the MEMI protocol. After I observed the significant roles that images and visceral and emotional feelings play in prolonging as well as desensitizing trauma symptoms, I decided to quantitatively assess these reactions after each set for two reasons. First, the I-Score's assessment of the intensity of reactions to images and feelings provides quantitative data clients can consider when asked to provide a SUD Score. Second, correlation tests of qualitative data—descriptive responses to sensory and feelings questions—and I-scores could provide additional validation of the therapy's effectiveness.

Each time images or visceral or emotional feelings are reported and recorded during the pretest, you will ask your client for an Intensity Score (I-Score). To reiterate, this score measures the strength of your client's reaction at that time to an image or feeling associated with the memory, using a range of scores from 0 (no intensity) to 4 (the highest intensity) as seen here:

I-Score

0	1	2	3	4
No intensity	Low	Moderate	High	Highest

During the pretest, if your client reports an image has no intensity (0) or low intensity (1), improvements following eye movement sets will not be significant. With scores that low, the potential for improvement is limited. Neither will there be corresponding room for significant improvement to the Subjective Units of Distress Score (SUD Score), because the I-Scale and SUD Scale each measures the strength of reactions to the problem state. An I-Score of 0 or 1 also indicates the qualities of the image are not particularly distressing to a client. On the other hand, if an I-Score is high (3) or highest (4) during the pretest, and is lowered following eye movement sets, a corresponding decrease in the SUD Score can be predicted. And remember, I-Scores only apply to sensory information (images and sometimes sounds) and visceral, emotional, or tactile feelings, not to context or thoughts.

Specific instructions for assessing and recording I-Scores on the MEMI Worksheet are included in Step 9.

Subjective Units of Distress (SUD) Scale Score

The SUD Scale is a 10- or 100-point measure of pain or distress commonly used in medicine and mental health treatment. In MEMI, the SUD Score is fixed at 100% during the pretest by making an assumption that the problem state at that time is as distressing as it's usually experienced by a client. If the problem state improves, the percentage will go down; if it gets worse, it could go over 100%. A SUD Score represents a client's overall perception of distress based on all changes to a problem state following each eye movement set. Ask your client to consider all the changes to the elements, including I-Scores, and rate the whole experience on a scale from 0-100%, with 0% representing no distress at all and 100% representing the worst possible distress. Clients usually have no difficulty understanding this.

When explaining I-Score and SUD Score instructions to clients, you can use the following script:

"After each eye movement set, I will ask you for two different scores. The first will be a score from 0-4 that expresses how intense your reactions are to just the visual images and feelings associated with this memory. Zero equals no intensity at all, and 4 is the highest intensity. I'll explain further how that works as we go along.

"The second score will measure how distressing or troubling the whole memory is following each eye movement set. This is a percentage score from 0-100%, with zero representing no distress at all and 100% the worst possible distress.

"Before we begin, we'll arbitrarily set the overall score at 100%—meaning the memory, as a whole, is as distressful as you usually recall it. After each eye movement set, I'll ask you if the memory is the same or different, what changed, and if those changes made it better or worse. If it's better, your overall score will go down to 90%, 80%, or 70%. If worse, it could go up."

Although a SUD Score higher than 100% indicates a client's overall response to a trauma has worsened, in practice this is a very rare occurrence. If it should occur, you ask what made it worse, and your client's response will determine the focus of the next eye movement set.

After the last eye movement set, a final SUD Score is requested. Here is what you can ask:

"OK, Bill, considering all the changes that have occurred with this memory** (name a few)**, if you compare what the experience was like when we began to what it's like now, what score would you give it?"

It's not unusual for a SUD Score to drop dramatically—from 100% to 50% or 40%—after only one or two sets. To mark the importance of a change that dramatic, you might ask, **"What caused it to go down so much?"** If, for example, your client answers, "The tightness in my chest is not there anymore, it's gone!," the response is an indication of how prominent a role that particular symptom played in their trauma symptomology. There should also have been a corresponding decrease in the I-Score for that visceral feeling. By eliciting the reason for the drop in score, you are also highlighting the importance of its extinction.

Practitioners often ask how to decide when to discontinue the eye movements or what the target score should be. In eye movement integration, rounds of eye movements were continued until symptom reduction had plateaued and no further gains were made, or until clients reported they were satisfied with the results. A SUD Score could conceivably go all the way down to 0%, when your client would report no distress at all related to the problem state. In classic EMDR, this is the target.

MEMI considers such a result both unnecessary and ill-advised, just as eliminating all fear of water moccasins in a client with a snake phobia would be inappropriate. Fears are triggered by limbic reactions to perceived threats in our environment.

These are defense mechanisms designed to protect us from danger. Removing all fears of perceived threats makes us vulnerable as humans. In MEMI, the goal is not to erase memories (it's not possible anyway) or resolve fears altogether, but to reduce them to within a normal, tolerable range for each client.

Although when to stop the eye movements will vary from client to client, a SUD Score target no higher than 50% is recommended. This score usually results in a problem state being at or near the point where its symptoms will be tolerable. Your client should also believe their reaction to the memory after treatment (i.e., their symptoms) will be manageable without undue stress. The strength of this belief is tested in Step 10 with the future rehearsal, which is discussed in greater detail later in this chapter.

If the score has been reduced to 50%, you can ask, **"Do you think the symptoms will be manageable now?"** or **"Do you think you will be able to manage your reactions to this experience when you think about it in the future?"** In any case, the final authority in deciding when to stop eye movement sets should be your client. If a score of 50% has been achieved but your client would like to do another set, you should always accommodate that request.

If after two or three sets your client has already reported a SUD Score of 20-30%, you could make a comment such as, **"Wow! That's a big change—from 100% all the way down to 20%!,"** and perhaps add, **"Do you want to stop here, or do you** *want to do another round?"* There's no harm in performing another set; often there's no further change anyway.

Some clients are quite conservative when estimating SUD Scores, especially if they believe the therapy will not work, or the improvements achieved will be short-lived. Even after showing substantial improvements in somatic and sensory responses, your client might still score the experience a 90% or 95%. Of course, there will be occasions when responses to a trauma lessen only slightly, and a score that high is commensurate with the severity of the symptoms.

If your client is still reporting a SUD score over 90% after the second set, even after feelings and imagery reactions and I-Scores have been reduced, this may be evidence of a conservative response. Rather than question the accuracy of the score, you can ask, *"What about that experience would need to change in order for the score to go down to . . . say about 50%?"* A discussion can ensue about the most pressing aspect of the experience that, if desensitized, would make the memory more tolerable. That aspect would then become the focus of attention during the next eye movement set. This discussion may also reveal a client's cautions, doubts, or misgivings about the therapy for you to address.

In addition, you should be prepared to respond to clients who ask whether continuous treatment will be required to prevent the symptoms from returning. Should that occur, you could make a statement like the following:

> *"In my experience, it's very unlikely your symptoms will go back to the way they were. After the eye movements, it's as if the brain recasts the memory without some of its negative aspects. You will always have a memory of that event, but you will most likely remember it the way you are thinking about it now. Over the next few weeks, you might check and recheck to see if that's true. But as time goes by, you will develop confidence that the change is permanent."*

When your client's symptoms have been successfully desensitized, and a decision to discontinue the eye movements has been made, it's important to celebrate that victory, even in some small way. At that point you can simply say, *"Congratulations"* or *"Great job!"* You might ask, *"Do you give high fives?"* If the answer is yes, you can raise a hand high to celebrate your work together. The high five reinforces the accomplishment and almost always brings a smile to a client's face.

STEP 9. RECORD RESULTS ON THE MEMI WORKSHEET

Recording results on the MEMI Worksheet (Appendix B) might appear more complicated than it will actually be in practice. Because clients usually report only one response for Thoughts and one or two responses each for Feelings and Sensory Information, you will usually have a limited number of reactions to track. For example, when no sounds or tactile feelings are associated with a memory, which is usually the case, that part of the worksheet is left blank. And if not readily reported by your client, you should not push to capture more information. Furthermore, it's unnecessary to detect and track all aspects of a memory's structure to achieve desensitization. Addressing two or three of the most distressing elements will usually reorganize the problem state to your client's satisfaction.

As you proceed through the sets, there will be a certain amount of jumping back and forth between sections of the worksheet because clients sometimes report changes in elements out of sequence. For instance, you might be asking about changes in Feelings when your client reports a change in the Context instead. If this occurs, you should take a moment to record their response in the appropriate section of the MEMI Worksheet before returning to the section being discussed.

Protocol Steps 7-9 are not purely sequential either, in the sense that you always finish one before moving on to the next. In other words, you will be following your client's lead by recording results in appropriate sections of the worksheet, even if they are out of sequence. Again, although the recording process may seem cumbersome at first, when you become accustomed to MEMI procedures, the amount of time devoted to recording responses will significantly diminish.

Recording Changes in Context or Thoughts
If a change in Context or Thoughts should occur after an eye movement set, you will write the nature of that change on the line corresponding to that set on the MEMI Worksheet under

THOUGHTS

THOUGHTS
❷ **Problem State**   Pretest   What did you say to yourself? *"I should have stopped it."*   Changes   Set 1: *"It wasn't my fault."*   Set 2: _____   Set 3: _____   Set 4: _____

Figure 9.1

the Thoughts or Context heading. *Figure 9.1* depicts how a change in Thoughts would be recorded. In the example, the thought during the pretest was: "I should have stopped it!," a self-critical statement. After Set 1, the client reports a different thought: "It wasn't my fault!," which is more self-affirming. The new thought was recorded on the line next to Set 1. If another thought was reported after the next set, it would be written on the line under Thoughts and to the right of Set 2.

SENSORY INFORMATION

SENSORY INFORMATION
❸ **Visual**   Pretest: *(circle one from each pair, if applicable)*   High ◄-----► Low   (Movie)/Still photo   Color/Black & white   (Near)/Far away   Fuzzy/(Clear)   Bright/Dark   I-Score: 4 ③ 2 1 0   Set 1: _____   I-Score: 4 3 2 1 0   Set 2: *"Less clear."*   I-Score: 4 3 ② 1 0   Set 3: *"Not a movie anymore, farther away."*   I-Score: 4 3 2 ① 0   Set 4: _____   I-Score: 4 3 2 1 0

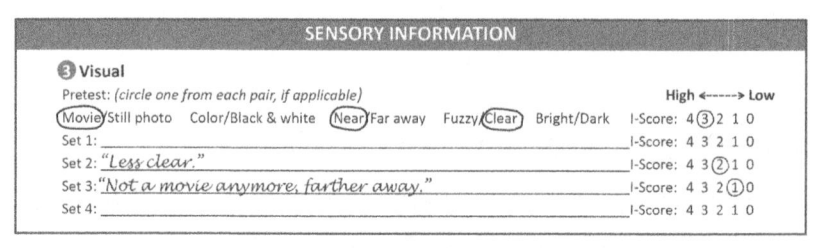

Figure 9.2

Recording Changes in Sensory Information

Changes in images and sounds are recorded under the Sensory Information heading of the worksheet. As previously indicated, clients do not usually report sounds associated with problem states, but they can be significant if present.

If your client says an image is different after a set, ask how it's different and write the nature of the change on the MEMI Worksheet to the right of the corresponding set number. After asking your client for a new I-Score, circle the corresponding I-Score number for that set on the same line. *Figure 9.2* shows how that might occur with a visual image. In the example, during the pretest the client reported the image was "a movie," was "near" (not far away), and was "clear." The I-Score reported during the pretest was 3 (high intensity). There was no change in the image after Set 1, so that line was left blank. After Set 2, the client reported the image was "less clear" and gave an I-Score rating of 2 (moderate intensity). After Set 3, the client reported the image was "Not a movie anymore and is farther away." This changed the I-Score from 2 (moderate) to 1 (low intensity).

Recording Changes in Feelings

Changes in Feelings (visceral, emotional, or tactile) are recorded on the worksheet in the same fashion as Sensory Information, with one exception. Instead of circling polar opposite qualities in the pretest as you would with images (near/far away), ask your client to self-report specific feelings, prompting with examples if necessary. *Figure 9.3* depicts how that might be accomplished.

FEELINGS

FEELINGS	
❸ **Visceral** *(stiff neck, nausea, etc.)*	
Pretest: *"Head throbbing at temples."*	I-Score: ④ 3 2 1 0
Set 1: _____	I-Score: 4 3 2 1 0
Set 2: *"Head throbbing less."*	I-Score: 4 3 ② 1 0
Set 3: *"Head throbbing gone."*	I-Score: 4 3 2 1 ⓪
Set 4: _____	I-Score: 4 3 2 1 0

Figure 9.3

In the pretest example, when the client was asked what visceral feelings were associated with the problem state, the reply was, "My head is throbbing at the temples." This statement was then written under the headings Feelings and Visceral on the line next to the word Pretest. When the client reported an I-Score for the head throbbing of 4 (highest intensity), the number 4 was circled next to "I-Score" on the same line. There was no change after Set 1, so the line was left blank. After Set 2, the client responded, "My head is throbbing less." That was written on the line next to Set 2, and an I-Score of 2 (moderate intensity) reported by the client was circled. After Set 3, the client reported the head throbbing was gone, and an I-Score of 0 (no intensity) was circled. This reduction in I-Scores represents a dramatic improvement in this client's experience of that visceral feeling—from the highest intensity to no intensity at all—in only three sets.

As expected, I-Scale Scores are normally the highest (3 or 4) during the pretest and decrease to their lowest point by the end of the fourth eye movement set. Although only four sets of eye movements are normally conducted, there are occasions when

MEMI Protocol Steps 7-10

you might decide to conduct a fifth set. In those instances, you will write client responses in the space beneath Set 4 and write in and circle the appropriate I-Score number to the right, where the I-Scores are recorded.

Recording SUD Scores

Lower I-Score responses usually result in corresponding set by set reductions in SUD Scores as well, because they measure similar variables. The I-Score assesses changes in individual somatic and sensory symptoms, while the SUD Score is a cumulative measure taking into account all the changes in context, thoughts, sensory information, and feelings.

SUD SCORES

SUD SCORES
Pretest = 100%　Set 1: __85__%　Set 2: __60__%　Set 3: __30__%　Set 4: ____%　Set 5: ____%
© 2020 Trauma Counseling & Training of Tucson

Figure 9.4

Figure 9.4 shows how SUD Scores are recorded on the worksheet. In the example, the SUD Score during the pretest is set at 100% and preprinted on the form. After Set 1, the client reported a SUD Score of 85%. After Set 2, the SUD Score reported was 60%. After Set 3, the score went down to 30%. No SUD Score was reported after Set 4 because the eye movements were discontinued following Set 3's score below 50%. The option exists to request and record a fifth SUD Score, should an extra eye movement set be conducted.

STEP 10. CONDUCT FUTURE REHEARSAL AND SELF-APPRECIATION

The last step in the protocol has two parts. In the first, you will test your client's reaction to the problem state in some imagined scenario in the future. This is a final test of treatment effectiveness and durability. The second part of the protocol's last step creates an opportunity for you and your client to review all the changes (improvements) that have been achieved during the session and honor those accomplishments.

Future Rehearsal

To introduce this first part of Step 10, you might make the following statement:

> *"Before ending a session, I like to ask clients how they think they will do after leaving. We test this with an activity called the future rehearsal. In a minute, I'm going to ask you to use your imagination to place yourself in some situation in the future when those negative feelings and sensations you used to have might be triggered. Can you think of a time or place when that might happen?"*

   Wait for a yes response.

> *"OK. Now, please take up to 30 seconds to imagine yourself in that future situation. You can do this with your eyes open or closed. Pay attention to how you will think and feel about it then. When you are done, tell me what your experience was like."*

Clients usually report their reactions are dramatically improved—the same as they were following the last eye movement set. If anxiety remains, related to the future event (it would normally be minor in nature), another eye movement set can be performed focusing on that future situation.

Madeline, a client with PTSD, had been sexually abused by a cousin 20 years before she began her therapy with me. At times, Madeline would still encounter the cousin at family gatherings, and she'd always been very anxious about seeing him until we conducted her only MEMI session. After two eye movement sets and a reported SUD Score of 50%, she described her reaction to the problem state (the abuse) as just "the thought of it." She no longer had the somatic and emotional reactions she'd always experienced. I suggested we conduct a third round of eye movements focused on a family gathering in the future, when she might encounter her cousin. This was her future rehearsal. Following that round, she reported a SUD Score of 40% and described her response to the imagined encounter as very manageable.

Self-appreciation

The second part of Step 10 provides an opportunity for you to reinforce all the improvements made during the session, help your client honor what they have achieved, and fire the resource anchor one last time. The following script is an example of what you might say during this final step in the protocol:

"We have one more brief exercise before finishing today. It's called self-appreciation. What I would like you to do is close your eyes and think about all the changes you've made today. You still have a memory of that event, but it's different now."

Cite a few of the changes made to the problem state.

"I encourage you to honor those changes you've made. You did this simply by learning to think about, feel, and experience that event in a different way. Take a moment to appreciate all you have accomplished."

Allow a few seconds to pass.

"And always remember the <u>Powerful</u> feeling you can create in yourself whenever you want."

Fire the anchor again.

"... That's right. <u>Powerful</u>. <u>Powerful</u>. Now, as you open your eyes, bring all those resources back here with you. Good, good. Very good."

To close out the session, you have the option of asking what your client thinks about the work you've done together. Clients sometimes ask how MEMI works. If you think an explanation will benefit your client, you might make a statement such as the following:

"MEMI is based on a belief that eye movements work together with our thoughts, feelings, and physical reactions to our experiences. So if your eyes go up here... you might be processing an image from the past."

Point to the visual past position.

"If your eyes are down there... you might be talking to yourself."

Point to the self-talk position.

"Let me give you an example. If you think about a car accident you had, and see broken glass all around you, like you're right back there again, your eyes will likely move to a particular location each time you recall that experience. The originators of this therapy theorized that if you were to think about a difficult memory while your eyes followed a pen moving around in front of you, it would interrupt the way your brain processes that information, and your reaction to the experience might actually improve. And that's exactly what happens. Of course, it's a bit more complicated, but that's it in a nutshell."

When bringing a session to a close, especially if a severe trauma has been desensitized, your client should be encouraged to practice self-care for a day or two. Although symptom regression is highly unlikely, memory integration could continue for a few days. Your client will be testing and retesting their reactions to the trauma and the session, replaying previous scenarios and considering the implications of the changes. My practice is to ask if I can check in with clients by phone, text, or email in a few days to see how they're doing. I tell them if they have questions or concerns, they can contact me.

Although these MEMI procedures have been presented in some detail, it's impossible to anticipate (much less incorporate) all the situations you will encounter in a session. And because the protocol, basic eye movements, and eye movement sets with illustrations required several chapters in this book to convey, they have been reproduced in Appendix C for easy reference. Additional information and considerations to keep in mind when using this therapy are discussed in Chapter 10.

The procedures presented in this guide represent almost two decades of development and experimentation, but there are many other eye movements, sets, reframes, and embedded commands that could be developed and used within the rubric of this approach. Those undertakings are encouraged, as are practical clinical trials and controlled studies of MEMI's effectiveness. I believe they would further affirm what I have found to be the case: MEMI is a safe, effective, limbic therapy for PTSD, acute stress disorder, and "little 't' traumas."

CHAPTER 10

MEMI Facts and Features

Getting started with MEMI is an exciting venture, especially after you discover how easy, effective, and safe this short-term therapy for trauma and other forms of anxiety is to learn and use. There's no expensive equipment to purchase, no cryptic theoretical models to decipher, and no extended period of supervision. With only 12 hours of training and this guide as a supplement, you will be equipped to successfully treat trauma. To add to what you have already learned, this chapter presents a number of facts, features, and clarifications about MEMI for the practitioner new to the therapy.

"THOUGHTS" IN MEMI VERSUS COGNITIVE RESTRUCTURING

In cognitive therapies, an individual's irrational narratives (beliefs) are thought to be the cause of emotional pain. Ellis (1994, 1996) theorized that faulty beliefs are responsible for adverse physical, emotional, and behavioral reactions to events. He argued that if beliefs become more rational and helpful, rather than self-defeating, client symptoms will improve. In order to encourage the adoption of more rational beliefs, Ellis and others pioneered the use of an approach called *cognitive restructuring*. With this technique, three skills are imparted to clients by therapists: 1.) how to examine their internal narratives; 2.) how to identify negative self-talk; and 3.) how to replace self-defeating thoughts with more positive ones (Spiegler, 2012). Cognitive restructuring is a key strategy used in cognitive behavioral therapies. A lot of therapy time is devoted to teaching and using these skills—principally stopping, redirecting, or replacing irrational thoughts with more affirmative narratives. In other words, clients are encouraged to engage in self-improvement by identifying irrational beliefs and adopting more rational self-talk instead (Ellis, 2008).

Cognitive restructuring can be thought of as an active strategy, whereas changing thoughts with MEMI should be considered a more passive one. Changing irrational thinking in MEMI is not a goal, a strategy, or a prerequisite for memory reorganization. Neither is it assumed that thought distortions are the sole cause of physical or mental distress. Instead, consistent clinical evidence confirms that thoughts naturally self-adjust in response to changes in somatic and sensory reactions following the eye movements and accompanying interventions. Stated another way, cognitions are automatically reorganized and become more rational—without redirection—after the visual, physical, and emotional reactions to problem states are desensitized.

MEMI is not considered cognitive nor behavioral, but more aptly described as organic, limbic, sensory, neurological, linguistic, and systemic. All modalities are engaged as a memory is reflexively desensitized during the eye movements and spoken commands. MEMI presuppositions assume the body's cognitive and neurological systems will achieve desensitization naturally as a result of strategic pattern interruptions in the form of eye movements, reframes, and embedded commands.

During the pretest, when you ask clients what thoughts occur to them about the trauma, or what they say to themselves about it, as you might expect, the thoughts are often inaccurate, irrational, or self-limiting. But you need not point that out. You could comment that their thoughts might change following the eye movements, along with their feelings, sensory information, and the context of the experience. During posttests, you ask if their thoughts (self-talk) about the experience are the same or different. If different, you ask if the new thoughts make it better or worse. In this manner, cognitive adjustments are not actively manipulated but passively elicited following eye movement sets. It is theorized that thought distortions are actually revised *in response to* the desensitization of somatic and sensory reactions. In my experience, this is what usually happens. Further study could validate this clinical finding.

van der Kolk et al. (2007) cautioned there is still much to learn about the treatment of traumatic stress. He conceded there were no studies showing that effective treatment of one trauma area (e.g., re-experiencing) would also yield improvements in other areas (e.g., hyperarousal or negative cognitions). Nevertheless, he wrote:

... it is likely that effective treatment of one problem, such as psychological reactivity, will have widespread beneficial effects on the overall system, and can secondarily decrease intrusions, concentration problems, numbing, and the ways victims experience themselves and their surroundings (p. 17).

Cognitive restructuring is used infrequently during MEMI treatment. For example, it might be employed when trauma resolution is impeded by what is called a *moral injury*. This phenomenon occurs when an individual believes they have caused or witnessed an event so horrendous it cannot be forgiven or forgotten. A soldier who mistakenly takes the life of a civilian or witnesses a gruesome tragedy might adopt a belief that resolution is not possible or even permissible due to its dreadful nature, or because they were somehow at fault. Litz et al. (2009) describe a moral injury as "perpetrating, failing to prevent, bearing witness to, or learning about acts that transgress deeply held moral beliefs and expectations."

Ann, a mother whose preadolescent son had died suddenly from an undetected cardiac anomaly, was refusing trauma therapy. Not only could she not forgive herself for failing to discover the defect, she also believed she would be denying her son's existence if she sought relief from her symptoms. Her anxiety was a way of holding onto him. Six years after his passing, she still preferred to live with the pain. This belief of hers came to light while discussing the "contract for change." When asked if she wanted to be free of the anxiety and dysphoria she experienced whenever she thought of her son's death, she responded with ambivalence. When asked what her son would think, she was certain he would not want her to suffer. This realization prompted a two-session discussion ending with an agreement that her son's death was not her fault. She was then able to express a commitment to proceed with treatment.

One other clarification should be made about Thoughts in MEMI versus cognitive restructuring. In eye movement Set 2 of the protocol, an embedded command is used to stimulate changes in thoughts about traumatic experiences. The therapist says, **"Still thinking about that experience, but you may find that ... _Your thoughts about this will change_."** The second half of the statement—the subliminal prompt to stimulate a cognitive shift regarding the experience—is a pattern interruption á la NLP. As such, the opportunity then arises for thought reorganization, but no direction is given about why the thoughts held at that time are irrational or how they should change. Thus, the command should not be confused with cognitive restructuring, which teaches clients how to identify distorted thinking and consciously adopt more rational internal narratives.

DEFINITION OF MEMI TREATMENT SUCCESS

Much has been written about the number of sessions required by various approaches to satisfactorily reduce or resolve the symptoms associated with PTSD. Since the shift to managed care decades ago, and the resultant need for short-term mental health therapies, the amount of time and the number of sessions required for symptom improvement have received inordinate attention. Interestingly enough, the development of NLP as a field of study occurred at a time when the profession was forced to deal with restrictions imposed by insurance companies on the number of reimbursable therapy sessions. But what does it really mean when proponents of a particular approach report it takes three, five, or even 15 sessions to successfully treat PTSD?

Unfortunately, confusion still exists about what constitutes PTSD treatment success. Chapters 2 and 3 explored the controversies surrounding misleading interpretations of therapeutic efficacy, as well as the unwarranted influence of randomized controlled trials (RCTs) and evidenced-based practices (EBPs) on treatment evaluation standards. The RCT is still touted as the gold standard in PTSD research, even though the validity of results produced with this method continue to be questioned. For example, although RCT studies of cognitive behavioral therapies for PTSD report the approaches are more effective than others, closer scrutiny reveals this is not the case. True tests of symptom resolution should confirm not only that certain results are statistically significant, but that a predetermined thresh-old for overall PTSD symptom resolution has been attained.

In MEMI, four types of assessments are used. The first measures perceptual changes after each eye movement set in the context, thoughts, feelings, and sensory information associated with the targeted memory. These changes recorded on the MEMI Worksheet are both qualitative (descriptive) and more quantitative (I-Score). The second assessment is the SUD Score, also taken after each set, which measures the cumulative effects of treatment considered as a whole. The third assessment is a subjective yes or no judgment from the client about whether they believe the memory will be manageable going forward.

The fourth assessment is the PTSD Checklist for DSM-5 (PCL-5), a standardized measure of therapeutic effects taken before MEMI treatment and two to four weeks after. Items on this checklist are aligned with the PTSD diagnostic clusters contained in the DSM-5 (re-experiencing, negative cognitions and mood, avoidance, and arousal). The PCL-5 also sets internal standards: a threshold score for confirming a provisional PTSD diagnosis (31-33); statistically determined ranges that confirm when score reductions represent changes not based on chance (5-10 points), and score reductions considered clinically significant (10-20 points) (Weathers et al., 2013). A copy of the checklist can be found in Appendix A. The PCL-5 is an updated version of the original checklist designed for use with the DSM-IV diagnostic criteria. One of the DSM-IV checklist forms (PCL-C) was used in a pilot study of MEMI treatment effects described in Appendix D. The PCL-C is in Appendix E.

The PCL-5 is used with individuals as a diagnostic tool, but it's also employed in RCT comparative studies to measure significant reductions in group symptoms. For reasons discussed in this chapter and Chapter 2, the sole use of RCTs as the most valid measure of treatment effectiveness obscures the importance of other goals—namely, treatment remission, client satisfaction, and improvements in broader health outcomes. Not elevating measures of these other variables to a more prominent role in determining treatment effectiveness is a disservice to those who struggle with PTSD.

Symptom resolution in MEMI requires a final SUD Score of 50% or less, client satisfaction with the results, client affirmation that reactions to the problem state will henceforth be manageable, and a PCL-5 Score below 33. Not to be confused with symptom reduction, these are absolute standards to be met when determining treatment success. Of course, other measures are sometimes used in concert with these assessments to supplement the MEMI standards, such as depression inventories or standardized measures of anxiety or trauma.

In the best of worlds, MEMI would work immediately with every client, without exception. If that were the case, there would be no need for other trauma therapies. Regardless of the embroidered claims made about certain therapies as the "best practice" or "premier treatment" for PTSD, there is a demonstrated need for other options, particularly approaches designed to calm limbic reactions in the brain. No therapy should be used exclusively or claim to be the treatment of choice, as evidenced by extant research. Not to pursue a variety of methods is decidedly short-sighted.

EYE MOVEMENTS ELICIT TRANCE STATES

Because the eye movements in MEMI are smooth pursuit—rhythmic and slow—this sometimes causes clients to relax so much that their eyes glaze over and their eyelids start to close. This is evidence of a calm, natural state induced by the eye movements and the voice of the therapist. There is no harm to the client, and this level of relaxation can also be interpreted as evidence of symptom reduction. However, clients who become too relaxed cannot continue to follow the movements of your pen or finger, and their minds might wander away from the problem state. If this happens, you can briefly stop the eye movements and say, **"Look at the pen, Bill."** This will bring your client back to a more alert state so the procedure can continue. You can also explain at the end of the eye movement set that relaxation is a natural result of the eye movements.

HANDLING ABREACTIONS

Merriam-Webster Medical Dictionary (2020) defines *abreaction* as... "the expression and emotional discharge of unconscious material (as repressed idea or emotions) by verbalization, especially in the presence of a therapist." This definition implies that these emotional outbursts only arise when memories that have been *repressed* are suddenly recalled. However, the expression of strong reactions during trauma treatment occurs more frequently when conscious but *suppressed* memories are verbalized.

Although the terms *repression* and *suppression* are often used interchangeably, they are not the same. Repressed memories are those blocked from conscious recall as a result of a traumatic experience. If a memory of childhood abuse is repressed, the person would have no recollection of the experience. A suppressed memory, on the other hand, involves an experience a person can remember but intentionally avoids. The case study of "Rebecca" in this guide is a good example. She had refused to talk about her assault with three different therapists before agreeing to MEMI treatment. She remembered everything, but for several years she systematically suppressed her rape-associated distress with her silence, alcohol abuse, dissociations, and withdrawal from her surroundings. In MEMI, the term abreaction is used to describe emotional outbursts in therapy related to repressed and suppressed memories.

While great care is taken in MEMI to avoid abreactions, there is always the chance your client will express overwhelming emotions when reacting to certain aspects of a recalled trauma, whether repressed or suppressed. You must be prepared for these situations. By carefully observing facial expressions and body language during the pretest and throughout the eye movements, you can assure that the resource anchor and therapeutic dissociation are securely in place before accessing the problem state. This will provide your client adequate protection *in most situations.*

Be mindful that abreactions are often preceded by subtle signs a client is decompensating. In advance of an abreaction, client facial muscles may tighten, their cheeks may flush or lose color, their jaws may clench, or their eyes may mist. These are called micro behavioral cues. Gentry (E. Gentry, personal communication, January 18, 2017) cites additional signs of abreactions: legs shaking; wringing hands; fetal posturing; eyes fixated downward; flat or pressured speech; and use of first-person language when describing the trauma.

Being prepared for strong client reactions is as important as knowing how to intervene when necessary. Tears are a normal and manageable response to re-exposure, even with protections, as long as they do not escalate into sobbing, erratic breathing, wailing, or calling out. Redness or misting in and around the eyes will be noticed before the first tear begins to form. If this happens, you might say: *"It looks like your eyes are misting. Are you all right to continue?"*

If your client's reactions should escalate, you can pause the eye movements, have them make eye contact, and ask them to take a few long, slow, deep breaths. You can also fire the resource anchor once again. Drawing your client's attention away from the experience projected across the room is another way to hinder their connection to the problem state. Instructing your client to *"Look at me"* or *"Come back here now"* are two more examples. There are many ways to distract clients for brief moments, and you should have several in mind for when they are needed.

I sometimes use another approach for de-escalating abreactions, proposed by Gentry (E. Gentry, personal communication, January 18, 2017). This technique leads clients through three sensory exercises designed to diminish reactions to traumatic memories. First, get your client's attention by whistling, waving your hands, or calling out their name. Then ask if they would like help in getting out of the emotional state. Seek a yes response. Once affirmed, do the following:

1. Ask your client to describe three objects above eye level in the room (an elevated view to avoid problem state visualizations).
2. Ask your client to identify three real sounds in the room or the vicinity.
3. Hand your client three different objects one at a time (e.g., a pencil, a binder clip, and a rubber band) and ask them to describe the shape and texture of each.

These visual, auditory, and tactile activities can be repeated, if necessary. Finally, ask your client what's different about what they are experiencing, compared to when the abreaction was occurring. Clients usually describe significant changes in their feelings, thoughts, and images related to the experience. This series of sensory exercises is a nonintrusive pattern interruption for abreactions as well as dissociations, should an intervention be needed.

Exercises like this are called *grounding* or *stabilization* techniques designed to reduce the intensity of one's reaction. The activity would also be branded a *bottom-up* strategy because it uses the senses and not cognitions to reverse the stress response and induce a more relaxed state. Diaphragmatic breathing, progressive relaxation, and the NLP anchoring technique are other bottom-up strategies. On the other hand, cognitive techniques to calm the dysregulated body (e.g., asking a client to imagine a safe place or a favorite relative at their side) are called *top-down* strategies (J. Sweeton, personal communication, November 5, 2019). Whether cognitive or sensory-based (top-down or bottom-up), the goal is to activate the parasympathetic (relaxation) response and de-escalate an abreaction, interrupt a dissociation, or prepare your client for re-exposure to a traumatic experience.

I can think of only three situations in the 20 years I have been using MEMI, during which client abreactions involved the emergence of repressed memories. Daniel was a 30-year-old artist who had a conscious memory of a trip to a remote cabin with a priest and two friends, where the preteen boys were provided alcohol. Daniel had been becoming increasingly anxious from flashbacks, nightmares, and memory fragments related to that event. He was referred to me for trauma treatment by his regular therapist. After establishing a resource anchor and therapeutic dissociation, we began the first set of eye movements. Without any warning, he stopped watching the pen and stared straight ahead (visualizing) before suddenly crying out, "No! No! No!" I asked what was happening, but he was unable to respond. He closed his eyes, continued to call out, and rocked forcefully from side to side in his seat. His head snapped back, his feet shot straight out, and his legs shook convulsively.

With a firm but calm voice, I said, *"Daniel, you're here in the present with me now. Leave that situation over there in the past and return here. Open your eyes and look at me. Look at me now."*

When he made eye contact, I said, *"Now, if it's all right with you, would you allow me to shake your hand? I would like to shake your hand. Give me your hand. Shake my hand."*

When offered, I clasped his hand firmly, shook it gently like I was greeting a friend, and said, *"Now, keep looking at me. You're here now. Take a deep breath. That's right. You're here. Good."* Daniel blinked away the stare and nodded, signaling his return.

Daniel's familiarity with the separator state established previously by therapeutic dissociation aided in the de-escalation of the abreaction. He slowly calmed himself and continued to make eye contact with me. Rarely do I touch clients, but in this case, and in one other case with a military veteran, a handshake helped stall the abreaction, yet did not compromise client integrity. A handshake represents an emotionally positive and personally neutral form of touch between men and women in our culture. At the same time, if either client had declined to shake my hand, I would have honored their response. Whenever I work with clients who express very strong emotions, or tend to dissociate, I inform them beforehand that I might ask them to maintain eye contact with me or even shake my hand, should it be necessary. In those cases, I do a dry run of the handshake before beginning and confirm the appropriateness of that method in making a connection during emotional upheaval. If they are uncomfortable with the idea of a handshake, I ask how they would like me to re-establish and maintain their attention, if needed.

Daniel regained his composure within about a minute. I maintained the handshake and eye contact until he showed signs of his "return" and was no longer associating into the past experience. He was horrified about what he had just recalled, of course. He described "seeing" how he had been separated from the other boys and led to a room at the back of the cabin, where he had been penetrated by the priest. A perception of rectal pain accompanied the recollection. Daniel recalled feeling that sensation a number of times over the years, sometimes seemingly out of the blue. Now, he said, he knew why.

This new information was understandably overwhelming. We postponed discussing the implications of this revelation until the next session, but only after Daniel demonstrated a clear orientation to his surroundings and expressed confidence that he could delay further discussion until our next meeting. After extreme expression of emotions, it's important for clients to be restored to a resourceful state before ending a session. Sometimes this means going overtime or delaying work that might be done in order to allow a client's emotions to return to an integrated state.

There's no way of knowing how accurate Daniel's recollections were, but the strong somatic and sensory reactions accompanying recall lent credence to his memory. Following a critical debriefing of this new information at his next session, Daniel was able to return to the eye movement work. The memory was desensitized to a manageable level, and he was referred back to his therapist of record for follow-up after a total of three sessions.

THE IMPORTANCE OF EYE CONTACT

Because eye movements are inherently associated with neurophysiological responses to human experiences, one way of interrupting habitual reactions to a trauma is by establishing eye contact. This technique is used to break state—shift a client's focus away from traumatic imagery and disrupt physical and emotional reactions.

This guide—Multichannel Eye Movement Integration—has also demonstrated how eye contact can be used in other ways when treating trauma. For example, eye contact is used when giving instructions for establishing therapeutic dissociation. You discourage your client from prematurely connecting to the traumatic material by saying, *"In a minute, you will project an image of that experience on the wall across the room, but don't look out there yet. Look at me now."* Or, if your client begins dissociating by staring down or to the side, you simply say, *"Look at me, Bill."* Finally, you can initiate eye contact to mitigate the effects of an abreaction, as described in the last section. When interrupting Daniel's abreaction, I said to him, *"Open your eyes and look at me."*

MEMI therapists accept responsibility for regulating client exposure to traumatic content through the use of dynamic protections not seen in other PTSD therapies. The intentional use of eye contact is one of those mechanisms.

WHEN REPRESSED INFORMATION EMERGES

Clients may spontaneously recall information that was previously blocked during MEMI treatment, even though this is rare and not a goal or expectation. The now well-worn statement "the body doesn't lie" expresses a principle that illuminates, in part, the circumstances under which new information may be recalled. Participants in MEMI seminars have asked how they can determine whether this emerging information is authentic and not imagined or fabricated. Since the false memory syndrome brouhaha two decades ago, the mental health profession has grown in its understanding of the nature of recalled memories and has demonstrated responsibility in clarifying how to view this phenomenon. Given the interconnectedness of the elements in the structure of an experience, the recall of previously blocked material will be corroborated by parallel information from the thoughts, feelings, and sensations of a given problem state. And, as indicated, recall is almost always accompanied by strong sensory and somatic reactions.

An example of a young man who began to recall information about a negative childhood experience during a MEMI session will demonstrate this principle. Jeremiah was a tall, strapping business executive who explained in his first session that he might have been sexually abused by a Little League coach when he was seven years old. He had a vague but conscious memory of an afternoon at the man's home, but could only recall a few details about that day. He could remember looking at a pornographic magazine and the coach calling a picture of an erect penis a banana. Jeremiah remembered being afraid of the man, and he was concerned something else he could not recall might have happened that day. He decided to seek treatment because he experienced a flood of disturbing images and emotions about the childhood experience after he learned the man had moved back to his family's neighborhood. Whenever Jeremiah thought of the man, he became agitated, balled his fists in rage, began breathing rapidly, and his thoughts would race. Most troubling to him were the fantasies he was entertaining of tracking the man down and "shoving a butcher knife into his gut and twisting it." Before we got started, I secured a commitment from him that he had no intention to act on those thoughts.

I explained to Jeremiah that it was quite possible he would not recall any new information relevant to the event during our work together. He might get clarification about certain aspects of the memory, but we had no way of predicting the outcome. After the first eye movement set, his image of just the magazine changed to a wide-angle view of the man's dining room. Jeremiah was no longer associated into the scene, looking down with his own eyes at the picture. Instead, he was watching himself in the scene from a vantage point across the room, a dissociated view. He was seated in a plastic chair, held together with tape, next to a kitchen trash container. These are details he had not previously recalled. His anger and somatic symptoms had subsided slightly, but he still reported a SUD Score of 80%. It seemed the memory was beginning to reorganize.

During the second set, however, he recalled a completely different memory from the same period of his life. He remembered being in his bedroom with a girl two years younger than him. If he was about eight years old, she would have been five or six. "I'm exposing myself," he said. Then he added, "I'm using language, but it's not my own. It doesn't make any sense. I told her, 'It's like a piece of fruit. You can touch it.'" He then briefly dissociated, staring down at the floor. When he looked up, he asked what I had just said. I had not said anything. I asked him where he'd been. "I'm not sure," he replied, "but I escape like that a lot."

I had Jeremiah look out at the original problem state again and questioned whether it was the same or different. His eyes widened, and he said, "There are two guys there now." When asked who the other person was, he responded, "The assistant coach, he's grinning at me, like mocking me over his shoulder." The context had changed. He added, "I can also hear the legs of the chair creaking as it's being pushed with me in it across the hardwood floor"—new (auditory) sensory information. At that point, his fists were tightly balled and he was breathing rapidly again. His SUD Score was back to 90%.

This brief case description shows the interplay among the elements in the structure of a memory when new information is emerging—the human neuropsychological system at work. After the first eye movement set, the associated image changed to dissociated, but Jeremiah's feelings and sensory responses remained strong (80% SUD Score). After the second set, however, he recalled a completely different experience that happened in his childhood bedroom. Why? Evidence suggests it was linked to the experience with his coach, because Jeremiah used comparable language to describe the two events. The coach's description of the penis in the magazine as a "banana" had become "a piece of fruit" when Jeremiah described his own penis to the girl. Further, and possibly because of what the coach might have done to him, he tells the girl "you can touch it." One could surmise this is where he got the idea to expose himself in the first place. It's also plausible the memory of the incident with the girl was pushed forward by his subconscious, while he was thinking about the incident with the coach, because of an implicit link between the two events. To extend this analysis, Jeremiah insisted the language he recalled using with the girl was not his own! If it wasn't *his* language, whose was it? Children are not born with knowledge of sexual acts, they are taught. The body and mind keep parallel, cross-referenced records, and they do not lie.

Jeremiah did not recall if anything else had happened to him at his coach's house that day, at least not during our work together. We did, however, proceed with desensitization of the primary memory, and he was able to address what he did remember in a productive manner. After his anger had subsided, he no longer had thoughts of accosting the man. Years later, I learned he was happily married with children and running for elective office. I also learned that when he told his mother about the abuse, she remembered suspecting something might have happened to him at that time. There were reports of other children being abused by the same man—who happened to be a pillar of their church.

There are times when clients will not remember the entire context of an event, but this does not preclude the existence of negative thoughts, sensory information, or feelings related to it. In these cases, the elements other than the context can nevertheless be successfully desensitized.

USING MEMI WITH DEAF AND HARD OF HEARING CLIENTS

Deaf and hard of hearing (DHoH) people comprise a unique linguistic and cultural community coalesced around the use of American Sign Language (ASL). Whereas this group used to be defined based on medical and pathological perspectives (hearing and speech deficits requiring speech training and auditory amplification), the DHoH community has defined itself as bilingual and bicultural for decades. This means the MEMI practitioner working with these clients must adhere to expectations this population has for the provision of appropriate mental health services. Not all DHoH clients are proficient lip-readers; in fact, many are not. Not all DHoH individuals are proficient English speakers—some are, many are not—although many are proficient readers and writers of English. However, almost all are proficient users of ASL, their natural language.

Practitioners should not expect to rely on lip-reading and spoken English when working with these clients. Most adult members of this community use ASL as their preferred language. This means ASL should be used when working with DHoH clients, preferably delivered by an ASL proficient therapist or, secondarily, through the use of a certified ASL interpreter. All states and most local communities where deaf people reside have agencies or businesses that provide interpreter referral services. Having a family member or friend who knows some sign language act as an interpreter is not appropriate, for reasons that should be obvious.

MEMI is an excellent therapy for DHoH clients because they are a population that research has demonstrated are visual learners and information processors. Most aspects of the therapy need little or no adjustment for these clients, with three important exceptions. First, it's important that the process be thoroughly explained to DHoH clients before beginning the eye movement sweeps. If a hearing client has a question in the middle of an eye movement set, the therapist can often respond verbally without interrupting the sweeps. If a question arises while working with a DHoH client, the eye movements must stop to allow the client to sign the question and the therapist to respond in ASL. Although interrupting the eye movements may be necessary sometimes, complete explanations prior to beginning each set will minimize interruptions.

Second, the strategic verbal reframes and embedded commands cannot be spoken as they would with hearing clients. Instead, before beginning each set, the therapist must explain the comments to the client by demonstrating exactly how and when key signs will be used to convey the commands and reframes during the eye movements. The therapist then executes the signs with the hand used as the focal point during the eye movement set.

Third, the therapist uses an index finger for the eye movements when working with DHoH clients, not a pen held in the hand. This allows for the smooth integration of signs into the eye movement sets. It is difficult to adequately explain in written directions alone how MEMI is adapted for DHoH clients. Therapists working with DHoH clients can learn this technique through demonstrations in MEMI trainings.

Here's a script you can use (translated into ASL, of course) when explaining the Figure 8 set:

"In a minute, we will do another sweep that includes the drawing of a figure 8 in the center of your field of vision–starting right about here."

Raise an index finger to the top-center position.

"I will first 'draw' the '8' like this."

Draw the "8" in one direction first.

"Then I will reverse it and go in the opposite direction."

Draw the "8" in the opposite direction.

"You will always focus your eyes on my finger and whatever I sign in the foreground, while at the same time thinking about that experience and everything related to it in the distant background. You will never look out there while watching my finger in the foreground, but you will keep thinking about the experience as if it is out there."

With the exceptions described above, MEMI works in basically the same fashion with DHoH clients as it does with hearing clients, and it is every bit as effective with this population.

OTHER MEMI TIPS

The experienced therapist will determine in which situations and under what circumstances MEMI therapy is most helpful. It should not be used in each session with every client. MEMI is a short-term therapy designed to address client anxiety and dysphoria related to specific problem states exhibited via thoughts and physical and sensory distress. It is critical to identify a specific problem state that is representative of the larger negative experience for focus during the eye movements. Simply telling a client to think about a problem that causes anxiety and then starting the eye movements without first specifying the target and its associated structure misses the heart of the therapy.

I am always surprised when I read cases in which a therapist has used EMDR with a client at each session for as long as a year or more. It appears some practitioners use eye movements simply as a relaxation technique, without a specific, targeted problem state. This is a stop-gap measure, not a solution to the deeper problem. Such a practice represents a misconception of the original purpose of these therapies. It's true that guided eye movements can induce relaxed states in individuals, but to make this the only goal ignores the incredible power of eye movements to target and heal the symptoms of trauma.

Clients occasionally ask how many MEMI sessions will be required for the therapy to work. The number of sessions will depend on the nature of the trauma—whether it's related to a single event or a series of offenses, who was involved, the severity of the offense(s), and the impact on the client's life. It could be as simple as persistent anxiety about having slighted a friend, or as severe as complex trauma from multiple sexual assaults. In addition, not all individuals react in the same way to threatening experiences; some respond with more resilience than others.

In general, though, the answer to how many sessions will be needed depends mostly on *how many problem states there are to resolve*. A client with PTSD from a single incident that lasted a few seconds (a tornado that eclipsed their house) might require only one to three sessions. However, a client with complex trauma from several separate incidents might have many distinct problem states to resolve. In these cases, it may be necessary to space out the MEMI sessions to allow you and your client time to process changes in the structure of each experience. The case report of "Kevin" in the next chapter is an example of complex trauma and how MEMI was used at critical junctures in his therapy to address specific problem states.

MEMI practitioners acknowledge that a thorough evaluation is integral to the successful treatment of mental health problems, but aspects of a trauma can also be resolved before taking a full case history. When clients are referred to me from other therapists for short-term PTSD work, the goal is often to desensitize the structure of the trauma—to diffuse re-experiencing and arousal symptoms using MEMI, not to provide comprehensive, long-term treatment.

If a new client presents with trauma-related symptoms, an initial evaluation and complete case history should be taken as soon as feasible. But if your client's condition is acute, MEMI might be initiated before taking a full case history. An ethical issue arises when a client is suffering from debilitating psychic pain and there is an effective cure, but treatment is delayed. You should, nevertheless, ask your client to complete the PCL-5 before beginning. It takes only a few minutes. Combined with the MEMI pretest data, you will have the critical information necessary to proceed with treatment.

Phobias

MEMI is an effective treatment for most phobia types because images or sensory reactions to the feared object or situation are easily identified. For example, if your client presents with a fear of bees, the approach would be similar to that used with an accident or assault victim. You would ask your client to think of a specific experience involving a bee that occurs frequently in their thoughts or images, is the most troublesome, or is the most difficult to ignore. Because several phobia types have childhood onsets, the focus could be a on the first event that gave rise to the phobia. There are times, however, when a later event is recalled as more threatening, even though there is a childhood referent. In any case, the experience chosen should be at or near the most intense—at the top of the phobic chain, so to speak—unless that choice would jeopardize client security.

Personal Failures, Slights, or Affronts

Most clients can think of an event from the past that still causes significant shame, guilt, disappointment, sadness, or remorse (sure evidence of our humanity). It could be something your client has done or not done that harmed another person. It could be persistent psychological pain after being betrayed by a friend or family member. It could be a mistake your client regrets or a missed opportunity that negatively affected their future. It could be a negative belief about self or others adopted as a result of adverse childhood experiences.

Most individuals harbor burdens of this sort, from which they would like to be free. Although these situations may not be classified as severe trauma, and would probably not qualify for a PTSD diagnosis, they can nevertheless be life-limiting and the cause of severe anxiety. Problems like these are called little 't' traumas in EMDR—what I call *lesser traumas*. MEMI is an excellent technique for resolving personal failures or disappointments that continue to cause distress in a person's life.

Substance Abuse

MEMI can be very helpful with two aspects of substance abuse work. First, many substance abusers harbor guilt from having harmed others, pain from being abused, or shame from negative self-characterizations that bind them to their addictions. The substances then help mask their guilt or shame. And individuals who have had adverse childhood experiences are much more likely to develop substance dependency as adults (Dube et al., 2005). Substance abuse treatment specialists sometimes argue that clients must have sustained periods of sobriety before traumatic experiences can be addressed. In my opinion, this is an incorrect assumption. If a conscious memory of abuse has never been desensitized, the physical and mental discord from that experience will impede substance abuse recovery.

Even if an addict is still abusing a substance, trauma treatment can proceed *under certain conditions*. Using any experiential technique with a client who is under the influence of a substance is contraindicated, but clients who have been clean and/or sober for one week (perhaps longer, depending on the substance) can benefit from MEMI treatment. The case report of Kevin, in the next chapter, reveals how traumatic experiences can be resolved even if a client has not achieved complete sobriety. Substance abuse rehabilitation programs should take note of this finding.

Marty was another client I worked with who was cross-addicted to benzodiazepines and amphetamines. In our discussions, he talked a good game, but he was unable to stay clean for more than a few days or commit to a recovery program. He had attended two inpatient rehabilitation programs and relapsed each time within weeks after finishing treatment. During his intake evaluation, I asked if he had any traumatic experiences in his past. He jokingly responded, "Not unless you count the time my dad kicked down the bedroom door, punched my mother, and drove off with me!" This incident occurred during a contentious custody battle when Marty was seven years old.

Marty's PCL-5 score produced evidence that the memory was a cause of significant anxiety whenever recalled, although he did not qualify for a PTSD diagnosis. A frightening visual movie of his father's cowboy boot kicking through a door's lower panel, his mother's screams, and the thought that he was going to die were accompanied by a nauseated feeling. After one eye movement set, the image changed from a fast-action movie to slow motion. Marty became less nauseated, but he still thought he "could have died." He reported a SUD Score of 75%. After the second set, the movie shrunk in size and became a still photo. Marty could no longer hear his mother's screams. When asked, "What do you think about the experience now?" he said, "That was a long time ago." A resourceful change in thoughts. His SUD Score was then 40%.

Marty's commitment to recovery soon improved. Within weeks he had begun to increase his amount of sober time, found a sponsor, and was regularly attending 12-step meetings. As of this writing, he has been clean for seven years. Of course, no one can say how instrumental MEMI treatment was in breaking his addiction cycle. However, Marty continues to say he's not sure he would have gotten clean if that memory had not been desensitized.

Addictive Cravings

MEMI is also an effective treatment for stopping addictive cravings, particularly with clients who express a sincere desire to stop using their preferred substance. Again, if there is no contract for change, the chances for success are diminished. But if your client says they want to stop using, and verbal and nonverbal responses are congruent with that statement—even if they're not sure it's possible—this demonstrates an adequate commitment to proceed with treatment.

When the goal is to desensitize cravings, you will elicit a specific memory of a time when your client was having a strong desire to use their substance of choice, conduct a pretest of the context, thoughts, feelings, and sensory information, and begin the eye movements. When working to resolve cravings, the most critical structural elements to address are the emotional and somatic feelings generated by their cravings. Clients get anxious with anticipation (emotional feelings) and bodily memories of somatic feelings are triggered (e.g., a rush through the nervous system or a dulling of the senses) each time they have a craving. The occurrence of and interplay between these two types of feelings are what constitute addictive cravings. I know. I've been there. Of particular importance when working with these clients is the future rehearsal, because overcoming cravings is critical to recovery. MEMI treatment can help clients move thoughts, feelings, and sensory information associated with cravings from negative to resourceful, and strengthen resistance to cravings when they occur.

This therapy can also be very helpful with process compulsions or addictions, like gambling, sex, or pornography, as long as your client has expressed a sincere desire to address the problem through the contract for change. In these cases, you would ask your client to select a past experience when they were engaged in the compulsive or addictive behavior that is distressing to them. The chosen experience should be the one they find most disturbing, the one that comes up in the thoughts most often, or the one that is the source of the most guilt or shame. This experience then becomes the problem state of focus during the eye movements.

This chapter was not intended as an exhaustive review of all possible uses of MEMI. No doubt, there is much more to be learned about the therapy's effectiveness in treating a wider array of mental health disorders. And because MEMI offers a very promising method for alleviating PTSD, lesser traumas, phobias, and other forms of anxiety, its responsible use with other disorders is encouraged. However, I would like to add one caution. Highly effective approaches are sometimes carelessly overapplied or misapplied in other treatment areas. This is what I believe happened with the use of randomized controlled trials (RCTs) in treatment effectiveness studies of PTSD. That research method is not a good fit for use with severe or long-term psychological disorders. The overapplication of EMDR in too many treatment areas is also a concern. At the same time, MEMI has proven to be much more than an effective standalone approach to treating trauma. With all of its capabilities, it should at least be adopted as an important component in comprehensive mental health treatment programs.

CHAPTER 11

MEMI Case Reports

As anyone who provides therapy knows, client disclosure of sensitive information does not unfold evenly or in a sequenced fashion. Some experiences, too embarrassing or frightening to mention at first, are withheld until client-therapist trust is established. Understandably, this delays psychotherapeutic outcomes. Progress in trauma treatment can be slow, uneven, and arduous, with false starts and pesky distractions along the way.

The case studies in this chapter illustrate how MEMI was used successfully with four clients diagnosed with PTSD. The details are authentic and accurate, but the cases have been edited to create clearer narratives and to protect client confidentiality. In each case, the therapy was completed before the Intensity Scale was used in the MEMI protocol, so scores from that measure are not included in these reports.

CASE 1. "REBECCA" — RAPE AND STALKING

> **Age**: 32
>
> **Presenting Symptoms**: alcohol and over-the-counter pill abuse; extreme agitation; frequent dissociations; agoraphobia
>
> **Precipitating Events**: rape and stalking that ended three years ago
>
> **Treatment History**: aborted therapy twice since the rape three years ago; refuses to discuss events with referring therapist; unmedicated; substance abuse is current focus in treatment
>
> **PCL-C (DSM-IV) Pretest**: 79
>
> **Provisional Dx**: PTSD
>
> **PCL-C (DSM-IV) Posttest**: 24

It's not uncommon in trauma work to encounter clients who are locked in habitual behavioral responses to either deaden overwhelming experiences or to escape reliving them. Individuals sometimes alter their mood with alcohol, drugs, food, or sex. Others withdraw from social settings and create insular lives to keep themselves safe from harm. Still others develop dissociations—ranging from hardly noticeable momentary lapses in awareness to the creation of alter egos with two or more distinct personality states, as in Dissociative Identity Disorder. Recognizing dissociation, in all its forms, is essential for effective trauma treatment. Rebecca's case exhibits a combination of substance abuse, dissociations, and stalwart avoidance of traumatic memories.

Background Information

I received a call from a counselor colleague of mine who had attended a MEMI training session I conducted. She was calling on behalf of a social worker friend of hers who was seeking help with a client. My acquaintance described the case of a battered woman who had been raped and stalked for more than a year by an ex-lover. Rebecca was attending therapy, but only sporadically, and not improving. Her therapist was unable to address the traumatic experiences with her because Rebecca would not discuss them. Instead, she was locked in a cycle of daily substance abuse with extended periods of dissociative behaviors. I was told Rebecca was likely suffering from PTSD. The situation sounded serious. I was asked to consult with Rebecca's therapist.

During the consult, I learned Rebecca was abusing a variety of substances, principally combinations of alcohol and over-the-counter pain-killers, sleep aids, and allergy medications—anything to dull her senses. The therapist informed me she was the third mental health professional to work with Rebecca over the previous three years. Any attempt to discuss what had happened to Rebecca was met with resistance.

The first therapist told Rebecca she wasn't ready to discuss the incidents; she was too distraught and needed more time. Her second therapist proposed using EMDR to address the trauma, but warned the technique might initially give rise to intense emotions about the assaults. Rebecca had no intention of discussing the trauma, so she ended treatment.

Her therapist at the time asked if I would accept a referral for short-term trauma treatment because they were not making progress. Although Rebecca professed a desire to resolve her struggle and agreed to the referral, I was informed she would probably be unwilling to explain what had happened to her. I was also told Rebecca was likely an alcoholic, so they had been working on substance abuse issues in lieu of addressing the trauma. After I agreed to work with Rebecca, she had to be prodded several times by her therapist and a family member to make the first appointment. Even then, she cancelled that appointment and rescheduled.

Initial Evaluation

Although only 32 years old, when she arrived with her new husband for the appointment, Rebecca could have been mistaken for a much older woman. Her attire was disheveled and she presented as extremely distractible. A very high pretest score on the PCL-C (DSM-IV) of 79/85 qualified her for a provisional PTSD diagnosis. (A score of 44 or above confirms the diagnosis.)

When we sat down, Rebecca began rocking slowly and rhythmically from front to back in her chair, which I assumed was a self-soothing behavior. She could only make eye contact for seconds at a time, examining her fingernails and picking at her cuticles in between. I began by telling Rebecca I knew from her therapist why she had come to see me. I promised she would not have to talk about what happened to her unless she was willing. She said she was not. Occasionally, she would stare down-center for extended periods, perhaps collapsing into the dissociative state she experienced whenever triggered by thoughts of the rape. I asked her to try to maintain eye contact with me, as that would make it easier for her.

Because I had promised Rebecca she would not have to discuss what happened to her, I simply asked how she had been doing recently, what her days were like. She reported having flashbacks and nightmares during which she would see a vivid, movielike re-enactment (visual sensory information) of one aspect of her multiple traumas. She would also get a knot in her stomach and her legs would tremble (visceral feelings). In her thoughts, Rebecca would berate herself for not having done more to stop what happened. She was not telling her trauma story, but describing her reactions whenever she thought about it. She volunteered this information. Our agreement to avoid telling her story was intact; she was leading the discussion.

Rebecca explained how she frequently hid in her closet while at home, held her knees to her chest, and rocked (apparently like she was doing in my office) for hours. She would only come out when her husband was expected home. She admitted having a drink or two to numb her feelings, but denied having an alcohol problem. She did not mention the over-the-counter substances I knew she'd been taking. Rebecca was able to meet her public obligations as a part-time worker, yet was very anxious whenever she left home.

I commented about how fearful she had to be when she was in the closet. She explained in detail what that was like for her—the thoughts she had and the associated feelings, which presented a baseline for future comparisons. We were not discussing the rape but her habitual response to it—her ritual in the closet. I asked if she would like to feel less fearful when in the closet, and she said yes. This was her contract for change, her agreement to proceed with treatment of the dissociative behavior in the closet. At the same time, I was confident that if the dissociative pattern could be desensitized, it was quite possible aspects of the central trauma might also be reorganized.

Diagnosis
PTSD with dissociative symptoms (309.81)

Treatment
I explained to Rebecca how MEMI might help and how it worked. I told her my number one goal would be to keep her as safe as possible while we worked together. I also confirmed I would never ask her to do anything she was unwilling to do. Because Rebecca described herself as feeling very unsafe while in the closet, we chose to anchor her in a feeling of safety based on a past experience of perceived security. She chose a time before the rape, when she was alone at the beach, no one knew where she was, and she felt completely at ease. Establishing therapeutic

dissociation with Rebecca was especially important because she was terrified of reliving those experiences.

I asked Rebecca to select a recent time when she was rocking back-and-forth in the closet, a time typical of those experiences or one that stood out as especially difficult while going through it. When she had such an event in mind, we did a pretest of her thoughts, feelings, and sensory information to determine the structure of the experience. I emphasized the distance between her and the memory projected on the wall all the way across the room (spatial reframe).

When we finished the first eye movement set, I asked Rebecca to look out at the experience again and tell me if it was the same or different. It was different. "I have less of a reaction to it," she said (visceral and/or emotional feelings). I asked if that made it better or worse. She said, "Better." The SUD Score she reported was 80%. We conducted a second set. "It's even less of a problem," she replied. The SUD Score was then 65%. We went through a third set. Rebecca looked more relaxed—less tense in the face, shoulders, and arms, and she was breathing more evenly. "I'm feeling more positive," she stated. "It would be nice if I could go for walks like I used to." These were new thoughts, beneficial cognitive shifts. The SUD Score after this third set was 50%, a very good sign. Rebecca questioned whether these effects would last. I told her they often did, but we would find out when I saw her the next time.

At her second appointment, Rebecca reported she was still less fearful when she thought of her ritual in the closet. She also reported feeling more confident since our first session. In fact, she had stopped retreating to the closet altogether after our appointment. "In general, I'm not as afraid," she said.

I explained what we had done during the first session was a Band-Aid, because we had not addressed the real problem. She said she understood. She was exhibiting so much resilience at that moment, I decided to assess whether she was ready to address the central problem state—the rape and stalking. When I asked Rebecca whether she would be willing to address the real problem with MEMI if she didn't have to talk about it, she said yes, with some conviction. Her face was exhibiting almost no tension, she was breathing calmly, and nodding in assent. This was her agreement to change.

I anchored her again in the secure experience from her past. With therapeutic dissociation in place, she then identified the associated images, feelings, and thoughts (the structure of the memory) she experienced each time she recalled the real problem. We did not discuss the context; I was not asking her to describe what happened with a first-person narrative. So our agreement not to discuss the details of the trauma was still intact.

After the first eye movement set, I asked Rebecca if her reaction to the experience was the same or different. She said it was less than it was before, therefore, obviously different. I asked what that meant. "I have less of a reaction to it," she said. I asked if that was better and she said yes. The SUD Score she reported was 85%. After the second set, Rebecca said the image was "farther away." A visual image moving farther away is usually beneficial. The SUD Score she reported this time was 70%. After the third set, Rebecca said the knot in her stomach was not as tight and her legs were not trembling (reductions in visceral reactions). She also said the memory, for the first time, felt like it was in the past. Moving farther back in time is almost always beneficial as well, a kind of time related reset, when the intensity of a recalled experience diminishes. "I want to move on," she added, another positive and intentional cognitive shift. At this point, Rebecca reported a SUD Scale Score of less than 50%, a very good sign.

What happened next was typical of MEMI work with clients. Rebecca spontaneously described the worst part of the rape, complete with details—the information she had been holding inside for years. I did not ask her to tell me. She was surprised when I pointed out she had explained everything without tears or the level of anxiety she'd always experienced. She asked how I could change her thoughts and feelings about the rape so quickly.

Before our third treatment session, Rebecca wrote in an email that she had something important to share with me. When she arrived, we did not do another MEMI session. Instead, she talked for the entire hour, explaining more details about the rape, how she was stalked, and her long journey through the legal system. *She also told me she was angry with me because I had spoiled her plan to commit suicide.* Rebecca had been planning her death for weeks before our first appointment. She had not wanted to see me at all. "What's the use?" she'd told herself. She was still considering suicide when she came for her second session, but had begun to question her plan. After that session, she changed her mind. Rebecca also said she had poured all the alcohol in the house down the kitchen sink; she had no desire for a drink. She thanked me for helping her.

I saw Rebecca twice more, once with her husband to help him understand the trauma work we had done and to explain her dramatic improvements. Rebecca told him about the planned suicide. She also explained how guilty she felt about planning to end her life, lying about her drinking and pill abuse, and her neglect of him while she was suffering. Rebecca's fifth treatment session was designed to help her let go of the guilt she still harbored for her past actions. We conducted MEMI therapy for the third and final time.

Results

Two weeks after her last session, Rebecca scored 24 on the PCL-C, 55 points lower than her pretest. A 10-20-point change is considered clinically significant, so her results were remarkable. Because other PTSD diagnostic criteria were in remission, Rebecca no longer qualified for the diagnosis. I referred her back to her regular therapist for follow-up. I can add that, although her score on the pretest was very high, Rebecca's case is not unique, but rather a good example of the effectiveness of MEMI as a short-term therapy (from 2-5 sessions) for PTSD.

Months after our final session, I received this email from Rebecca's referring therapist:

I finally met with Rebecca and her husband this morning, and we had a closure session. She told me about her treatments with you. It is amazing what you were able to accomplish with your skills. She seems like a different person and her husband agrees. She said that she goes to the mall alone now and went to the beach by herself. She is beginning to smell the roses. She thanked me for being here for her these past few years and for referring her to you. I feel confident that she will be okay now. However, I did encourage her to get another therapist to continue working on getting to know herself.

CASE 2. "KEVIN" – CHILDHOOD PHYSICAL AND SEXUAL ABUSE

> **Age**: 45
> **Presenting Symptoms**: frequent dissociations; depressed mood; moderate anxiety; disappears overnight without explanations; possible substance abuse
> **Precipitating Events**: mother's death one year ago; mother's history of bipolar disorder; childhood physical and sexual trauma and homelessness; violent, alcoholic father who left the home when Kevin was seven
> **Treatment History**: several months of weekly therapy with the same provider since his mother's death; childhood sexual abuse and possible substance abuse were not discussed; unmedicated
> **PCL-C (DSM-IV) Pretest Score**: 58
> **Provisional Diagnosis**: PTSD with dissociations; r/o substance dependence disorder; r/o major depressive disorder
> **PCL-C (DSM-IV) Posttest Score**: 36

Individuals who are exposed to traumatic experiences may not develop PTSD symptoms for months, years, or even decades after the incident. This is now specified in the *Diagnostic and Statistical Manual of Mental Disorders*, fifth edition as "delayed onset" or "delayed expression" PTSD. This case study is a disturbing tale of physical, sexual, and emotional violence, and demonstrates the characteristics of complex trauma. Because the onset of Kevin's symptoms occurred many years after the events, the study illustrates the long-term effects of trauma. But, as one would hope, it also exemplifies the stalwart resilience of the human spirit.

Background Information

I first became aware of Kevin's problems when his partner came to see me for a consultation. Although they had been in a loving, harmonious relationship for 10 years, Kevin was feeling like a stranger to him. He described Kevin as severely depressed, emotionally distant, and exhibiting bizarre behaviors following the death of his mother several months earlier. Kevin had begun to disappear at night and would not answer his cell phone while gone, claiming when he returned that he'd been walking around the city all night. When pressed for details, Kevin gave dubious explanations about where he'd been and what he'd done. I suspected a substance abuse problem or an affair, but did not convey those thoughts to his partner. Kevin had been attending weekly counseling sessions with another therapist, but in his partner's opinion was not making progress. At his partner's urging, Kevin agreed to see me for a consultation the following week.

Initial Evaluation

Kevin was a handsome, intelligent, well-groomed, and well-spoken gay man in his mid-40s with a good job as a white-collar professional. He had been in therapy for almost a year, ever since the death of his mother. He presented as anxious, shifting frequently in his chair and crossing and uncrossing his legs. His responses were guarded, giving a minimum amount of information when answering questions. He was also dissociating for brief moments, staring off to his right, seemingly occupied in thought and losing track of our conversation.

Kevin was the oldest of five children, raised in severe poverty (homeless on several occasions) by a bipolar, single mother. His father had been a violent alcoholic who physically abused him when he was young. Once, after a wine bottle was broken over his head, Kevin had to have glass shards removed from his scalp in the ER. His dad lived separately from the family from the time Kevin was seven.

Kevin reported being sexually abused twice by his mother before the age of 12. After one incident, she beat him severely. His partner was generally aware Kevin had been abused, but Kevin had never discussed the events in detail with anyone, not even his therapist at the time. Kevin's siblings had also been sexually abused by their mom and/or an uncle, acts which undoubtedly provoked a pattern of intersibling abuse that followed.

Kevin was mistreated in other ways as well. On many occasions, he was the target of his mother's physical and emotional abuse. He was beaten in public once and shamed in front of a crowd. On another occasion, she stabbed his hand with a fork at the dinner table. Kevin also had been sexually abused by an older man near a playground at the age of eight, and by a male friend of his mother's when he was nine. When he began working as a teenager, Kevin's mother would force him to surrender all his earnings. Any one of these incidents could have resulted in a PTSD diagnosis, all of them taken together must have been overwhelming for him. However, nothing would compare to two other repulsive acts of abuse Kevin would disclose to me later.

One would expect a child so severely abused to develop serious problems as an adolescent or adult—depression, anxiety, obesity, drug or alcohol addiction, health problems, relationship issues, legal difficulties, suicide, and the like. On the one hand, and against the odds, after finishing high school and leaving home, Kevin demonstrated a remarkable ability to earn a living and care for himself. From an hourly wage earner, he worked his way up to a management position. When he had risen as far as he could without further education, he entered and finished college, and eventually earned a graduate degree.

At the same time, there were familiar markers in his history as a result of the abuse. From the time he was first molested until he reached the age of 30, Kevin chose self-isolation over engagement, evidence of dissociative tendencies that sometimes mask conscious responses to ill-treatment. At 16, he began exercising obsessively in response to a weight problem, a habit he would maintain with intensity until his mother's death. Between ages 20 and 40, he often worked 60-plus hours per week, even while a full-time student, perhaps distinctive overcompensation to offset feelings of inadequacy.

Kevin also reported being exploited for sex during those same years, another trait common among survivors of sexual violence. He described two long-term relationships as dysfunctional. The first was with an alcoholic who was both physically and mentally abusive, and the second he reported as unstable and fueled by alcohol. However, he denied having an alcohol problem. By that time, Kevin's dissociative defenses were well-honed. But in his late 30s, Kevin met the partner he was in a relationship with when he began therapy with me. Although his relationship had been balanced and healthy, he was still wrapped in various obsessions—cleaning, exercise, and work were the most pronounced. The pattern held steady for years, until his mother's death triggered a dramatic change.

At the end of the consultation, I informed Kevin I was willing to work with him, and with his permission we would explore the abuse in his history. Although his nighttime disappearances pointed to substance abuse, he denied having a problem of any kind. We discussed the possible use of MEMI to help resolve his trauma symptoms. Two weeks later, we began our sessions, after Kevin had terminated counseling with the other therapist. Kevin's score on the PCL-C (DSM-IV) before beginning treatment was 58. That was 14 points above the cutoff score of 44 to confirm a PTSD diagnosis.

Kevin became a long-term client; there was much to unravel. Like many complex trauma cases, his did not unfold neatly.

Diagnosis

PTSD with delayed onset and dissociative symptoms (309.81); stimulant use disorder, amphetamine-type, severe (304.40)

Treatment

In our first session, I asked two things of Kevin—that he be honest with me and that he show up for all appointments. He agreed. In the end, he didn't always do either until he was firmly established in recovery, but progress, not perfection was the message I conveyed to him.

It was important to determine what he was doing when he stayed out all night. I explained my personal and professional experiences with addictions. I did not ask <u>if</u> he was using a substance. Asking that question is a trap for addicts; it's too easy for them to lie. Instead, I observed that anyone who is disappearing overnight, especially for days at a time, must be using something or having an affair. He vehemently denied an affair. This was my opening. "So, what are you using?" I asked. His answer was crystal methamphetamine, a form of "speed," with a rapid downward spiral to addiction.

I made it clear we could not do eye movement therapy if he was drunk or high. He agreed to abstain from all substances for the two weeks leading up to our first MEMI treatment session. I was confident Kevin had kept his promise the day we began. However, addicts do lie, and there were several times early in our work when he withheld information about using. When he eventually got honest about when he used, where, and with whom, he had taken an important step in his recovery.

Kevin explained he'd become despondent and inconsolable after his mother died. Memories from his past flooded the present, connecting him once again to blocked childhood emotions. Given his tendency to isolate, he started taking long walks over great distances, leaving the house in the late afternoon and not returning until morning. During one of those outings, a stranger offered Kevin the drug. It allowed him to escape the depression, briefly replacing the pain with heightened euphoria. And like other addicts, he thought the drug was designed for him, until his cravings for it became uncontrollable.

Based on his partner's reports, Kevin was probably exhibiting clinical symptoms of delayed onset PTSD before he started using crystal meth. I explained this to Kevin, who agreed with the observation. I added that his mother's passing could have triggered previously compartmentalized memories and feelings associated with the abuse. Because he was frequently staring off to his right, dissociating, I also described the historical role of dissociation in his response to his experiences. There were three treatment priorities to be addressed with Kevin: 1.) the memories of abuse; 2.) crystal meth dependence; and 3.) his frequent dissociative behaviors.

When I asked Kevin to select the most difficult memory from his experiences, he described an as yet undisclosed instance of sexual abuse he'd never told anyone. When he was 14 years old, his mother pressured him into having intercourse with her lesbian girlfriend, a heinous form of mistreatment because of all of its implications. We performed two sets of eye movements focused on the problem state associated with the sex act. After the first eye movement set, Kevin reported the image had "moved far away." He also felt less of a physical connection to it (less intense visceral and emotional feelings). Both of these changes made the memory better. His SUD Score at the end of the second set was 50%, a response which usually indicates a memory will be manageable going forward. But we were both surprised by what happened next.

The third eye movement set he had requested was interrupted when I observed Kevin stiffen in his chair, hold his breath, and widen his eyes—a shift from his more relaxed state. I explained that I noticed the change and asked what was happening. Spontaneously, an image of another event had appeared and eclipsed the one of him in bed with the woman. In its place, he recalled a discussion with his mother and her girlfriend at the dining room table, during which he was forced to agree to abort the child he had fathered. When a different memory suddenly supplants a targeted memory like this, it often signals the importance of the new memory. I imagine it's a way for the unconscious mind to push more significant aspects of a trauma to the forefront. Kevin had not realized how troubling that decision had been for him, not until that moment. Filled with emotion, tears in his eyes, he described this memory as devastating—evidence of its primacy and impact. This memory would prove more difficult to desensitize than the first.

After the third MEMI set, the visual image of the abortion discussion had improved, but not as much as the image of the sexual act had. The discussion image was less vivid (visual imagery) than before the eye movements, but the picture was not as diffused as the first memory. At the same time, his visceral reactions were less severe. Accordingly, these changes made the memory seem better to him. His final SUD Score (after four sets) in relation to the second, more troubling memory was 60%. We ended the session there at his request, even though we had not reached the desired 50% SUD Score.

When Kevin returned the following week, his opinion about the previous session was decidedly positive. He declared how amazed he was that, no matter what he did, he was unable to "bring back" either of the troubling memories after our eye movement work.

Kevin's abuse experiences were addressed first (even though he was using crystal meth every week to 10 days) because his traumatic memories were intertwined with his addictive behaviors. The memories triggered dissociations, and dissociations were a portal to his drug use. If a client's internal narrative is tied to traumatic experiences that carry guilt or shame, it's possible, even wise, to first neutralize the disruptive memories early in substance abuse treatment. Waiting until the substance dependence is under control could take a long time, sometimes years. Traumatic memories can be successfully resolved as long as the client is substance-free at the time of treatment. Of course, if a client does not agree to abstain from their substance of choice prior to a planned MEMI session, or shows up for the appointment high, treatment cannot go forward.

We would use MEMI a number of times during the course of Kevin's treatment, but it was not used frequently. Once the harsh effects of the first two memories had been resolved, there was no need to revisit them unless and until his response to them changed. It never did. Kevin's score on the PCL-C two months after treatment was 36, a decrease of 22 points from his pretest of 58. Although he still had a moderate level of concern about falling asleep, feeling distant from people, and avoiding thoughts about past experiences, his score no longer reached the threshold for a PTSD diagnosis. Other PTSD symptoms also receded to within a normal range.

We used MEMI with other memories Kevin identified as strong and intrusive. We also used the therapy for events in the present that triggered emotional responses similar to those from his past. In one situation, contractors doing renovations on his house walked off the job and would not return his calls. For a brief time, it seemed the work would never be completed. Kevin's reaction was extreme; he became anxious and was frequently dissociating again. When we conducted a MEMI session focused on this new situation, his arousal symptoms (anger, racing thoughts, and shortness of breath) were successfully desensitized. It was also an opportunity for him to understand how his reactions to the contractor were similar to those he experienced when recalling acts of childhood abuse, even though the circumstances were entirely different.

I was asked by the editor of this book, why, if the circumstances were so different, would the feeling and sensory reactions be similar? This is an important question. As has been pointed out, when traumatic experiences are recalled, the distressing somatic, emotional, and sensory reactions that occurred at the time of the event are reactivated in individuals diagnosed with PTSD, even under seemingly unrelated circumstances.

In Chapter 1, the functions of the amygdala and hippocampus, and the differences between *explicit* and *implicit* memories were explained. Explicit memories are factual, autobiographical accounts of our experiences (e.g., who was there, how long an event lasted, and what happened). These memories are conscious and easily recalled. As the explicit memory center of the brain, the hippocampus responds to queries from the amygdala about potential threats using its store of explicit memories as a reference. Implicit memories are unconscious sensory impressions: a car backfiring nearby will cause a startle; a stranger's imposing stare might generate fear. When the amygdala receives sensory input about potential threats from the thalamus, it quickly checks its store of implicit memories before initiating the stress response.

In Kevin's case, his explicit memory of the abuse had been desensitized with MEMI, so that recalling the experience no longer triggered disturbing symptoms. He still had a memory of the event, but it was no longer as threatening or intense. However, his subliminal impressions of people—his view of their trustworthiness and goodness—had been distorted by years of childhood mistreatment and would cast a long shadow. Survivors of rape or sexual assault often become suspicious of, distrust, or closely examine the actions and motivations of others, even years after memories of abuse have been desensitized. These reactions become the default when responding to life's experiences. Even when a situation bears little resemblance to an original trauma, the structure of the reaction can be very similar.

After Kevin's reactions to his early trauma were resolved to his satisfaction, we began to address his drug dependence and dissociative behaviors. It had taken only three sessions to calm his most threatening memories of abuse, but it would take many more to completely reintegrate all of his painful experiences and to conquer his addiction.

A year into our work together, Kevin was lamenting his dissociations, saying all the partitions that had kept things separate in his mind were gone; everything was swirling around and memories were constantly rearranging as he recalled more. We had neutralized the difficult memories at the top of the chain, but fragments of other times he had been victimized dropped into consciousness in piecemeal fashion over the next two years. The cycle from memory to pain to dissociation to drug use would require more time to be dismantled.

With a long history of self-isolation, active participation in 12-step programs was excruciatingly uncomfortable for Kevin. The thought of talking to a potential sponsor was even worse. However, in 12-step meetings you can choose to be silent and listen. You can arrive and leave without saying a word to anyone.

Results

Kevin's posttest score of 36 on the PCL-C following three MEMI sessions at the very beginning of our work together was 22 points lower than his pretest of 58. Because the score was well below the PTSD threshold of 44 points, and because other trauma symptoms were within normal ranges, he no longer warranted a PTSD diagnosis. This did not change during five years of treatment.

Kevin's recovery from crystal meth, on the other hand, was long and onerous. After many slips and two different local, outpatient rehab programs, he eventually entered residential treatment where he began to get his bearings. His number of days clean in a row began to grow from slip to slip. From one week to several, to a month, then 90 days and more. The trajectory was slow, but steadily upward.

He also began to demonstrate the wisdom of 12-step thinking in his life's daily dealings. About three years into our work, Kevin changed our schedule from weekly to biweekly sessions, evidence of his growing confidence. He had begun to dissociate less and to recognize the triggers tempting him to emotionally disappear. He finally secured a 12-step sponsor and began attending a regular meeting he found comfortable. In our final year of work together, more than five years after his first session, Kevin reduced his sessions to once a month.

During his recovery, Kevin had faced a major challenge at work, sought and secured a new position where he felt valued and respected, and repaired the damage done to his primary relationship. In our final sessions before termination, Kevin celebrated one year of sobriety. He spoke about how he was making friends and was able to laugh and joke with others. Although he said he was still working on overcoming a fear of talking to people, Kevin was, in all respects, a new man.

CASE 3. "ASHLEY" — SEXUAL ABUSE AND ABANDONMENT

> **Age**: 55
>
> **Presenting Symptoms**: depressed mood; mild to moderate anxiety
>
> **Precipitating Events**: childhood sexual assault; domestic violence and abandonment
>
> **Treatment History**: attended therapy a few times when younger, but never discussed details of the sexual assault
>
> **PCL-5 Pretest Score**: 70
>
> **Provisional Diagnosis: PTSD**: r/o mood disorder
>
> **PCL-5 Posttest Score**: 15

Revelations about the pervasiveness of systematic physical and sexual abuse in institutions of all types has been covered widely in the media over the last two decades. As survivors have come forward and reported dreadful patterns of mistreatment, assaults and cover-ups, few organizations have escaped the resulting scrutiny and upheaval. Churches, private schools, political groups, large companies, and even the movie industry have all had their day in the spotlight. Ashley's case depicts an example of childhood sexual abuse at a private, residential school. Complicating her situation was a history of domestic disturbance at home that she would not fully comprehend until MEMI treatment was completed.

Background Information

In a phone consultation before our first session, Ashley introduced herself as a management coach with graduate-level training in mental health and human development. She said it was time for her to address several traumatic events from her past, hinting that one or more of them involved sexual violence. She had attended individual therapy to address the trauma a few times, but she believed there was more work to be done. In preparation for our first session, I asked Ashley to make a prioritized list of all the traumatic events in her life based on level of severity, with the most troubling at the top.

Initial Evaluation

When we met, Ashley presented as an attractive, composed, well-groomed, and articulate 55-year-old woman. In spite of her troubled history, she had reached the peak of her profession and was beginning to plan for retirement. I was impressed by her confidence and calm demeanor as she sat opposite me—barely a hint of weakness or vulnerability. That would all change when she began to describe the most challenging of the several negative experiences she'd endured as a child. The two most difficult had rarely been discussed, much less resolved, even though each was a constant source of anguish.

By the age of 11, Ashley had already witnessed multiple disturbing incidents at home, been physically assaulted twice at school, and been raped more than once at another school she attended. She'd also been abandoned by her mother following a series of domestic disputes. In all, Ashley had listed 12 separate traumatic experiences, but the violence at home and the rape were at the top of her list.

Ashley was one of my first clients to be administered the PCL-5, the revised version of the PTSD Checklist introduced in 2013. Studies have demonstrated the instrument's validity and reliability, and confirmed the questionnaire is psychometrically sound (Blevins et al., 2015; Wortmann et al., 2016). Ashley scored 70 out of a possible 80 points on the checklist pretest, a very high score. All of her answers indicating frequency or level of intensity in response to PTSD problem statements were either "quite a bit" (10 items) or "extremely" (10 items). With a minimum of 31-33 points required for a provisional PTSD diagnosis, her score was 37 points above that threshold. All other criteria required for confirmation of a PTSD diagnosis were also met. Although Ashley was reporting abuse from her childhood, she did not qualify for a delayed onset diagnosis because she had been experiencing severe symptoms throughout her life, a marvel considering her appearance and accomplishments.

Diagnosis

PTSD (309.81)

Treatment

At our initial session, we agreed to first use MEMI to address the violence Ashley had witnessed at home as a child. During the MEMI pretest, she described an image of violence in the kitchen. It was a dim, close-up shot of just her mom ranting at the table while the children looked on (visual sensory information). Ashley chose to focus on one particular kitchen incident that had triggered her mother's flight from the house and an absence of several days. Although her parents would reunite from time to time after that, Ashley remarked, "It would never be the same." Following the incident, her mother was often gone for extended periods.

When asked about her physical sensations, Ashley described a dense heaviness in her upper torso, from her shoulders to her waist and down her arms (visceral feelings). Although she remained composed, her eyes began to mist, indicating an emotional reaction. She was breathing rapidly and shallowly (visceral feelings). When asked for her thoughts about the experience, Ashley talked about being confused when the incident occurred and wondered why her mother was so angry. A resource anchor was established, Ashley was reminded the kitchen image was across the room in the past, and she would remain in the present. I explained she would be viewing her younger self going through the experience from a distance. She agreed she was ready to begin the eye movements.

After the first set, even with the protections afforded by the resource anchor, Ashley broke down in an outpouring of grief as she re-envisioned her mother yelling at the table. She later said she'd always connected this particular event with the breakup of her family. As she cried in response to the memory, she said, "No little girl should have to live through that!" Her thoughts had changed, from being confused at the time to a reflection of its effect on her as a child. She then complained about the severe heaviness in her arms, something she'd felt before when under stress, but it was especially pronounced after the first eye movement set. Nothing else had changed about the experience. The SUD Score remained at 100%.

When Ashley was fully prepared for the second set, I suggested she focus on the heaviness in her arms. She would still think about the image in the kitchen, but I asked her to be especially mindful of those visceral feelings. When the eye movements were well underway, Ashley's facial muscles began to exhibit less tension. She also took a deep breath in the middle of the set, an auspicious sign of change. When we finished the eye movement set, Ashley spontaneously closed her eyes. She did not appear upset or in distress. Under her lids, her eyes shuttled back and forth in saccades (rapid, horizontal movements), reminding me of a computer in search of data.

When she opened her eyes, Ashley said both the image and the context had changed. She had a wider-angle view of the entire kitchen and could see her mother and father standing and arguing with each other. But this did not seem to distress her. "I feel lighter!" she said. Ashley began flapping her arms up and down at her sides like a chicken. She then lifted both arms straight over her head, grabbed one wrist with the other hand, and stretched upward. Lowering her arms, she crooked them in front of her chest, shook her hands at the wrists, and began to laugh heartily. The heavy, visceral feelings in her arms were gone. She laughed and laughed and laughed. We both did, and for a long time.

When I asked for her thoughts about what she had just seen, Ashley said her mom had always been a very strong woman, and instead of the conflicting feelings she had about her before the session, she sensed only warmth when thinking about her. When I asked for a location of the warmth in her body, Ashley raised a hand and tapped her sternum three times, quite a change from the heaviness located there before. On the other hand, for the first time she observed only coldness from her father in the scene—a change in context. She was beginning to consider how her mother might also have been a victim. Her thoughts about both her parents had changed.

When asked for a SUD Score, Ashley rated the experience at 30%. I remarked that was a big change. I then asked, if her response to the trauma were to remain at that level going forward, did she think it would be manageable? She answered Yes. When asked if she would like me to conduct another eye movement set, Ashley said she thought she'd be okay without it. Just to be sure, we did a future rehearsal. I asked her to think of a time in the future when she would likely think about the scene in the kitchen again. While imagining that future event, there was no heaviness in Ashley's upper torso, just a warmth in her chest when she thought about her mother. We exchanged high fives.

Ashley was very aware, however, of the more serious memory she wanted to confront. She expressed nervousness and fear about addressing the rape she experienced when she was 10. I assured her that we would not address that experience until she was ready.

At the beginning of our second session, I asked Ashley how she had been feeling since our first session. She was pleased to report the gains she had achieved were the same as when she left the session. She still had warm feelings when thinking of her mother, and the scene in the kitchen was no longer a concern. Just as I was beginning to transition the discussion to the second traumatic memory we had agreed to address, Ashley said she wanted to tell me something. "What's that?" I asked. "I've never divulged the details of this experience to anyone—not anyone," she said emphatically. Although still composed, the strain in her voice was palpable.

I assured Ashley she would not have to explain what happened or divulge any of the details of the assault, if that's what she preferred. Nevertheless, as soon as she was anchored in her resource state, and therapeutic dissociation had been re-explained and established, she launched into a description of the rape that took place after hours in the high school gymnasium, perpetrated by a boy several years older than her. The school she was attending at the time was a private, K-12 residential program. As such, the children were supervised in the evening by residential staff.

During the pretest, it was clear Ashley's behavioral responses to this memory were much more taxing than her reaction to the kitchen trauma during our first session. Her eyes were already tearing up; her fingers were gripping the edge of her seat; her upper body was stiff; she was breathing erratically, holding her breath at times; and her facial muscles were taut. I saw what I thought was a look of anguish on her face. Ashley commented three times about how sad and ashamed she felt because she had experienced pleasure during the rape. A statement such as "I'm so ashamed" would have characterized it well, although those were not her exact words. That shame had been a source of guilt all her life and would need to be addressed at some point. I refired her anchor to diminish her symptoms to a more manageable level before accessing the negative imagery and somatic reactions associated with the memory.

When asked about sensory information associated with the memory, Ashley said there were no sounds. The picture of the rape had muted colors and was narrowly focused on the act itself (visual imagery). When asked about feelings, she said her body was tight and felt restrained (visceral feelings). That made sense, given what might have happened. The rigidity in her body and facial expressions were consistent with that description. She also described being unable to breathe freely, as if her windpipe was constricted (visceral feelings).

After the first eye movement set, Ashley reported little had changed, but she nevertheless gave her reaction an 85% SUD Score. Following the second set, similar to our first session, Ashley closed her eyes and searched the memory, her eyes moving rapidly back and forth behind her lids. When she opened her eyes, she again reported a change in the image. The incident had "come back to life," she said, with the colors in the gym the way they were back then. "Now I can see the whole scene as it was, but I'm not afraid of it anymore," she added. The changes in the image and her thoughts seemed to make it less threatening. I asked Ashley how she knew she was unafraid, what evidence did she have? She reported her reaction to the memory was not as harsh, that she didn't feel as tense as before. She said her windpipe "had loosened a bit, but not much."

But that was not all. Ashley looked up to her left, then straight ahead, where her eyes widened then narrowed, like she was bringing an image into focus. She told me she'd just remembered something she'd forgotten. The night of the rape, she had been taken to the gym by a dormitory supervisor and left with the older boy. Ashley then commented that the rape might have been planned and not happenstance. "Why else would a supervisor walk me to the gym after dark and leave me there with an older boy—just the two of us, alone?" she asked rhetorically. She then realized she'd been raped more than once there!

Based on this new information, Ashley's thoughts about the experience changed, becoming more analytical. Instead of shame and self-blame, her thinking shifted to an objective observation of what happened in the gym. This reinterpretation of the events, the change in her thoughts from self-blame to a more reasoned perspective, may have been prompted by the change in context—when the memory expanded to include her being ushered to the gym by a supervisor. Ashley's SUD Score after this second set of eye movements dropped to 60-65%. Although her thoughts had become less self-critical, her visceral reactions were still pronounced—based on the tightness in her body and breathing difficulty.

Before beginning the third eye movement set, I asked Ashley to hold in her awareness the constricted windpipe as she engaged the image across the room. At the end of the eye movement set, she took a deep breath, looked across the room, and said, "It's different. I feel lighter now." She took another deep breath and said, "I can feel cool air going all the way down into my lungs and a warmth across my chest." The rigidity in her body had also relaxed. Although the image from the second set of eye movements had not changed after completing the third set, the changes in her physical symptoms were enough for her to report she felt unafraid.

We reviewed all the changes to Ashley's memory from start to finish. First, Ashley's thoughts about the rape had shifted from self-critical to analytical. In spite of the troubling realization that she had been raped more than once, her emotional feelings had changed; she was no longer afraid. Her visceral feelings had changed as well; she was much more relaxed, and her windpipe was no longer constricted. The memory's visual representation had also changed—from a narrowly framed picture of the act, the image had become a panoramic view of the entire gym, with the colors no longer muted as they had been. For some unknown reason, that particular change had calmed Ashley's reactions to the memory. Given all these changes, I asked, "What score would you give the memory now?" "It's low," she responded, "around the 20s."

Before deciding to discontinue the eye movements, I asked if Ashley wanted to address the shame she felt about having experienced pleasure during the rape. She nodded in agreement. I explained that shame and self-condemnation are common reactions among victims who have experienced pleasure during sexual assaults, or believe they were somehow at fault for what happened. Ashley was surprised to hear my comment. She said she fought the rape the first time, but at some point she gave up. I explained she was likely forced or threatened with physical violence at the time, and suggested the constricted breathing and body rigidity might have been evidence of that. "You shouldn't hold yourself responsible," I said. "It's not what you chose, and there was nothing you could have done to stop it." I expressed hope that one day Ashley would be able to release any self-criticism, guilt, or shame for what had been done to her. She acknowledged that hope as well.

I questioned Ashley. Was she satisfied with the improvements following the eye movements, considering the changes in thoughts (less self-critical), images (from a close-up to a panoramic view), and visceral feelings (reduced muscle tension and relaxed breathing)? She said she was. As part of the future rehearsal, I asked whether she believed her reactions to the experience would be manageable going forward. She answered yes. We shared a high five and ended the session.

When Ashley returned for her third session two weeks later, she reported her reactions when thinking about both experiences were the same as at the end of each session, although she resented that those events had occurred at all. She continued with therapy for several more sessions. During those meetings, her comments reinforced the impact our eye movement work had on her life. Ashley said she was much more contemplative, had new energy, and she experienced dramatic improvements in sleep. She also mentioned making better choices. Even her spouse remarked how much lighter she seemed. Six months after our MEMI work, Ashley opened the session by saying, "I feel ebullient! I have so much more clarity now and the ability to see things differently. Everything is easier."

Results

Ashley's before and after scores on the PCL-5 demonstrated a dramatic reduction in symptoms. Prior to treatment, she scored 70 on the checklist and all of her answers to PTSD problem statements were either "quite a bit" (10 items) or "extremely" (10 items). Following treatment, Ashley scored 15/80 points, and all responses except one were rated either "not at all" (7 items) or "a little bit" (12 items). Her posttest score was 16 points below the threshold for a PTSD diagnosis and 55 points lower than before MEMI treatment. She no longer met the criteria for a PTSD diagnosis. Because a reduction of 10-20 points or more indicates a significant treatment effect, her after-treatment score also strongly reinforced the SUD Score results and the changes in context, thoughts, sensory information, and feelings related to the two traumatic memories that had received focus.

Months later, Ashley explained an insight that came to her as she was relaxing on a beach—what she called a "memory bubble." While thinking about the events at her school, she recalled something else about one of the nights she was raped. It had to be past bedtime; the halls were dark as the supervisor led her away from her residence. She'd also remembered the gym was dimly lit. Ashley concluded there must have been a silent conspiracy of abuse going on back then because at least one supervisor was involved. This insight of hers was later corroborated. Numerous reports of sexual abuse made by her contemporaries in the alumni association led to an investigation of sexual assaults at the school.

CASE 4. "MIGUEL" — WITNESS TO DAUGHTER'S OPIOID OVERDOSE

> **Age:** 58
>
> **Presenting Problems:** severe anxiety; insomnia; negative self-assessments
>
> **Precipitating Events:** teenage daughter's two near-fatal drug overdoses
>
> **Treatment History:** family therapy with a substance abuse counselor, but no previous therapy to address his trauma-related symptoms
>
> **PCL-5 Pretest Score:** 52
>
> **Provisional Diagnosis:** PTSD
>
> **PCL-5 Posttest Score:** 32

The conditions under which PTSD can be diagnosed are spelled out in the DSM-5 diagnostic criteria for the disorder under Criterion A. In order to receive the diagnosis, an individual must have been exposed to an actual death threat, serious injury, or sexual violence in one of four ways. The person must have: directly experienced a trauma; been a witness to a trauma; heard about a trauma happening to a close family member or friend; or received repeated or extreme exposure to traumas (e.g., police, first responders, or child protective services personnel). Without satisfying one or more of these requirements, PTSD cannot be diagnosed. Miguel's case is an example of an individual who developed PTSD after witnessing several life-threatening events related to his daughter's drug addiction.

Background Information

Miguel was referred to me by a therapist colleague of his who was aware of MEMI therapy's potential to help him with the problems he was facing. The referral source described Miguel as extremely distressed about certain events he had witnessed when his daughter had overdosed—experiences he could not get out of his mind. During our conference call, Miguel indicated he would prefer to wait and discuss details of his situation when we met. An appointment for an initial session was scheduled for the following week.

Initial Evaluation

Miguel was a tall, slim, 58-year-old physician and father of three who was experiencing severe anxiety after his daughter had overdosed multiple times on the drugs she was injecting. Like many young people with opioid addictions, "Shana" had been hospitalized twice, in and out of day treatment, and had attended two in-patient rehabilitation programs. In two situations, emergency responders had to use drastic measures to resuscitate Miguel's nonresponsive daughter. He characterized his reaction to Shana's drug use as a mix of super cop, when he scrutinized her every move, and gullible enabler, (based on the times he had believed the lies she told him). The result, he said, was a level of anxiety he had never experienced as an adult.

At our initial session, Miguel's before-treatment score on the PCL-5 was 52 out of 80, exactly 20 points above the threshold of 31-33 to confirm a PTSD diagnosis. All other requirements were also satisfied. It was apparent how upset Miguel was about Shana's addiction. As a physician, he understood the danger she was in, but like many parents with substance abusing adolescents, he and his wife felt powerless over their daughter's drug addiction.

Diagnosis
PTSD (309.81)

Treatment
During his MEMI pretest, Miguel reported two traumatic experiences related to Shana's addiction as the most troubling. The one he considered worse—a time when he discovered Shana sprawled on her bed at home with a needle protruding from her arm—became the focus of his therapy. The second experience occurred in a hospital room, when an attending physician told Miguel and his wife that Shana's condition would be touch and go for the next 24-48 hours. For the first time, Miguel was facing the possibility Shana might not survive.

When asked what thoughts he had about watching his daughter with a needle in her arm, Miguel said, "This is painful," and wondered aloud what part he played in Shana becoming a drug addict. It later became clear that he blamed himself for contributing to her addiction, believing he'd been too hard on her when she was young. This idea was confirmed on the PCL-5 pretest, when Miguel answered "extremely" to the question about blaming yourself or someone else for the stressful experience. In another foreshadowing of what was to unfold during treatment, he also responded "extremely" to the question about having strong physical reactions when something reminded him of the stressful experience. These were two of only three "extremely" responses on his pretest.

Miguel reported both visceral and emotional feelings related to the memory. The visceral feelings he described were tension in his jaw, shoulders, and the small of his back. The emotional feelings were sadness about his daughter's plight, which he described as connected to a physical heaviness around his heart, and shame about the fact he had a daughter who was an addict. In combining the sadness with the heart heaviness, he was conflating a visceral feeling with an emotion. In NLP, this blending of inner representations is called a synesthesia (Dilts & DeLozier, 2000).

Miguel also stated he "saw" a movie of the experience, with intermittent still photos of Shana sitting on the edge of her bed in a stupor, the needle stuck in her arm (visual sensory information). The clear images were mostly black and white, but had hints of color. There were no sounds associated with the memory.

After the first eye movement set, Miguel said his reaction to the memory was different. The visceral and emotional feelings he'd reported—the tension in his jaw, back, and shoulders, and the sad heaviness around his heart—had diminished. This, he said, made the visual memory of Shana on the bed better, easier to tolerate. In addition, the image of her had moved a little farther away, "making it slightly harder to distinguish, less clear," he said. However, Miguel's thoughts about the experience and the context remained the same. After considering the changes to the memory, he gave it a SUDS Score of 85%. I remarked he was going in the right direction.

Following the second eye movement set, Miguel reported his visceral and emotional feelings had improved compared to the first set. The shape of the heart heaviness had changed from a circle around the organ into a rectangle. Miguel believed the change made it feel better, not worse. The tension in his jaw and upper torso had also diminished. The visual image of the experience had moved even farther away and off to his left, causing it to be even less clear. The context and thoughts remained as they were during the pretest. Considering the most recent changes, he gave his reaction to the memory a SUD Score of 65%, so it was continuing to improve.

I asked Miguel to pay particular attention to the rectangle of heart heaviness during the third round of eye movements. After that set he reported the sad, heart-heavy sensation, the mixture of visceral and emotional feelings about the memory, had changed its shape again. It was smaller—a narrow, horizontal strip across his chest—with a bulge on the right side he interestingly labeled "resistance." When asked what the visual image was like, he responded with surprise, "It's not there. I can't get it back!" Considering these additional changes, Miguel gave the entire experience a SUD Score of 55%. But he was not yet satisfied with the results.

Before the fourth eye movement set, I asked Miguel if he wanted to decrease the sad, heart-heavy feelings even more. This was a way of recontracting with him to achieve greater desensitization. Curiously, instead of answering the question, he responded by saying he'd always had negative feelings about himself. I wondered why he responded with self-criticism when asked whether he wanted to perceive his daughter's overdose with less reactivity.

We reviewed all the changes to the memory. The visual image had completely disappeared; Miguel couldn't get it back. The heart-heavy feeling had diminished with each eye movement set, and its shape had changed—from a circle to a rectangle, to a narrow strip across his chest, with a bulge on one end that he considered resistance. Metaphorically speaking, while the narrow strip's thinness could infer less heart-heavy feelings/sadness, the bulge on the right end might be thought of as a threat (resistance) to Miguel's healing trajectory, like a hose swelling at its weakest point before it bursts.

Because he responded with self-criticism when asked if he wanted to reduce the reaction even more, I considered whether Miguel's resistance might be tied to guilt he felt for mistreating Shana when she was younger—a personal failure, a type of moral injury. He might then be blaming himself for his daughter's addiction. Agreeing to further diminish his own reactions to the memory might therefore be unacceptable and a cause for the resistance. This was an educated guess on my part. When asked if the bulge's resistance might represent guilt from his treatment of Shana, perhaps a reason why he should not heal more from the experience, Miguel agreed the observation was plausible.

I then used a cognitive restructuring technique to help Miguel reframe his perspective on the matter, away from self-blame to a more productive outlook. I pressed him for a more direct response to my question about whether he wanted to further reduce the heart-heavy reaction he was experiencing. "It would be better for me and for Shana if I released the resistance to decreasing those feelings," Miguel responded. In other words, if he were less sad and heavy-hearted, he could be more resourceful in dealing with Shana's addiction.

The focus during the fourth eye movement set became the "bulge of resistance" on the right side of Miguel's chest. Following the set, he reported the bulge had shrunk in size. In response to a question about what thoughts he then had about seeing Shana on her bed in a stupor, Miguel said, "It's better." That was a positive, cognitive shift from the pretest, when his response was "This is painful." We reviewed all the changes in his reactions to the experience. The visual image was gone; the sad, heart heaviness was greatly diminished; the tension in his jaw and lower back were gone; and his thoughts about Shana's overdose were more benign. When I asked Miguel for a final SUD Score, he rated his response to the problem state below 50%.

Results

Two weeks after our first session, Miguel was seen for a follow-up appointment. He confirmed the changes in the imagery, and his physical and emotional reactions to the memory were as they had been at the end of his first appointment. The PCL-5 was readministered and yielded a posttest score of 32 out of 80. This was a 20-point reduction from Miguel's pretest score of 52, representing evidence of significant clinical improvement as a result of MEMI therapy. Although a score of 32 was exactly at the threshold for a PTSD diagnosis (31-33), the reduction in his SUD Scores as well as the changes in visual imagery and emotional and visceral sensations supported a discontinuation of the PTSD diagnosis. Finally, his PCL-5 Score on the cusp of the cutoff point was also understandable. Miguel's daughter was still an addict, and there was no way to predict if the future would be relapse-free or not.

Miguel attended just two sessions with me, so there was no opportunity to address the second memory he had discussed. He was encouraged to join a local Al-Anon support group for family members and friends of alcoholics and addicts. Several months later, he reported he was attending weekly Al-Anon meetings and finding them meaningful and helpful. By working the Al-Anon steps with his sponsor, he was able to respond more resourcefully when Shana relapsed. He told me he was certain the MEMI experience was a turning point for him in his own recovery. The therapy had been instrumental in defusing his strong visual, emotional, and somatic reactions, allowing him to deal more calmly and thoughtfully with his family's struggle with addiction.

APPENDIX A

PCL-5 (DSM-5)

PCL-5

Instructions: Below is a list of problems that people sometimes have in response to a very stressful experience. Please read each problem carefully and then circle one of the numbers to the right to indicate how much you have been bothered by that problem in the past month.

In the past month, how much were you bothered by:	Not at all	A little bit	Moderately	Quite a bit	Extremely
1. Repeated, disturbing, and unwanted memories of the stressful experience?	0	1	2	3	4
2. Repeated, disturbing dreams of the stressful experience?	0	1	2	3	4
3. Suddenly feeling or acting as if the stressful experience were actually happening again (as if you were actually back there reliving it)?	0	1	2	3	4
4. Feeling very upset when something reminded you of the stressful experience?	0	1	2	3	4
5. Having strong physical reactions when something reminded you of the stressful experience (for example, heart pounding, trouble breathing, sweating)?	0	1	2	3	4
6. Avoiding memories, thoughts, or feelings related to the stressful experience?	0	1	2	3	4
7. Avoiding external reminders of the stressful experience (for example, people, places, conversations, activities, objects, or situations)?	0	1	2	3	4
8. Trouble remembering important parts of the stressful experience?	0	1	2	3	4
9. Having strong negative beliefs about yourself, other people, or the world (for example, having thoughts such as: I am bad, there is something seriously wrong with me, no one can be trusted, the world is completely dangerous)?	0	1	2	3	4
10. Blaming yourself or someone else for the stressful experience or what happened after it?	0	1	2	3	4
11. Having strong negative feelings, such as fear, horror, anger, guilt, or shame?	0	1	2	3	4
12. Loss of interest in activities that you used to enjoy?	0	1	2	3	4
13. Feeling distant or cut off from other people?	0	1	2	3	4
14. Trouble experiencing positive feelings (for example, being unable to feel happiness or have loving feelings for people close to you)?	0	1	2	3	4
15. Irritable behavior, angry outbursts, or acting aggressively?	0	1	2	3	4
16. Taking too many risks or doing things that could cause you harm?	0	1	2	3	4
17. Being "superalert" or watchful or on guard?	0	1	2	3	4
18. Feeling jumpy or easily startled?	0	1	2	3	4
19. Having difficulty concentrating?	0	1	2	3	4
20. Trouble falling or staying asleep?	0	1	2	3	4

PCL-5 (14 August 2013) National Center for PTSD

Multichannel Eye Movement Integration

APPENDIX B
MEMI WORKSHEET Page 1

MEMI Worksheet

Client Name: _____ Date: _____ Therapist: _____

PCL-5 Pretest: _____   PCL-5 Posttest: _____

CONTEXT

① Problem State
Pretest
Who was there? _____
When/Where? _____
What happened? _____

Changes
Set 1: _____
Set 2: _____
Set 3: _____
Set 4: _____

THOUGHTS

② Problem State
Pretest
What did you say to yourself? _____
_____
_____

Changes
Set 1: _____
Set 2: _____
Set 3: _____
Set 4: _____

NOTES: _____
_____
_____
_____

© 2020 Trauma Counseling & Training of Tucson

Multichannel Eye Movement Integration

MEMI WORKSHEET Page 2

SENSORY INFORMATION

❸ Visual
Pretest: *(circle one from each pair, if applicable)*   High ←-----► Low
Movie/Still photo   Color/Black & white   Near/Far away   Fuzzy/Clear   Bright/Dark   I-Score: 4 3 2 1 0
Set 1: _____ I-Score: 4 3 2 1 0
Set 2: _____ I-Score: 4 3 2 1 0
Set 3: _____ I-Score: 4 3 2 1 0
Set 4: _____ I-Score: 4 3 2 1 0

❹ Auditory
Pretest: *(circle one from each pair, if applicable)*   High ←-----► Low
Loud/Soft   Close/Far away   High/Low-pitched   Rhythmic/Random   Words/Sound   I-Score: 4 3 2 1 0
Set 1: _____ I-Score: 4 3 2 1 0
Set 2: _____ I-Score: 4 3 2 1 0
Set 3: _____ I-Score: 4 3 2 1 0
Set 4: _____ I-Score: 4 3 2 1 0

FEELINGS

❺ Visceral *(stiff neck, nausea, etc.)*   High ←-----► Low
Pretest: _____ I-Score: 4 3 2 1 0
Set 1: _____ I-Score: 4 3 2 1 0
Set 2: _____ I-Score: 4 3 2 1 0
Set 3: _____ I-Score: 4 3 2 1 0
Set 4: _____ I-Score: 4 3 2 1 0

❻ Emotional *(anger, fear, etc.)*   High ←-----► Low
Pretest: _____ I-Score: 4 3 2 1 0
Set 1: _____ I-Score: 4 3 2 1 0
Set 2: _____ I-Score: 4 3 2 1 0
Set 3: _____ I-Score: 4 3 2 1 0
Set 4: _____ I-Score: 4 3 2 1 0

❼ Tactile *(scratch, burn, etc.)*   High ←-----► Low
Pretest: _____ I-Score: 4 3 2 1 0
Set 1: _____ I-Score: 4 3 2 1 0
Set 2: _____ I-Score: 4 3 2 1 0
Set 3: _____ I-Score: 4 3 2 1 0
Set 4: _____ I-Score: 4 3 2 1 0

SUD SCORES

Pretest = 100%   Set 1: _____%   Set 2: _____%   Set 3: _____%   Set 4: _____%   Set 5: _____%

© 2020 Trauma Counseling & Training of Tucson

APPENDIX C

MEMI PROTOCOL AND EYE MOVEMENT SUMMARY

10 Steps in the MEMI Protocol

1. Administer PCL-5 and establish rapport
2. Secure agreement to change
3. Pretest elements of structure
4. Anchor resource state
5. Introduce therapeutic dissociation
6. Conduct eye movements
7. Test Structure of Experience elements
8. Take I-Score and SUD-Score readings
9. Record results on MEMI Worksheet
10. Conduct future rehearsal and self-appreciation exercises

MEMI BASIC EYE MOVEMENTS

1. Above the Horizon
2. Standing Triangle 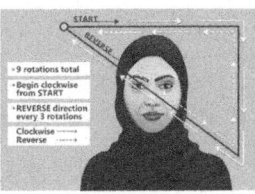
3. Sitting Triangle 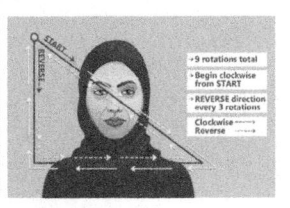
4. Figure 8 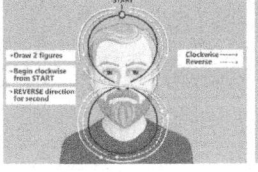
5. Shrinking Circles

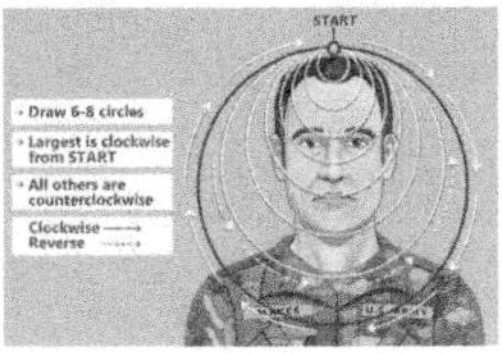

MEMI EYE MOVEMENT SETS

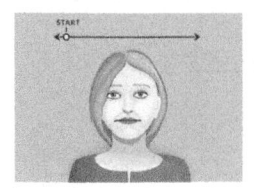

Set 1. Above the Horizon

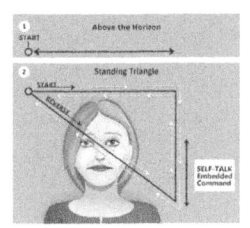

Set 2. Standing Triangle and SELF-TALK command

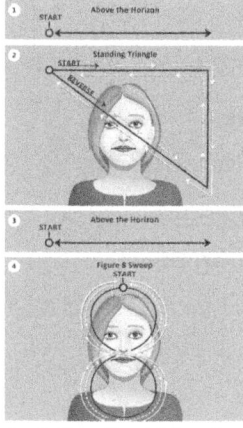

Set 3. Standing Triangle and Figure 8 sweeps

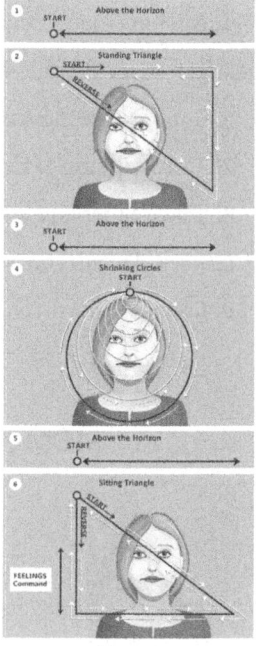

Set 4. Both triangle sweeps, circles, and FEELINGS

APPENDIX D

MULTICHANNEL EYE MOVEMENT INTEGRATION EFFICACY USING PCL-C

Abstract

This pilot study of Multichannel Eye Movement Integration (MEMI) treatment effects was conducted using the PTSD Checklist civilian version (PCL-C) for DSM-IV with five PTSD clients seen for treatment in a private practice setting. The purpose of the study was twofold: 1.) to determine whether the PCL-C would be compatible with the MEMI protocol and 2.) to test whether the protocol produced significant improvements in PTSD symptoms. The results of the study were reported at the Annual Conference of the American Mental Health Counselors Association in 2012. Although the number of subjects was small, the study demonstrated the measure was a viable addition to other assessments used with MEMI. Pre and posttest results also indicated MEMI treatment was effective in reducing PTSD symptoms.

Multichannel Eye Movement Integration (MEMI)

Eye Movement Integration is a brief, solution-focused eye movement approach for PTSD and other forms of anxiety conceived by Steve and Connirae Andreas (1993). Despite its simplicity and efficiency, structured evaluations of its effectiveness were never undertaken. The therapy's procedures were also insufficiently documented. Consequently, it received much less attention than Eye Movement Desensitization and Reprocessing (EMDR) even though the two approaches share a history.

In 2002, I began documenting procedures for EMI. During that process, it became clear the technique, as originally conceived, could be enhanced, and several new features were added to the approach. Following a few years of development, the original technique was transformed into a fully-formed therapy called Multichannel Eye Movement Integration, with a theoretical model, standard protocol, procedures, and assessment techniques.

The PTSD Checklist

The PTSD Checklist (PCL) was developed by the U.S. Department of Veterans Affairs National Center for PTSD. The Center has demonstrated exceptional leadership in creating, evaluating, and disseminating notable, practitioner-friendly measures for assessing and monitoring PTSD treatment effects. The Center developed and disseminated assessments based on the DSM-IV PTSD diagnostic criteria that were in use until 2013, when revised versions based on DSM-5 criteria were introduced (American Psychiatric Association, 2013). This study utilized a DSM-IV version of the measure known as the PTSD Checklist, civilian version (PCL-C).

The PCL-C for DSM-IV

When the PCL was developed by Weathers et al. (1993), it had three distinct forms. The PCL-C (civilian form) was used

Appendix D

in this pilot study. The other two versions were a military form (PCL-M) and a form designed for a specific traumatizing event (PCL-S). Each form is a 17-item checklist with five possible Likert-type responses to different problem statements associated with the DSM-IV PTSD diagnostic criteria. Response options on the Checklist range from one to five and indicate increasingly severe reactions to each problem statement, from "not at all" (1) to "extremely" (5). Here is one example from the Checklist:

13. Feeling jumpy or easily startled?

Not at all   A little bit   Moderately   Quite a bit   Extremely
(1)   (2)   (3)   (4)   (5)

The higher the score, the more severe an individual's reaction is to a problem statement. A total severity score on the Checklist is obtained by summing the scores for each of the problem statements. With 17 items on the Checklist, and a range of possible scores from one to five, symptom severity totals can range from 17 to 85. A score of three or higher on an individual item represents an endorsement of that particular PTSD symptom, meaning its presence has been confirmed. A score of one or two means the problem statement is not endorsed. A total severity score of 44 or higher on the PCL-C results in a PTSD diagnosis, as long as the other PTSD diagnostic criteria are also met. In addition, at least one PCL-C item representing Cluster B (questions 1-5), three items representing Cluster C (questions 6-12), and two items representing Cluster D (questions 13-17) must be endorsed. A copy of the PCL-C can be found in Appendix E.

Evaluation studies of the PCL for DSM-IV have established that a 5-10-point reduction in pre and posttest scores represents change "not due to chance" and considered reliable. A reduction of 10-20 points represents clinically significant change. The Checklist developers, therefore, recommend that 5 points be used as a minimum threshold for determining if a client is responding to an intervention and at least 10 points to determine whether improvements are clinically meaningful (U.S. Department of Veterans Affairs, 2020e).

The PCL-C is in the public domain and can be downloaded by practitioners from the U.S. Department of Veterans Affairs website. However, it's important to note that the PCL-C is an older version of the Checklist and the PCL-5 should now be used because it's based on DSM-5, the current version of the statistical manual. Therapists who would like to evaluate treatment effects using the National Center's measures will find the directions provided on the Center's website to be clear and concise. The PCL-C and the PCL-5 can be downloaded using this link: **https://www.ptsd.va.gov/professional/assessment/ adult-sr/ptsd-checklist.asp**

Subjects

Study participants ranged in age from 38 to 55. Three were men and two were women. All but one had previously been in therapy. Three of the subjects had been sexually abused by family members; one had lost a late-term baby from an *in utero* infection; and one was a military veteran who had been injured in the Middle East. Two of the subjects had substance abuse problems. While all subjects also suffered from moderate to severe depression and/or anxiety, only three were taking antidepressant medication.

Procedures

Subjects were administered the PCL-C prior to treatment to confirm or reject a PTSD diagnosis. They were also assessed for the presence of other DSM-IV PTSD diagnostic criteria. Subjects then attended either two or three treatment sessions, during which the MEMI protocol was used. One month after each final session, subjects were readministered the PCL-C, and pre and posttest results were compiled and analyzed.

Results

During the diagnostic phase, each of the five subjects in the study met all the criteria for a PTSD diagnosis using the PCL-C and based on other DSM-IV requirements. Here are the before treatment PCL-C scores for the five subjects:

1.) 55
2.) 57
3.) 79
4.) 51
5.) 57

Each score was above the threshold (44) for confirming a PTSD diagnosis. Cluster A, B, C, and D endorsements required for a positive diagnosis were also confirmed. Individual posttest scores were as follows:

1.) 29
2.) 32
3.) 24
4.) 27
5.) 36

Posttest scores ranged from 8 to 20 points below the 44-point cutoff for a PTSD diagnosis. Based on these results, none of the pilot test subjects qualified for a PTSD diagnosis after MEMI treatment.

Subjects scored between 21 and 55 points lower on the posttest, strongly exceeding the threshold decrease of 10-20 points for determining significant clinical improvement. The actual differences in pre and posttest scores for each subject were:

1.) 26
2.) 25
3.) 55
4.) 24
5.) 21

Comparison of pre and post mean scores was ruled out due to the small sample size and the ordinal nature of checklist data. In lieu of pre and post mean tests, a histogram was constructed summarizing the frequencies and percentages of reported pretest

Appendix D

and posttest scores (1-5) for all subjects and all 17 problem statements. With five subjects and 17 items on the Checklist, a total of 170 problem statement ratings were given by subjects during the study—85 during the pretest and another 85 posttreatment. *Figure 1* shows these results. For example, the first column on the left indicates subjects responded "not at all" to problem statements only 10 times during the pretest. The number 10 represents 12% of all 85 pretest responses. During the posttest, subjects responded "not at all" 38 times, representing 45% of all the 85 posttest responses.

FREQUENCIES AND PERCENTAGES OF PCL-C RESPONSES PRE AND POST MEMI

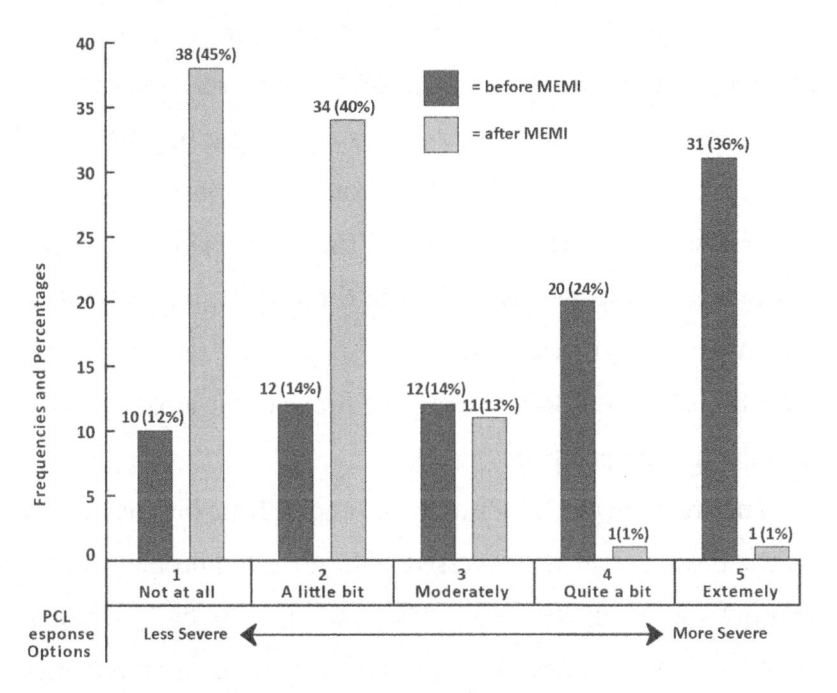

Figure 1

Before treatment scores on the PCL-C were rated severe much more frequently than after treatment scores. An analysis of the pretest responses reveals problem statements were rated "moderately" 12 times, "quite a bit" 20 times, and "extremely" 31 times, accounting for 74% of the 85 before MEMI treatment ratings. On the other hand, problem statements were rated "not at all" only 10 times during the pretest and "a little bit" 12 times, accounting for only 26% of the before responses. A higher percentage of severe ratings during a pretest is what would be expected of PTSD subjects prior to treatment.

A review of posttest responses indicates statements were rated much less frequently as severe than pretest responses. Items were rated "moderately" 11 times, "quite a bit" just once, and "extremely" only once as well, altogether accounting for just 15% of the posttreatment ratings. Conversely, "not at all" ratings were given 38 times (45%) and "a little bit" 34 times (40%), accounting for 85% of the posttest responses. In effect, the pretest and posttest profiles had flipped. Subjects responded "quite a bit" 20 times (24%) during the pretest, but only once (1%) during the posttest. In addition, "extremely" responses were reported 31 times (36%) during the pretest, but also just once (1%) during the posttest.

The frequency of the "not at all" and "a little bit" responses on the posttest had also reversed. Subjects rated problem statements "not at all" 38 times (45%) and "a little bit" 34 times (40%). In other words, 85% of the time problem statements were not endorsed during the posttest, inferring the particular

PTSD symptoms described in the statements had been rated asymptomatic.

Another way to assess the pre and post differences depicted in *Figure 1* is to compare how many times the items (symptoms) were endorsed in each test. An item rated "moderately," "quite a bit," or "extremely" on the PCL confirms the presence of the symptom represented by that item. By comparing frequencies and percentages for the combined endorsed items, one can discern to what extent the item endorsements changed pre and posttreatment. In the pretest, subjects rated items "moderately," "quite a bit," or "extremely" 63 times (74%). Yet in the posttest, subjects gave those ratings only 13 times, representing just 15% of all the 85 ratings given. This means that items were endorsed 50 fewer times (59% less) in the posttest when compared to the pretest.

Discussion

This pilot study provides evidence that the PTSD Checklist and the MEMI protocol are compatible when used to treat PTSD. Following these findings, the Checklist became a standard part of the MEMI protocol until the PCL-5 was introduced in 2013. Although these results are noteworthy, considering the ranges recommended for determining significant outcomes when using the PCL-C, they cannot be generalized beyond the scope of this study due to the small sample size and statistical limitations.

However, analyses of the PCL-C response frequencies and percentages do provide evidence of MEMI's effectiveness in producing lasting improvements in PTSD symptoms. Now that the PCL-5 is the current standard for PTSD assessment and treatment monitoring, more extensive evaluations of MEMI's effectiveness could provide further insight into the benefits of this protocol in treating PTSD.

APPENDIX E
PCL-C (DSM-IV)

INSTRUCTIONS: Below is a list of problems and complaints that people sometimes have in response to stressful life experiences. Please read each one carefully, then circle one of the numbers to the right to indicate how much you have been bothered by that problem <u>in the past month</u>.

	Not at all	A little bit	Moderately	Quite a bit	Extremely
1. Repeated, disturbing *memories, thoughts,* or *images* of a stressful experience from the past?	1	2	3	4	5
2. Repeated, disturbing *dreams* of a stressful experience from the past?	1	2	3	4	5
3. Suddenly *acting* or *feeling* as if a stressful experience *were happening again* (as if you were reliving it)?	1	2	3	4	5
4. Feeling *very upset* when *something reminded you* of a stressful experience from the past?	1	2	3	4	5
5. Having *physical reactions* (e.g., heart pounding, trouble breathing, sweating) when *something reminded* you of a stressful experience from the past?	1	2	3	4	5
6. Avoiding *thinking about* or *talking about* a stressful experience from the past or avoiding *having feelings* related to it?	1	2	3	4	5
7. Avoiding *activities* or *situations* because *they reminded you* of a stressful experience from the past?	1	2	3	4	5
8. Trouble remembering *important parts* of the stressful experience from the past?	1	2	3	4	5
9. *Loss of interest* in activities that you used to enjoy?	1	2	3	4	5
10. Feeling *distant* or *cut off* from other people?	1	2	3	4	5
11. Feeling *emotionally numb* or being unable to have loving feelings for those close to you?	1	2	3	4	5
12. Feeling as if your *future* will somehow be *cut short*?	1	2	3	4	5
13. Trouble *falling* or *staying asleep*?	1	2	3	4	5
14. Feeling *irritable* or having *angry outbursts*?	1	2	3	4	5
15. Having *difficulty concentrating*?	1	2	3	4	5
16. Being *"super alert"* or watchful or on guard?	1	2	3	4	5
17. Feeling *jumpy* or easily startled?	1	2	3	4	5

PCL-C for DSM-IV (11/1/94)   Weathers, Litz, Huska & Keane   National Center for PTSD - Behavioral Science Division

REFERENCES

Abou, E., & Goldwaser, G. (2010). Effective psychological treatments for posttraumatic stress disorder: Prolonged exposure therapy. *Naval Center for Combat & Operational Stress Control.* https://archive.org/details/prolongedExposure2

Abramovitch, A., & Schweiger, A. (2015). Misuse of cognitive neuropsychology in psychiatry research: The intoxicating appeal of neo-reductionism. *the Behavior Therapist, 38(7), 187-191.* https://www.researchgate.net/publication/282879653_Misuse_of_Cognitive_Neuropsychology_in_Psychiatry_Research_The_Intoxicating_Appeal_of_Neo-Reductionism

Akirav, I., & Richter-Levin, G. (2002). Mechanisms of amygdala modulation of hippocampal plasticity. *The Journal of Neuroscience, 22*(22), 9912-9921. https://doi.org/10.1523/JNEUROSCI.22-22-09912.2002

American Psychiatric Association. (1980). *Diagnostic and statistical manual of mental disorders: DSM-III* (3rd ed.). https://www.amazon.com/DSM-III-Diagnostic-Statistical-Manual-Disorders/dp/B000P1A7CK

American Psychiatric Association. (2013). *Diagnostic and statistical manual of mental disorders: DSM-5* (5th ed.). https://www.psychiatry.org/psychiatrists/practice/dsm

American Psychological Association. (2019). Clinical practice guideline for the treatment of posttraumatic stress disorder: Cognitive behavioral therapy (CBT). https://www.apa.org/ptsd-guideline/treatments/cognitive-behavioral-therapy#

Andreas, C., & Andreas, S. (1989). *Heart of the mind: Engaging your inner power to change with neuro-linguistic programming.* Real People Press. https://www.amazon.com/Heart-Mind-Engaging-Neuro-Linguistic-Programming-dp-0911226311/dp/0911226311/ref=mt_other?_encoding=UTF8&me=&qid

Andreas, C., & Andreas, S. (1993). Eye movement integration applied with a Vietnam veteran who had been experiencing intrusive memories. Video recorded at the 1993 Fifth International Congress on Ericksonian Approaches to Hypnosis and Psychotherapy in Orlando, FL. **http://j.mp/3ulsxV**

Andreas, S., & Andreas, C. (2015). Eye movement integration therapy. In E. S. Neukrug (Ed.), *The sage encyclopedia of theory in counseling & psychotherapy*. SAGE Publications, Inc. **https://www.amazon.com/SAGE-Encyclopedia -Theory-Counseling-Psychotherapy/dp/1452274126 #reader_1452274126**

Andreas, S., & Faulkner, C. (Eds.). (1996). *NLP: The new technology of achievement*. William Morrow and Company. **https:// www.amazon.com/NLP-New-Technology-Achieve ment-Comprehensive/dp/0688146198/ref=tmm _pap_swatch_0?_encoding=UTF8&qid=&sr=**

Austin, A. T. (2020, November 7). On the name of IEMT. The Association for IEMT Practitioners. **https://integraleyemovementtherapy.com/**

Bandler, R. (1985a, February). *Mind and body synthesis*. Paper presented at the Annual Conference of the Southern Institute of Neuro-Linguistic Programming, Clearwater, FL.

Bandler, R. (1985b). *Using your brain—for a change: Neuro-linguistic programming*. Real People Press. **https://www.amazon.com/Using-Your-Brain-Change- Neuro-Linguistic/dp/0911226273**

Bandler, R., & Grinder, J. (1979). *Frogs into princes: Neuro linguistic programming*. Real People Press. **https://www.amazon.com/Frogs-into-Princes-Linguis tic-Programming/dp/0911226192**

Beaulieu, D. (2003). *Eye movement integration therapy: The compre hensive clinical guide*. Crown House Publishing. **http://www .academieimpact.com/en/nouvelles_IMO.php**

References

Beck, C. E., & Beck, E. A. (1984). Test of the eye-movement hypothesis of neurolinguistic programming: A rebuttal of conclusions. *Perceptual and Motor Skills, 58*(1), 175-176. **https://journals.sagepub.com/doi/10.2466/pms.1984.58.1.175**

Benish, S. G., Imel, Z. E., & Wampold, B. E. (2007). The relative efficacy of bonafide psychotherapies for treating post-traumatic stress disorder: A meta-analysis of direct comparisons. *Clinical Psychology Review, 28*(5) 746-758. **https://www.sciencedirect.com/science/article/abs/pii/S0272735807001845?via%3Dihub**

Benson, H. (2000). *The relaxation response.* HarperCollins Publishers. (Original work published 1975) **https://www.harpercollins.com/products/the-relaxation-response-herbert-bensonmiriam-z-klipper?variant=32207490416674**

Bisson, J., Ehlers, A., Matthews, R., Pilling, S., Richards, D., & Turner, S. (2007). Psychological treatments for chronic post-traumatic stress disorder: Systematic review and meta-analysis. *The British Journal of Psychiatry, 190*(2), 97-104. **https://doi.org/10.1192/bjp.bp.106.021402**

Blevins, C. A., Weathers, F. W., Davis, M. T., Witte, T. K., & Domino, J. L. (2015). The posttraumatic stress disorder checklist for DSM-5 (PCL-5): Development and initial psychometric evaluation [Abstract]. *Journal of Traumatic Stress, 28*(6), 489-498. **https://doi.org/10.1002/jts.22059**

Bohart, A. C., O'Hara, M., & Leitner, L. M. (1998). Empirically violated treatments: Disenfranchisement of humanistic and other psychotherapies. *Psychotherapy Research 8*(2), 141-157. **https://www.ingentaconnect.com/content/routledg/psyres/1998/00000008/00000002/art00003**

Bothwell, L. E. (2014). *The emergence of the randomized controlled trial: Origins to 1980* [Doctoral dissertation, abstract]. Columbia University. **https://academiccommons.columbia.edu/doi/10.7916/D8K072V0**

Bothwell, L. E., Greene, J. A., Podolsky, S. H., & Jones, D. S. (2016). Assessing the gold standard—Lessons from the history of RCTs. *The New England Journal of Medicine, 374*, 2175-2181. **http://www.nejm.org/doi/full/10.1056/NEJMms1604593**

Bradley, R., Greene, J., Russ, E., Dutra, L., & Westen, D. (2005). A multidimensional meta-analysis of psychotherapy for PTSD. *The American Journal of Psychiatry, 162*(2), 214-227. **https://doi.org/10.1176/appi.ajp.162.2.214**

Bremner, J. D., Elzinga, B., Schmahl, C., & Vermetten, E. (2008). Structural and functional plasticity of the human brain in posttraumatic stress disorder [Abstract]. *Progress in Brain Research, 167*, 171-186. **https://www.ncbi.nlm.nih.gov/pmc/articles/PMC3226705/**

Buckner, M., Meara, N. M., Reese, E. J., & Reese, M. (1987). Eye movement as an indicator of sensory components in thought [Abstract]. *Journal of Counseling Psychology, 34*(3), 283-287. **https://doi.org/10.1037/0022-0167.34.3.283**

Cannon, W. D. (1915). *Bodily changes in pain, hunger, fear and rage: An account of recent researches into the function of emotional excitement.* D. Appleton & Company. **https://psycnet.apa.org/doiLanding?doi=10.1037%2F10013-000**

Carey, B. (2004, August 10). For psychotherapy's claims, skeptics demand proof. *The New York Times*, p. 43. **https://www.nytimes.com/2004/08/10/science/for-psychotherapy-s-claims-skeptics-demand-proof.html**

Carpenter, D. (2010). *Reputation and power: Organizational image and pharmaceutical regulation at the FDA.* Princeton University Press. **https://press.princeton.edu/books/paperback/9780691141800/reputation-and-power**

Carroll, M. (2020). A conversation John Grinder had with Francine Shapiro in the early 1980s. Posted on the John Grinder Facebook page. Retrieved July 10, 2020 from **https://www.facebook.com/RealJohnGrinder/**

References

Chambless, D. L., Sanderson, W. C., Shoham, V., Bennett Johnson, S., Pope, K. S., Crits-Christoph, P., Baker, M., Johnson, B., Woody, S. R., Sue, S., Beutler, L., Williams, D. A., & McCurry, S. (1996). An update on empirically validated therapies. *The Clinical Psychologist, 49*(2), 5-18. **https://cpb-us-w2.wpmucdn.com/web.sas.upenn.edu/dist/6/184/files/2017/03/Task-Force-1996_report-20t8hyh.pdf**

Clay, R. (2010). More than one way to measure. *Monitor on Psychology, 41*(8), 52. **https://www.apa.org/monitor/2010/09/trials**

Corey, G. (2013). *Theory and practice of counseling and psychotherapy* (9th ed.). Brooks/Cole, Cengage Learning. **https://www.academia.edu/41154389/Corey_9th_ed**

Cormier, S., Nurius, P. S., & Osborn, C. J. (2013). *Interviewing and change strategies for helpers* (7th ed.). Brooks/Cole, Cengage Learning. **https://www.cengage.com/c/interviewing-and-change-strategies-for-helpers-7e-cormier/9780840028570PF/**

Courtois, C. A., & Gold, S. N. (2009). The need for inclusion of psychological trauma in the professional curriculum: A call to action. *Psychological Trauma: Theory, Research, Practice, and Policy, 1*(1), 3-23. **https://doi.org/10.1037/a0015224**

Deacon, B. J. (2013). The biomedical model of mental disorder: A critical analysis of its validity, utility, and effects on psychotherapy research [Abstract]. *Clinical Psychology Review, 33*(7), 846-861. **https://doi.org/10.1016/j.cpr.2012.09.007**

Deacon, B. J., & McKay, D. (2015). The biomedical model of psychological problems: A call for critical dialogue. *the Behavior Therapist, 38*(7), 231-235. **https://www.researchgate.net/publication/283046589_The_Biomedical_Model_of_Psychological_Problems_A_Call_for_Critical_Dialogue**

Deninger, M. (2011). *Snakes in my dreams: A mental health therapist's odyssey from hardship to healer*. Unrivaled Books. **https://www.amazon.com/Snakes-My-Dreams-Therapists-Hardship/dp/1613601093**

DePrince, A., & Newman, E. (2011). Special issue editorial: The art and science of trauma-focused training and education [Abstract]. *Psychological Trauma: Theory, Research, Practice, and Policy, 3*(3), 213-214. **https://doi.org/10.1037/a0024640**

Dilts, R. B. (1983). *Roots of neuro-linguistic programming*. Meta Publications. **https://www.amazon.com/Roots-Neuro -Linguistic-Programming-Robert-dp-0916990125 /dp/0916990125/ref=mt_other?_encoding =UTF8&me=&qid=**

Dilts, R. B. (2006). Response to John Grinder (English translation). Institut Repere. Retrieved November 18, 2020 from **https://cc.bingj.com/cache.aspx?q=Robert+Dilts +response+to+John+Grinder+in+English&d=4589640807 298661&mk-t=en-US&setlang=en-US&w=4eKFpkpKV GenIKj5IlIYwC48Z4p-FVh7**

Dilts, R. B., & DeLozier, J. A. (2000). *Encyclopedia of systematic neuro-linguistic programming and NLP new coding*. NLP University Press. **http://nlpuniversitypress.com/**

Dilts, R. B., Grinder, J., Bandler, R. W., & DeLozier, J. A. (1980). *Neuro-linguistic programming: Volume I: The study of the structure of subjective experience*. Meta Publications. **https://www .amazon.com/Neuro-Linguistic-Programming -Structure-Subjective-Experience/dp/0916990079**

Dube, S. R., Anda, R. F., Whitfield, C. L., Brown, D. W., Felitti, V. J., Dong, M., & Giles, W. H. (2005). Long-term consequences of childhood sexual abuse by gender of victim. *American Journal of Preventive Medicine, 28*(5), 430-438. **https://www.ajp monline.org/article/S0749-3797(05)00078-4/fulltext**

Einstein Healthcare Network (2020, October 29). *Mental and behavioral health programs: Treatment options: Post-traumatic stress disorder treatment in Philadelphia*. **http://www.einstein.edu/mental-behavioral-health /prolonged-exposure-therapy/**

Ellis, A. (1994). *Reason and emotion in psychotherapy: A comprehensive method of treating human disturbances*. Citadel. **https://www.amazon.com/Reason-Emotion-Psycho therapy-Albert-Ellis/dp/1559722487/ref=tmm _hrd_swatch_0?_encoding=UTF8&qid=&sr=**

Ellis, A. (1996). *Better, deeper, and more enduring brief therapy: The rational emotive behavior therapy approach.* Brunner/Mazel. **https://psycnet.apa.org/record/1995-99068-000**

Ellis, A. (2008). Cognitive restructuring of the disputing of irrational beliefs. In W. D. O'Donohue & J. E. Fisher (Eds.), *Cognitive behavior therapy: Applying empirically supported techniques in your practice* (2nd ed.), 91-95. John Wiley & Sons, Inc. **https://www.amazon.com/Cognitive-Behavior-Therapy-Empirically-Techniques/dp/0470227788**

EMDR Institute. (2020a, November 7). *History of EMDR.* **http://www.emdr.com/history-of-emdr/**

EMDR Institute. (2020b, November 7). *Theory of EMDR.* **http://www.emdr.com/theory/**

Felitti, V. J., Anda, R. F., Nordenberg, D., Williamson, D. F., Spitz, A. M., Edwards, V., Koss, M. P., & Marks, J. S. (1998). Relationship of childhood abuse and household dysfunction to many of the leading causes of death in adults: The adverse childhood experiences (ACE) study. *American Journal of Preventive Medicine. 14*(4), 245-258. **https://doi.org/10.1016/S0749-3797(98)00017-8**

Ford, J. D., & Kidd, P. (1998). Early childhood trauma and disorders of extreme stress as predictors of treatment outcome with chronic posttraumatic stress disorder [Abstract]. *Journal of Traumatic Stress, 11*(4), 743-761. **http://www.trauma-pages.com/a/ford98.php#:~:text=Early%20Childhood%20Trauma%20and%20Disorders%20of%20Extreme%20Stress,may%20have%20minor%20differences%20from%20the%20published%20version**

Fredericks, R. (2011). *The relationship between EMDR and NLP.* Retrieved January 29, 2011 from **http://www.RandiFredericks.com/Randi/art/EMDR_nlp.cfm**

Frieden, T. (2017, August 2). *Why the "gold standard" of medical research is no longer enough.* STAT. **https://www.statnews.com/2017/08/02/randomized-controlled-trials-medical-research/**

Galin, D., & Ornstein, R. (1974). Individual differences in cognitive style-I. Reflexive eye movements. *Neuropsychologia, 12* (3), 367-376. **https://doi.org/10.1016/0028-3932(74)90052-9**

Gallagher, M. W., & Resick, P. A. (2012). Mechanisms of change in cognitive processing therapy and prolonged exposure therapy for PTSD: Preliminary evidence for the differential effects of hopelessness and habituation [Abstract]. *Cognitive Therapy Research, 36*(6), 750-755.
https://pubmed.ncbi.nlm.nih.gov/24363472/

Galovski, T. E, Norman, S. B., & Hamblen, J. L. (2020, October 31). *Cognitive Processing Therapy for PTSD*. U.S. Department of Veterans Affairs National Center for PTSD.
https://www.ptsd.va.gov/professional/treat/txessentials/cpt_for_ptsd_pro.asp

Goodman, K. W. (2003). *Ethics and evidence-based medicine: Fallibility and responsibility in clinical science*. Cambridge University Press. https://onlinelibrary.wiley.com/doi/abs/10.1046/j.1365-2753.2003.00429.x

Grand, D. (2013). *Brainspotting: The revolutionary new therapy for rapid and effective change*. Sounds True.
https://books.google.com/books/about/Brainspotting.html?id=B8iBMAEACAAJ

Grimley, B. (2014). Origins of EMDR—A question of integrity? *The Psychologist. 27*(8), 561.
https://thepsychologist.bps.org.uk/volume-27/edition-8/letters-men-and-mental-health-minefield

Grohol, J. M. (2020, October, 29). *Mental health professionals: US statistics 2017*. PsychCentral. https://psychcentral.com/blog/mental-health-professionals-us-statistics-2017/

Guyatt, G. H. (1991). Evidence-based medicine. *American College of Physicians Journal Club, 114*(suppl 2), A-16.
https://www.jameslindlibrary.org/guyatt-gh-1991/

Head, L. S., & Gross, A. M. (2008). Systematic desensitization. In W. T. O'Donohue & J. E. Fisher (Eds.), *Cognitive behavior therapy: Applying empirically supported techniques in your practice* (2nd ed.), pp. 542-549. John Wiley & Sons, Inc.
https://www.amazon.com/Cognitive-Behavior-Therapy-Empirically-Techniques/dp/0470227788

References

Herbert, J. D., Lilienfeld, S. O., Lohr, J. M., Montgomery, R. W., O'Donohue, W. T., Rosen, G. M., & Tolin, D. F. (2000). Science and pseudoscience in the development of eye movement desensitization and reprocessing: Implications for clinical psychology [Abstract]. *Clinical Psychology Review, 20*(8), 945-971. **https://doi.org/10.1016/S0272-7358(99)00017-3**

Hoobyar, T., Dotz, T., & Sanders, S. (2013). *NLP: The essential guide to neuro-linguistic programming*. HarperCollins Publishers. **https://www.scribd.com/book/163657873/NLP-The -Essential-Guide-to-Neuro-Linguistic-Programming**

Insel, T. (2015). Psychiatry is reinventing itself thanks to advances in biology. *New Scientist, 227*(3035), 5-57. **https://www.new scientist.com/article/mg22730353-000-psychiatr*y-is -reinventing-itself-thanks-to-advances-in-biology**

James, W. (1890). *The principles of psychology. Vol. 1.* Henry Holt and Company. **https://archive.org/details/theprinciples ofp01jameuoft**

Kessler, R. C., Berglund, P., Demler, O., Jin, R., Merikangas, K. R., & Walters, E. E. (2005). Lifetime prevalence and age-of-onset distributions of DSM-IV disorders in the National Comorbidity Survey Replication [Abstract]. *Archives of General Psychiatry, 62*(6), 593-602. **https://pubmed.ncbi.nlm.nih.gov/15939837/**

Kinderman, P. (2015). A psychological model of mental health and well-being: Rational but radical. *the Behavior Therapist, 38*(7), 227-231. **https://www.madinamerica.com/wp-content /uploads/2015/11/Behavior-Therapist-Oct-2015.pdf**

Kinsbourne, M. (1972). Eye and head turning indicates cerebral lateralization [Abstract]. *Science, 176*(4034), 539-541. **https://science.sciencemag.org/content/176/4034/539**

Klein, R. (2015). *Eye movement integration^{TM} (EMI^{TM}) manual* [Unpublished]. American Hypnosis Training Academy. **https://www.ahtainc.com/index_files/Page673.htm**

Kocel, K., Galin, G., Ornstein, R., & Merrin, E. L. (1972). Lateral eye movement and cognitive mode. *Psychonomic Science, 27*, 223-224. **https://link.springer.com/article /10.3758%2FBF03328944**

Lacasse, J. R., & Leo, J. (2015). Antidepressants and the chemical imbalance theory of depression: A reflection and update on the discourse. *the Behavior Therapist, 38*(7), 206-213. **http://purl.flvc.org/fsu/fd/FSU_migr_csw_faculty _publications-0084**

Landin-Romero, R., Moreno-Alcazar, A., Pagani, M., & Amann, B. L. (2018, August). How does eye movement desensitization and reprocessing work? A systematic review on suggested mechanisms of action. *Frontiers in Psychology.* **https://doi.org/10.3389/fpsyg.2018.01395**

Lanese, N. (2019, May 9). *Fight or flight: The sympathetic nervous system.* Live Science. **https://www.livescience.com /65446-sympathetic-nervous-system.html**

Lilienfeld, S. O., & Arkowitz, H. (2020, October). Taking a closer look: Can moving eyes back and forth help to ease anxiety? *Scientific American Mind, 17*(6), 80-81. **https://www.jstor.org/stable/24921634**

Litz, B. T., Stein, N., Delaney, E., Lebowitz, L., Nash, W. P., Silva, C., & Maguen, S. (2009). Moral injury and moral repair in war veterans: A preliminary model and intervention strategy [Abstract]. *Clinical Psychology Review, 29*(8), 695-706. **https://doi.org/10.1016/j.cpr.2009.07.003**

Logie, R. (2014a, July). EMDR—More than a therapy for PTSD? *The Psychologist. 27*(7), 512-516. **https://thepsychologist.bps.org.uk/volume-27 /edition-7/emdr-more-just-therapy-ptsd**

Logie, R. (2014b, September). EMDR—Origins and anomalies. *The Psychologist. 27*(9), 638-639. **https://thepsychologist.bps.org.uk/volume-27 /edition-9/letters-unequal-britain-and-more**

Mandal, A. (2019, February 26). *What is a biomarker?* News-Medical.net, Life Sciences. **https://www.news-medical .net/health/What-is-a-Biomarker.aspx**

References

Marich, J. (2011). *EMDR made simple: 4 approaches to using EMDR with every client.* Premier Publishing & Media. **https://www.amazon.com/EMDR-Made-Simple-Approaches-Client/dp/1936128063**

McFall, R. M. (1991). Manifesto for a science of clinical psychology. *The Clinical Psychologist, 44*(6), 5-88. **https://www3.nd.edu/~ghaeffel/McFall_Manifesto_1991.pdf**

McGlynn, E. A., Asch, S. M., Adams, J., Keesey, J., Hicks, J., DeCristofaro A., & Kerr, E. A. (2003). The quality of health care delivered to adults in the United States. *The New England Journal of Medicine, 348,* 2635-2645. **https://www.nejm.org/doi/full/10.1056/NEJMsa022615**

McSweeney, L. B., Rauch, S. A., Norman, S. B., & Hamblen, J. L. (2020, November 20). Treatment essentials. *PTSD: National Center for PTSD: Prolonged Exposure for PTSD.* U. S. Department of Veterans Affairs. **https://www.ptsd.va.gov/professional/treat/txessentials/prolonged_exposure_pro.asp**

Merriam-Webster. (n.d.). Abreaction. In *Merriam-Webster.com dictionary.* Retrieved November 8, 2020, from **https://www.merriam-webster.com/dictionary/abreaction**

Merriam-Webster. (n.d.). Visceral. In *Merriam-Webster.com dictionary.* Retrieved November 8, 2020, from **https://www.merriam-webster.com/dictionary/visceral**

Miller, G. A., Galanter, E., & Pribram, K. H. (2013). *Plans and the structure of behavior.* Barakaldo Books. (Reprint of the 1960 edition) **https://www.amazon.com/Plans-Structure-Behavior-George-Miller/dp/1614275203**

Miller, S. D., Hubble, M. A., Chow, D. L., & Seidel, J. A. (2013). The outcome of psychotherapy: Yesterday, today, and tomorrow [Abstract]. *Psychotherapy, 50*(1), 88-97. **https://doi.org/10.1037/a0031097**

Moncrieff, J. (2015). The myths and realities of drug treatment for mental disorders. *the Behavior Therapist, 38*(7), 214-218. **https://www.madinamerica.com/wp-content/uploads/2015/11/Behavior-Therapist-Oct-2015.pdf**

Monson, C. M., & Shnaider, P. (2014). *Treating PTSD with cognitive-behavioral therapies: Interventions that work*. American Psychological Association. **https://www.apa.org/pubs/books/4317339**

Morgan, M. A. (2017, July 10). *Biomarkers: The future of PTSD diagnosis and treatment monitoring?* Psychological Health Center of Excellence. Clinician's Corner Blog. **https://www.pdhealth.mil/news/blog/biomarkers-future-ptsd-diagnosis-and-treatment-monitoring**

National Institute for Mental Health. (2020, November 3). *Post-traumatic stress disorder: Treatments and therapies*. **https://www.nimh.nih.gov/health/topics/post-traumatic-stress-disorder-ptsd/index.shtml#part_145375**.

Norman, S., Hamblen, J., Schnurr, P., & Eftakari, A. (2020, October 31). *Overview of psychotherapy for PTSD*. U. S. Department of Veterans Affairs National Center for PTSD. **https://www.ptsd.va.gov/professional/treat/txessentials/overview_therapy.asp**

O'Connor, J. (2001). *NLP workbook: A practical guide to achieving the results you want*. Thorsons. **http://homepage.sns.it/falco/doc/intro_nlp.pdf**

O'Connor, J., & Seymour, J. (1990). *Introducing NLP: Neuro-linguistic programming: Psychological skills for understanding and influencing people*. The Aquarian Press. **https://doc.lagout.org/science/0_Computer%20Science/3_Theory/Neural%20Networks/Neuro%20Linguistic%20Programming%20WorkBook.pdf**

Peele, S. (2015). Why neurobiological models can't contain mental disorder and addiction. *the Behavior Therapist, 38*(7), 218-222. **https://www.madinamerica.com/wp-content/uploads/2015/11/Behavior-Therapist-Oct-2015.pdf**

Resick, P. A., Monson, C. M., & Chard, K. M. (2014). *Cognitive processing therapy: Veteran/military version: Therapist and patient materials manual*. U.S. Department of Veterans Affairs. **https://www.div12.org/wp-content/uploads/2015/07/CPT-Materials-Manual.pdf**

References

Rosenzweig, L. (2020, November 20). *Accelerated resolution therapy*. The Rosenzweig Center for Rapid Recovery. **https://acceleratedresolutiontherapy.com/**

Sackett, D. L., Rosenberg, W. M., Muir Gray, J. A., Haynes, R. B., & Richardson, W. S. (1996). Evidence-based medicine: What it is and what it isn't [Abstract]. *the BMJ, 312*, 71. **https://doi.org/10.1136/bmj.312.7023.71**

Schmidt, U., Kaltwasser, S. F., & Wotjak, C. T. (2013). Biomarkers in posttraumatic stress disorder: Overview and implications for future research. *Disease Markers, 35*(1), 45-54. U. S. National Library of Medicine: National Institutes of Health. **https://www.ncbi.nlm.nih.gov/pmc/articles/PMC3774961/**

Schnurr, P. P., Friedman, M. J., Engel, C. C., Foa, E. B., Shea, M. T., Chow, B. K., Resick, P. A., Thurston, V., Orsillo, S. M., Haug, R., Turner, C., & Bernardy, N. (2007). Cognitive behavioral therapy for posttraumatic stress disorder in women: A randomized control trial. *JAMA, 297*(8), 820-830. **https://jamanetwork.com/journals/jama/fullarticle/205769**

Seal, K. H., Maguen, S., Cohen, B., Gima, K. S., Metzler, T. J., Ren, L., Bertenthal, D., & Marmar, C. R. (2010). VA mental health services utilization in Iraq and Afghanistan veterans in the first year of receiving new mental health diagnoses [Abstract]. *Journal of Traumatic Stress, 23*(1), 5-16. **https://doi.org/10.1002/jts.20493**

Seidler, G. H., & Wagner, F. E. (2006). Comparing the efficacy of EMDR and trauma-focused cognitive-behavioral therapy in the treatment of PTSD: A meta-analytic study [Abstract]. *Psychological Medicine, 36*(11), 1515-1522. **https://doi.org/10.1017/S0033291706007963**

Shapiro, F. (1989). Efficacy of the eye movement desensitization procedure in the treatment of traumatic memories [Abstract]. *Journal of Traumatic Stress, 2*(2), 199-223. **https://doi.org/10.1002/jts.2490020207**

Shapiro, F. (1995). *Eye movement desensitization and reprocessing (EMDR): Basic principles, protocols, and procedures* (1st ed.). The Guilford Press. **https://emdria.omeka.net/items/show/17585**

Shapiro, F. (2001). *Eye movement desensitization and reprocessing (EMDR): Basic principles, protocols, and procedures* (2nd ed.). The Guilford Press. **https://www.amazon.com/Eye-Movement-Desensitization-Reprocessing-EMDR/dp/1572306726**

Shapiro, F. (2002). Paradigms, processing, and personality development. In F. Shapiro (Ed.), *EMDR as an integrative psychotherapy approach: Experts of diverse orientations explore the paradigm prism*. American Psychological Association Books. **https://www.apa.org/pubs/books/431797A**

Shapiro, F., & Forrest, M. S. (1997). *EMDR: The breakthrough therapy for overcoming anxiety, stress, and trauma*. Basic Books. **https://onlinelibrary.wiley.com/doi/epdf/10.1002/jts.20493**

Shedler, J. (2017, November 19). *Selling bad therapy to trauma victims: Patients and therapists should ignore new guidelines for treating trauma*. Psychology Today Blog. **https://www.psychologytoday.com/us/blog/psychologically-minded/201711/selling-bad-therapy-trauma-victims**

Spiegler, M. D. (2012). Behavior therapy II: Cognitive-behavioral therapy. In J. Frew & M. D. Spiegler (Eds.), *Contemporary psychotherapies for a diverse world* (pp. 320-359). Taylor & Francis Group. **https://www.amazon.com/Contemporary-Psychotherapies-Diverse-World-Revised/dp/0415898382#reader_0415898382**

Springer, S. P., & Deutsch, G. (1993). *Left brain, right brain: Perspectives from cognitive neuroscience*. W. H. Freeman and Company. **https://www.abebooks.com/products/isn/9780716723738/30715098600&cm_sp=snippet-_-srp1-_-PLP6**

Steenkamp, M. M. (2015, August 4). *Cures for PTSD often remain elusive for war veterans*. Quoted in NYU Langone Health News Hub. **http://nyulangone.org/press-releases/cures-for-ptsd-often-remain-elusive-for-war-veterans**

Steenkamp, M. M., Litz, B. T., Hoge, C. W., & Marmar, C. R. (2015). Psychotherapy for military-related PTSD: A review of randomized clinical trials [Abstract]. *JAMA, 314*(5), 489-500. **https://jamanetwork.com/journals/jama/article-abstract/2422548**

Stevens, J. S., Kim, Y. J., Galatzer-Levy, I. R., Reddy, R., Ely, T. D., Nemeroff, C. B., Hudak, L. A., Jovanovic, T., Rothbaum, B. O., & Ressler, K. J. (2017). Amygdala reactivity and anterior cingulate habituation predict posttraumatic stress disorder symptom maintenance after acute civilian trauma [Abstract]. *Biological Psychiatry, 81*(12), 1023-1029. **https://doi.org/10.1016/j.biopsych.2016.11.015**

Sweeton, J. (2019). *Trauma treatment toolbox: 165 brain-changing tips, tools and handouts to move therapy forward.* PESI Publishing & Media. **https://www.pesi.com/store/detail/26171/trauma-treatment-toolbox**

Tanenbaum, S. J. (2005). Evidence-based practice as mental health policy: Three controversies and a caveat. *Health Affairs, 24*(1). **https://doi.org/10.1377/hlthaff.24.1.163**

Tavris, C. (2003). Mind games: Psychological warfare between therapists and scientists. *Chronicle of Higher Education, 45*(25). **https://www.researchgate.net/publication/265540493_Mind_Games_Psychological_Warfare_Between_Therapists_and_Scientists**

Thomason, T. C., Arbuckle, T., & Cady, D. (1980). Test of the eye-movement hypothesis of neurolinguistic programming. *Perceptual and Motor Skills, 51*(1), 230. **https://doi.org/10.2466/pms.1980.51.1.230**

Tunis, S. R., Stryer, D. B., & Clancy, C. M. (2003). Practical clinical trials: Increasing the value of clinical research for decision making in clinical and health policy [Abstract]. *JAMA, 290*(12), 1624-1632. **https://jamanetwork.com/journals/jama/article-abstract/197353**

U. S. Department of Veterans Affairs (2020a, October 31). *How common is PTSD in adults?* National Center for PTSD. **https://www.ptsd.va.gov/understand/common/common_adults.asp**

U. S. Department of Veterans Affairs (2020b, October 31). *PTSD Checklist for DSM-5 (PCL-5).* National Center for PTSD. **https://www.ptsd.va.gov/professional/assessment/adult-sr/ptsd-checklist.asp**

U. S. Department of Veterans Affairs. (2020c, October 31). *Treatment essentials: Psychotherapy—Cognitive Processing Therapy for PTSD.* National Center for PTSD. **https://www.ptsd.va.gov/professional/treat/txessentials/index.asp**

U. S. Department of Veterans Affairs (2020d, November 22). *For providers: Trauma, PTSD and treatment:* 2017 clinical practice guidelines for the management *of PTSD.* National Center for PTSD. **https://www.ptsd.va.gov/professional/treat/txessentials/cpg_ptsd_management.asp**

U. S. Department of Veterans Affairs (2020e, November 28). *Using the PTSD checklist for DSM-IV (PCL).* National Center for PTSD [PDF download]. **www.ptsd.va.gov/professional/assessment/documents/PCL_handoutDSM4.pdf**

van der Kolk, B. A. (2015). *The body keeps the score: Brain, mind, and body in the healing of trauma.* Penguin Publishing Group. **https://www.barnesandnoble.com/w/the-body-keeps-the-score-bessel-van-der-kolk-md/1117229987**

van der Kolk, B. A., McFarlane, A. C., & Weisaeth, L. (Eds.) (2007). *Traumatic stress: The effects of overwhelming experience on mind, body, and society.* The Guilford Press. **https://books.google.com/books?hl=en&lr=&id=3hjHDwAAQBAJ&oi=fnd&pg=PP1&ots=qm6KNxOgSn&sig=QDUbqtvVYkRueZH7yIugpWghQvk#v=onepage&q&f=false**

Volkow, N. (2015, June 12, updated 2016, June 12). *Addiction is a disease of free will.* HuffPost. **https://www.huffpost.com/entry/addiction-is-a-disease-of_b_7561200**

References

Wampold, B. E., & Imel, Z. E. (2015, March). *What do we know about psychotherapy?—And what is there left to debate?* Society for the Advancement of Psychotherapy. **http://www.society forpsychotherapy.org/what-do-we-know-about-psychotherapy-and-what-is-there-left-to-debate**

Wampold, B. E., Imel, Z. E., Laska, K. M., Benish, S., Miller, S. D., Fluckiger, C., Del Re, A. C., Baardseth, T. P., & Budge, S. (2010). Determining what works in the treatment of PTSD [Abstract]. *Clinical Psychology Review, 30*(8), 923-933. **https://doi.org/10.1016/j.cpr.2010.06.005**

Weathers, F. W., Litz, B. T., Herman, D., Huska, J., & Keane, T. (1993). *The PTSD checklist (PCL): Reliability, validity, and diagnostic utility*. National Center for PTSD. [Scale designed for use with the DSM-IV PTSD criteria. Available for download from the Center's website.] **https://www.ptsd.va.gov/professional/assessment/adult-sr/ptsd-checklist.asp**

Weathers, F. W., Litz, B. T., Keane, T. M., Palmieri, P. A., Marx, B. P., & Schnurr, P. P. (2013). *PTSD checklist for DSM-5 (PCL-5)*. National Center for PTSD. [Scale available for download from the Center's website.] **https://www.ptsd.va.gov/professional/assessment/adult-sr/ptsd-checklist.asp**

Whitaker, R. (2015). Anatomy of an epidemic: The history and science of a failed paradigm of care [Abstract]. *the Behavior Therapist, 38*(7), 192-198.
https://psycnet.apa.org/record/2015-56839-006

Wlassoff, V. (2015, January 24). *How does post-traumatic stress disorder change the brain?* Brain Blogger. **http://brainblogger.com/2015/01/24/how-does-post-traumatic-stress-disorder-change-the-brain/**

Wolpe, J. (1954). Reciprocal inhibition as the main basis of psychotherapeutic effects [Abstract]. *AMA Archives of Neurology & Psychiatry, 72*(2), 205-226. **https://jamanetwork.com/journals/archneurpsyc/article-abstract/651819**

Wolpe, J. (1958). *Psychotherapy by reciprocal inhibition.* Stanford University Press. **https://books.google.com/books /about/Psychotherapy_by_Reciprocal_Inhibition .html?id=gJqaAAAAIAAJ**

Wolpe, J. (1969). *The practice of behavior therapy.* Pergamon Press. **https://books.google.com/books/about/The_Practice _of_Behavior_Therapy.html?id=2XtHAAAAMAAJ**

Wortmann, J. H., Jordan, A. H., Weathers, F. W., Resick, P. A., Dondanville, K. A., Hall-Clark, B., Foa, E. B., Young-McLaughan, S., Yarvis, J. S., Hembree, E. A., Mintz, J., Peterson, A. L., & Litz, B. T. (2016). Psychometric analysis of the PTSD checklist-5 (PCL-5) among treatment-seeking military service members. *Psychological Assessment, 28(11),* 1392-1403. Advance online publication. **https://doi.org/10.1037/pas0000260**

Young, P. (2004). *Understanding NLP: Principles & practice (2nd edition).* Crown House Publishing. **https://www .amazon.com/Understanding-Nlp-Principles -Peter-Young-dp-1904424104/dp/1904424104 /ref=mt_other?_encoding=UTF8&me=&qid=**

Zimerman, A. L. (2013). Evidence-based medicine: A short history of a modern medical movement. *AMA Journal of Ethics, 15*(1), 71-76. **https://journalofethics.ama-assn.org/article /evidence-based-medicine-short-history-modern -medical-movement/2013-01**

INDEX

A

Andreas, C., 1, 94, 101, 102-103, 105, 108, 111-112, 117, 121, 130, 138, 145, 335
Andreas, S., 1, 94, 101, 102-103, 105, 108, 110, 111, 117, 121, 138, 145, 175, 176, 196, 335
Abou, E., 69
Above the Horizon eye movement, 147-148, 192-194, 198-200, 204-205, 209-211, 210-211, 333, 334
Abramovitch, A., 50, 51
abreaction, 257, 260, 262
  definition of, 257
acute stress disorder, 39-40, 248
adaptive information processing (AIP) model, 97
addictive cravings, treating with MEMI, 278-279
adrenal glands, 30
adrenocorticotropic hormone (ACTH), 30
Adverse Childhood Experiences (ACE) study, 41-42, 52
Akirav, I., 33
American Hypnosis Training Academy (AHTA), 4
American Psychiatric Association, 9, 39, 336
American Psychological Association (APA), 48, 56, 58, 64, 67, 72
  PTSD clinical practice guideline, 10, 64
amygdala, 7, 26-29, 30-36, 302
anchoring: definition of, 176-177
anchoring, 13, 118-119, 135, 165-166, 172, 175-181, 260
anterior cingulate cortex, 26, 31-32
anxiety, related to personal failures, 275
Austin, A., 12
autonomic nervous system (ANS), 22, 24

B

Bandler, R., 12, 85, 89, 108, 183
Beaulieu, D., 12, 131, 195
Beck, C., 89
Beck, E., 89
Benish, S., 75
Benson, H., 24-25
biomarkers, 35, 51
biomedical model, 10, 45, 49-52
Bisson, J., 74, 75, 118
Bohart, A., 59
Bothwell, L., 52, 53, 55, 65
Bradley, R., 74
brain hemisphere activation studies, 82-83
breaking state, 108
Bremner, J., 33, 36
Buckner, M., 89-90

C

Carey, B., 58, 60
Carpenter, P., 53
Carroll, M., 95
Centers for Disease Control (CDC), 41, 54
central nervous system (CNS), 21-25
Chambless, D., 59
Children and Adults with Attention Deficit/Hyperactivity Disorder (CHADD), 51
cingulate cortex, 26, 31
Clay, R., 54, 55
client safety, 1, 11, 71, 118, 144, 165, 174
cognitive behavioral therapies, 8, 11, 36-37, 44-45, 64-65, 67-68, 70, 72-76, 77-78, 155, 250, 254
cognitive behavioral therapy (CBT), 3, 63-65, 67, 74, 99
cognitive processing therapy (CPT), 64-65, 67, 70, 100
cognitive restructuring, 16, 44, 64, 70, 113-114, 139, 249-253, 325

conduct future rehearsal and self-appreciation (Step 10), 244-248, 333
Corey, G., 70
Cormier, S., 70
corticotropin-releasing hormone, 30
Courtois, C., 42

D

Deacon, B., 49, 51, 53
deaf and hard-of-hearing people, 177, 269-272
DeLozier, J., 87, 95, 107, 122, 161, 183, 322
Deninger, M., 3
Depression and Bipolar Support Alliance (DBSA), 51
DePrince A., 42
desensitization (see also MEMI memory reorganization), 9, 65, 68, 90-92, 107, 112, 165, 166, 174, 223, 224, 239, 251, 268, 324, 336
Diagnostic and Statistical Manual of Mental Disorders, 5th edition, PTSD diagnostic criteria in, 37, 39, 292
Dilts NLP eye movement study, 84-86, 105
Dilts, R., 12, 83-90, 104, 105, 107, 122, 138, 161, 183, 322
direct commands, 131
dissociation, 13, 15, 94, 108, 119, 135, 157, 158, 166, 181-187, 206, 207, 258, 261, 262, 264, 282, 286, 288, 298, 303, 312, 333
Dube, S., 276

E

efficacy versus effectiveness, 60-62, 72-73, 77, 78
Einstein Healthcare Network, 69
Ellis, A., 113, 249, 250
embedded command, 14, 15, 131-133, 135, 138, 150, 199-203, 204, 209, 210-215, 251, 253, 270
Erickson, M., 4, 12, 107, 121, 162, 183
evidence-based practices (EBPs), 11, 56-65, 67, 99

explicit memories (see also implicit memories), 27-28, 302
exposure therapy, 3, 65, 67-72, 75, 99, 111, 118, 173
eye accessing cues, 83-90, 92, 104, 105, 130
eye contact, importance of, 259, 260-261, 262, 264, 282-283, 284, 285
Eye Movement Desensitization and Reprocessing (EMDR), 9, 12, 58, 64-65, 90-101, 103, 106-115, 118, 131, 148, 193, 219, 235, 275, 336
controversies, 93-101
eye movement integration, 12, 13, 14, 15, 117-121, 131, 136, 138, 139, 143-146, 155, 190, 191, 195, 219, 235
Eye Movement Integration (EMI), 1, 2, 11, 13, 101-103, 105, 106-115, 117-118, 121, 131, 231
Eye Movement Integration™ (EMI™), 1, 2, 117-120
eye movement sets, 14, 113, 121, 128, 143, 173, 187, 189, 190-216, 219, 220, 227, 231, 232, 233, 236, 237, 248, 271, 334
eye movements, 12-15, 30, 81-83, 85, 90, 98, 104, 190, 248
  and cognitive restructuring, 250-251
  and neurosensory processing, 9, 83, 85-90, 104-106, 138, 250
  and trance states, 256-257
  in Eye Movement Desensitization and Reprocessing EMDR, 9, 12, 91-92, 98, 100, 106, 110-111, 193
  in Eye Movement Integration (EMI), 12, 100-103, 106, 111-119, 13
  in MEMI, assumptions about, 137-139
  in MEMI, basic, 14-15, 143-154, 248, 333
  in MEMI, random versus strategic approach to, 13, 137, 139, 144, 146, 190
  in MEMI, when to discontinue, 235-238

in the NLP training exercise, 93-94
use with deaf and hard of hearing clients, 270-271

F

Faulkner, C., 122, 176
Felitti, V., 41, 52
fight or flight response (see also stress response),), 7, 8, 10, 25, 26-29, 31
Figure 8 basic eye movement, 151-153, 204-209, 271, 333, 334
Food and Drug Administration, 53, 54
Ford, J., 74
Forrest, M., 97
Fredericks, R., 95
Frieden, T., 54-55, 62, 65
functional magnetic resonance imaging (fMRI), 34
future rehearsal and self-appreciation (Step 10), 189, 244-248

G

Galin, D., 82, 83, 85, 87
Gallagher, M., 70
Gentry, E., 258, 259
Gold, S., 42
gold standard controversy, 52-56, 76, 254
Goldwaser, G., 69
Goodman, K., 58
Grimley, B., 96
Grinder, J., 12, 83, 86, 94-96, 108, 183
Gross, A., 68
Guyatt, G., 56

H

habitual eye movements, 88, 104, 115, 138
Head, L., 68
hemispheric language dominance, 88
Herbert, J., 93
hippocampus, 26, 27, 28, 29-30, 33, 302
Hoobyar, T., 122
horizontal sweeps, 147-148, 192-194
hypothalamus, 26, 30, 31
hypothalamic, pituitary, adrenal (HPA) pathway, 30

I

Imel, Z., 76, 77
implicit memories (see also explicit memories), 27-28, 302
Insel, T., 50
insula, 26, 32
Intensity Scale (I-Scale), 16, 156-157, 169-171, 231-233, 281
Intensity Score (I-Score), 170, 220, 230, 231-233, 235, 237, 241-243, 254, 333
internal narrative (see also "self-talk"), 87, 111, 137, 300
introduce therapeutic dissociation (Step 5), 158, 181, 185-187, 333

J

James, W., 81, 83

K

Kaiser Permanente, 41
Kessler, R., 39
Kidd, P., 74
Kinderman, P., 51
Kinsbourne M., 82, 83, 86, 88
Klein, R., 1, 2, 4, 12, 13, 94, 97, 112, 117-119, 135, 178
Kocel, K., 82, 84

L

Lacasse, J., 51
Landin-Romero, R., 99
Lanese, N., 7
Langley Porter Neuropsychiatric Institute, 82
Dilts NLP eye movement study, 84-86, 105
Langone Medical Center, 72
Leo, J., 51
Lilienfeld, S., 98
limbic system, 10, 21, 25, 26, 27, 33-37, 38, 78, 105, 115, 136, 139, 155, 235, 248, 250, 256
Litz, B., 252
Logie, R., 96

M

Mandal, A., 35
Marich, J., 91, 97, 100
McFall, R., 56
McGlynn, E., 58
McKay, D., 49, 51
Miller, G., 75, 76, 109
Moncrieff, J., 51
Monson, C., 63
Morgan, M., 35
Multichannel Eye Movement
 Integration (MEMI), 2, 7, 13-18, 117,
 119, 131-133, 139, 146, 175, 335-336
 accessing positions (see also NLP eye
  movement model), 86, 101, 104, 110,
  137, 138, 144-145, 147, 186, 191-
  192, 196, 200, 201, 209, 211, 216
 administer the PCL-5 and establish
  rapport (Step 1), 160-162, 333
 anchor a resource state (Step 4), 158,
  175-181, 333
 anchoring, 119, 135, 165, 166, 172,
  175-181
 basic eye movements, 14-15, 143-144,
  190-192, 248, 333
  Above the Horizon, 147-148, 192-
   194, 198-200, 204-205,
   209-211, 333-334
  Figure 8, 147, 151-152, 153, 204-
   209, 271, 333, 334
  Shrinking Circles, 147, 152-154,
   330, 333, 334
  Sitting Triangle, , 147, 150-151, 209,
   211, 212, 213, 214, 215, 333, 334
  Standing Triangle, 147, 149-150,
   198-199, 200, 202, 203, 204, 206,
   208, 209, 210, 211, 214, 333, 334
 case reports, 16, 281
  "Ashley," 306-318
  "Kevin," 292-305
  "Miguel," 319-327
  "Rebecca," 282-291
 clinical study of (Appendix D), 17, 137,
  156, 255, 335

conduct eye movements (Step 6),
 189, 190-218, 333
conduct future rehearsal and self-
 appreciation (Step 10), 189, 190,
 220, 236, 244-248, 316, 333
Context, 16, 124-126, 129, 155,
 176, 190, 220-221, 228-229, 233,
 239-240, 243, 251, 254, 267-269,
 278, 288, 310, 311, 314, 318, 323
effectiveness of, 17, 138, 190, 191,
 202, 219, 231-232, 244,
 248, 253-256, 279, 335
eye contact, 259, 261-262, 264,
 284, 285
Feelings, 13, 16, 89, 124-127, 129,
 138, 169, 176, 178, 190, 209, 212,
 215, 217, 218, 220, 225-228, 231-
 232, 238-239, 241-243, 251, 254,
 260, 265, 267, 269, 278, 285, 286,
 287, 288, 330, 334
gestures and vocalizations, 161,
 185-187
handling abreactions, 16, 257-263
hypnotic suggestions, 13, 132-133
introduce therapeutic dissociation
 (Step 5), 181-187, 333
limbic therapy, 136, 248
memory reorganization, 150, 212, 250
metaphors, 13-15, 132
"multichannel" approach, 13-14
origin of, 117
pattern interruption, 125, 129, 184,
 202, 207, 212, 251, 253, 260
presuppositions, 12, 13, 118, 121-131,
 251
pretest Elements of Structure (Step 3),
 158, 164-175, 333
protocol, 7, 13, 14-16, 118, 120, 121,
 131, 155, 156-157, 158, 189-190,
 219-220, 231, 238, 244, 248, 253,
 333, 335, 336, 339, 343-344
Step 1. administer the PCL-5 and
 establish rapport, 158, 160-162, 333
Step 2. secure agreement to change,
 158, 162-164, 333

Step 3. pretest Elements of Structure, 158, 164-175, 333
Step 4. anchor a resource state, 158, 175-181, 333
Step 5. introduce therapeutic dissociation, 158, 181-187, 333
Step 6. conduct eye movements, 189, 190-218, 333
Step 7. test Structure of Experience, 16, 189, 220-231, 333
Step 8. take I-Score and SUD Score, 16, 189, 220, 231-243, 333
Step 9. record results on MEMI Worksheet, 16, 189, 190, 220, 238-238, 333
Step 10. conduct future rehearsal and self-appreciation, 16, 189, 190, 220, 236, 244-248, 316, 333
reactivation, 124
record results on MEMI Worksheet (Step 9), 189, 190, 220, 238-243, 333
repressed information, 264-269
scripts, 15, 121, 125, 155, 177, 191, 196-197, 200-203, 207-209, 213-215
secure agreement to change (Step 2), 158, 162-164, 333
Sensory Information, 16, 124-130, 138, 176-177, 190, 194, 217, 218, 220, 223-225, 228, 233, 238, 240-241, 243, 278, 285, 287, 313, 318
sets, 14-15, 121, 128, 143, 150, 154, 187, 189-218, 219-220, 222, 224, 227, 231, 232-233, 234, 235, 236, 239, 242, 245, 251, 271, 299
Set 1, 192-198, 240, 243, 334
Set 2, 198-203, 240, 241, 242, 243, 253, 334
Set 3, 204-209, 241, 242, 243, 334
Set 4, 209-215, 243, 334
spoken command, 251
direct, 131, 135, 138, 150, 206
embedded, 14, 15, 131-133, 135, 138, 150, 199-203, 204, 209, 210-215, 251, 253, 270, 330

Steps 7-10, 16, 190, 217, 219-248, 333
Structure of Experience theoretical model, 13, 125-128
take I-Score and SUD Score readings (Step 8), 189, 231-238, 333
test for Structure of Experience (Step 7), 16, 189, 220-231, 333
therapeutic dissociation, 13, 119, 135, 157, 158, 165-166, 181-187, 206-207, 258, 261, 262, 264, 286, 288, 312, 333
therapist instructions, 15, 155
Thoughts, 114, 124-126, 129, 132, 133, 134, 135, 138-139, 165, 169, 178, 190, 200-201, 203, 209, 218, 222, 223, 229, 233, 238, 239-240, 243, 247, 249-253, 254, 260, 265, 266, 268, 269, 272, 274, 277, 278, 287, 288, 316, 318, 323, 325
treating phobias, 16, 184, 274-275, 279
Worksheet, 16, 121, 155, 170, 173, 189, 190, 198, 203, 209, 215, 220, 221, 224, 227, 233, 238-243, 331-332

N

National Alliance on Mental Illness, 51
National Center for PTSD, 40, 70, 72, 99, 336
National Conference of the American Mental Health Counseling Association, 175
National Institute of Mental Health, 10, 43, 49
National Institute on Alcohol Abuse and Alcoholism, 51
National Institute on Drug Abuse, 49, 50
National Institutes of Health, 54
Naval Center for Combat and Operational Stress Control, 69
nervous system, 21-25, 278
Neuro-Linguistic Programming (NLP) anchoring, 13, 118, 119, 175-181, 260

eye movement model, 12, 83-90,
91, 92, 94, 100, 101-103, 110-111,
126, 130, 144, 145, 191, 201
   origins, 12
   presuppositions, 12, 13, 94, 111, 118, 122-131
   strategies, 7, 9, 12, 94, 96, 107-109, 119-120, 133, 161, 175, 183, 260
neurotransmitters, 7
Newman, E., 42
New York Times, The, 58
nontrauma therapies, 3, 44, 45, 75

O

O'Connor, J., 108
Ornstein, R., 82, 83, 85, 87

P

parasympathetic nervous system (PaNS), 24-25, 261
pattern interruption, 129, 184, 202, 207, 212, 253, 260
Peele, S., 51
peripheral nervous system (PeNS), 22-25
Perls, F., 12, 121, 183
phobias, MEMI treatment of, 16, 184, 274-275, 279
post-traumatic stress disorder (PTSD), 9, 25, 37-46, 63, 279
   Checklist for DSM-5 (PCL-5), 40, 156-157, 158, 160, 255, 319, 329, 336, 338
   Checklist for DSM IV, 156, 255, 282, 284, 292, 296, 335, 336, 338, 339, 345
   diagnostic criteria, 10, 39-41, 156, 160, 290, 319, 336, 337, 339
   National Center for, 40, 70, 72, 99, 336
   practices, 7, 10, 65
   therapies for, 3, 30, 32, 35, 44-46, 50, 56-59, 60-66, 67, 78, 81, 106, 118, 119, 146, 155, 172, 173, 174, 197, 249-250, 253-254
   treatment, 7-8, 10-11, 35-37, 43-45, 48, 49, 51, 56, 58, 59-66, 74, 76, 78
   appropriateness, 35, 262
   effectiveness studies, 8, 11, 17, 57, 71, 77-78, 99, 255, 279
prefrontal cortex, 26, 31, 33, 36
   deactivation, 34, 36
presuppositions, definition of, 12, 119
   in MEMI, 13-14, 118, 121-131, 251
pretest elements of structure (Step 3), 158, 164, 333
problem state, 107-109, 133, 134, 135, 136, 137, 139, 154, 156, 157, 158, 167, 169, 172, 183, 187, 190, 194-197, 198, 200, 201, 203, 212, 215, 216, 220-221, 223, 227, 228, 231, 232, 233, 235, 236, 239, 242, 244, 245, 246, 250, 256-257, 258, 259, 260, 265, 267, 272-273, 279, 288, 299, 325
prolonged exposure therapy (PE), 64, 65, 67, 70, 100, 111

R

randomized controlled trials (RCTs), 10, 48, 52-59, 65, 76, 99, 117, 254, 279
   gold standard controversy, 52-56, 57, 76, 254
rapport, establishment of, 158, 160, 161, 333
Real People Press, 1
reciprocal inhibition, 68, 112, 118, 176
record results on the MEMI Worksheet (Step 9), 189, 190, 220, 238-243, 333
re-exposure, 35, 259, 261
reframing, 131-135, 207
relaxation response, 24-25, 261
repressed information, emergence of, 16, 264-269
Resick, P., 70
resource state, 118, 158, 172, 175-181, 185, 312, 333
Richter-Levin, G., 33
Rosenzweig, L., 12

S

Sackett, D., 57
safety mechanisms, 13, 112
Satir, V., 12, 121
Schnurr, P., 65, 75, 118
Schweiger, A., 50, 51
Seal, K., 74, 118
secure agreement to change (Step 2), 158, 162-164, 333
Seidler, G., 99
self-talk (see also internal narrative), 86, 87, 199-201, 209, 247, 250, 251, 334
separator state, 184, 262
Seymour, J., 108
Shapiro, F., 12, 58, 81, 90, 101, 107, 108, 109-110, 113, 219
Shedler, J., 65
Shnaider, P., 63
Shrinking Circles basic eye movement, 147, 152-154, 330, 333, 334
Sitting Triangle basic eye movement, 147, 150-151, 211, 212, 213, 214-215, 333, 334
somatic nervous system (SoNS), 22, 23
Spiegler, M., 250
Springer, S., 88
Standing Triangle basic eye movement, 147, 149-150, 198-199, 200, 202, 204-205, 206, 208, 209, 210, 211, 214, 333, 334
state of being, 167
Steenkamp, M., 65, 72, 73, 75
Stevens, J., 34-36, 38, 105, 115, 155, 175
Structure of Experience elements, tests of (Step 7), 16, 189, 220-231, 333
Structure of Experience theoretical model, 13, 121-131
Subjective Units of Distress (SUD) Scale, 16, 107, 120, 156, 170-171, 231, 232, 233-237
submodalities, 126-127, 129
substance abuse, MEMI treatment of, 275-277, 283-284, 292, 293, 296, 300, 339
SUD Score readings, taking (Step 8), 16, 189, 220, 231-238, 333
Sweeton, J., 9, 10, 30, 260
sympathetic nervous system (SyNS), 7, 24, 25
synesthesia, 322
systematic desensitization, 68, 107, 165-166

T

Tanenbaum, S., 58-62, 63, 73, 78
Tavris, C., 58, 93
test-retest procedure (see also TOTE model), 109
thalamus, 26-28, 30, 302
therapeutic dissociation, 13, 15, 119, 135, 157, 158, 165-166, 181-187, 206, 207, 258, 261, 262, 264, 286, 288, 312, 333
Thoughts versus cognitive restructuring, 16, 114, 139, 249-253
Tomason, T., 88-89, 104
top-down treatment strategies, 260
TOTE model, 109
trauma-informed care, 10, 41, 43
traumatic event, 21, 39, 108, 130, 135, 227, 307
  neurophysiology of, 8, 10, 21-38, 155
  processing of, 3, 9, 16, 21-23, 31-35, 81-90, 102, 104, 105, 130, 138, 145, 247
  re-experiencing, 11, 33, 35, 37-38, 40, 70-71, 111, 129, 131, 160, 174, 181, 251, 255, 274
  re-exposure, 1, 35-37, 67-72, 174-175, 259, 261
  responses to, 10, 21-25, 26-32, 33-38, 70, 227
trauma treatment, 11, 12-14, 17, 41, 49, 61-62, 64, 71-72, 74, 78, 257, 261, 276, 281, 282

controversies, 10, 48-49, 57-65, 93-101, 254
protection during, 36-37, 111, 118, 119, 131, 135, 158, 165, 173, 185, 195, 258, 259, 264, 309
research, 7-9, 10-12, 21, 33-37, 43-45, 47-62, 63, 65, 67, 72-78, 81-90, 99, 104-106, 279
Trauma Treatment Toolbox, 10
treating addictive cravings, 278
Tunis, S., 60

U

U. S. Department of Veterans Affairs, 17, 39, 40, 64, 67, 160, 336, 338

V

van der Kolk, B., 71, 73-74, 75, 79, 118, 173, 251
visual kinesthetic dissociation (V/K/D), 94, 108, 183-185
Volkow, N., 50

W

Wampold, B., 76-77
Weathers, F., 160, 255, 336
Whitaker, R., 51
Wlassoff, V., 33
Wolpe, J., 68, 107, 118, 120, 175
Wortman, J., 40, 308

Y

Young, P., 182

Z

Zimerman, A., 57

ABOUT THE AUTHOR

Mike Deninger, PhD, LPC, CCTP, CTNLP, CT-MEMI, NBCCH grew up in a large, working-class family in Western New York. As a college senior, he became interested in a career as an educator while working part-time as a supervisor in the boys' residence hall at Buffalo's St. Mary's School for the Deaf. With dedication and drive, by the age of 33, Mike rose to a leadership position in the education of deaf children.

After earning a PhD with distinction in special education administration, he was appointed Dean of Pre-College Programs at Gallaudet University in Washington, DC, the only liberal arts university for the deaf in the world. With this appointment, Mike had reached the pinnacle of his profession. However, despite these professional achievements, all was not right with him.

In his 2011 memoir, *Snakes in My Dreams: A Mental Health Therapist's Odyssey from Hardship to Healer,* Mike shared the candid truth behind his transition from a top position educating deaf children to a career as a therapist, author, and master trainer in mental health. He earned a graduate degree in counseling, trainer certifications in Ericksonian Hypnotherapy, Eye Movement Integration™ and Neuro-Linguistic Programming, and established a private counseling practice. During this transformation, Mike also confronted alcohol addiction, came out as a gay man, and triumphed over PTSD caused by childhood sexual abuse.

Mike knows what it's like to recover from trauma. Moreover, he's keenly aware of the renewal that's possible when one frees the mind, relaxes the will, and allows the body's neurological systems to heal traumatic wounds. In the spirit of "giving back," Mike now shares his trauma-related skills and knowledge with survivors of all types and the professionals who advise them. With enthusiasm and insight, he continues to counsel those suffering from PTSD and lesser traumas. And utilizing his background in education, Mike enjoys offering virtual seminars and consultations in Multichannel Eye Movement Integration—the methodology he developed—to therapists eager to utilize this effective approach.

Mike also has an interest in acting and theatre. An Equity member, he has performed off Broadway in New York and at the Kennedy Center and Arena Stage in Washington, D.C. Today Mike lives in Tucson, Arizona with his husband and partner, Michael Mayes, and their canine companion, Gracie.

Made in the USA
Las Vegas, NV
03 September 2021